Self-transcendence and Ego Surrender
A Quiet-enough Ego or an Ever-quieter Ego

**David Hartman, LCSW
& Diane Zimberoff, LMFT**

Self-transcendence and Ego Surrender
A Quiet-enough Ego or an Ever-quieter Ego

Ultimately, an individual brings all his/her splinter parts, that is to say subpersonalities, to awareness, and the ego recognizes itself to be a sibling rather than a parent or an overlord. Resolution of lifelong patterns of conflict lies in surrender to the ultimate organizing principle of the individual, the Self, the Archetypal Self, the Transpersonal Self, the creator of the grand illusion and the one within most capable of accessing the conflict-free center core resources.

Published by:

Wellness Press
The Wellness Institute
3716 - 274th Ave SE
Issaquah, WA 98029
800-326-4418
www.wellness-institute.org

ISBN 978-0-9622728-9-9

Self-transcendence and Ego Surrender
A Quiet-enough Ego or an Ever-quieter Ego

Table of Contents

Illustrations

Foreword

Transpersonal Psychology, Self-transcendence and Ego Surrender

The field of transpersonal psychology, a psychology encompassing realms of consciousness beyond the human ego, is by definition expansive. It includes discreet altered states of consciousness and the various psychotechnologies (meditation, parapsychology, shamanic journeying, sacred ceremony, holotropic breathwork, hypnosis, guided imagery, Carl Jung's active imagination, dream work, past life regression, near-death experience) and psychopharmacologies (psychoactive plants, psychedelics) used to achieve them.

It includes aspects of transpersonal anthropology, mapping the many multicultural approaches to the exploration of psychospiritual consciousness (Lahood, 2007).

Transpersonal psychology has unveiled illuminating maps of eudaimonic growth (Bauer, McAdams, & Pals, 2008), the potentials for advanced adult development (Loevinger, 1976, 1997), the stages, structures and states of consciousness available to human beings (Wilber, 2009).

It offers a unique transpersonal, non-medical model approach to psychopathology, its diagnosis and treatment, including spiritual emergencies, spiritual wounding and restoration, and the very concept of *basic sanity* (Chogyam Trungpa & Goleman, 2005) from a contemplative-phenomenological paradigm (Bradford, 2012).

Transpersonal coaching provides purposeful growth-oriented interventions beyond the therapeutic damage repair of psychotherapy (Hartman & Zimberoff, 2014).

Existential phenomenology falls within the purview of transpersonal psychology, relying primarily on contemplative thinking rather than a more conventional cognitive conceptual form of thinking (Thompson et al., 1989). Empirical science isolates variables and privileges objectivity and logical deduction, whereas phenomenology recognizes the connectedness of variables and privileges subjectivity and intuition.

Special and unique qualitative methods have been developed to facilitate research on areas of inquiry that cannot be studied through the scientific quantitative methods that have served psychology for the past hundred years (Wertz et al., 2011).

The authors of this book have selected a specific portion of that vast array of topics to focus on, namely the potential development to optimal functioning through transcendent states and stages of consciousness, beyond ego. We review the history of the field and the cross-cultural nature of its manifestations, assess existing maps of the known and unknown psychic terrain, suggest postgraduate curricula for training Higher Education students in the discipline, and explore eudaimonic growth, self-authorship and self-evolution.

In the words of Carl Jung (1967, para. 18), speaking of all the greatest and most important problems of life:

> They can never be solved, but only outgrown. I therefore asked myself whether this outgrowing, this possibility of further psychic development, was not the normal thing, and whether getting stuck in a conflict was pathological. Everyone must possess that higher level, at least in embryonic form, and must under favourable circumstances be able to develop this potentiality.

All the evidence from so many disciplines in the arts and sciences verifies that everyone, all human beings, have the potential to advance to higher levels of functioning, to develop beyond the everydayness to psychospiritual awakening. It is our intention and desire to promote such a development to optimal functioning through encouragement in education, therapy, and coaching.

Part 1. Transpersonal Psychology: What is it? How do we use it?

Chapter One

Introduction to Self-transcendence and Ego Surrender

In this book we will explore today's state of the art in transpersonal psychology, its historical roots and its many facets in practice. The basic premise for exploration revolves around the dominant notion that the journey of self-transcendence and ego surrender offers an antidote to self-limiting everyday beliefs.

Self-transcendence is the expansion of our self-boundaries to connect with dimensions beyond the typically discernible world. This signals a direct appeal to one's soul to awaken and engage.

How do we approach such a task? Transpersonal psychology and therapy welcome the imminent and transcendent dimensions of human experience: exceptional human functioning and achievements, the nature and meaning of deep spiritual and mystical experiences, non-ordinary states of consciousness, and how to develop our highest potentials as human beings.

The self-concept becomes increasingly transparent to itself, becoming both observer and observed, a witness to the dynamic flow of psychic events. This 'witness consciousness' and the self-transcendence upon which it is based are foundational ingredients of higher stages of human development.

One's ego surrenders by quieting, recognizing itself to be a sibling to other aspects of the psyche rather than a parent or an overlord, and acknowledging the rightful leadership of the ultimate organizing principle within, the Transpersonal Self. The quieting can follow the course of balance, seeking a "quiet-enough ego", or of growth, seeking an "ever-quieter ego." Either choice brings increasing tranquility amidst the challenges of life in today's world because, paradoxically, an experience of ego surrender and of letting go *increases* an individual's internal locus of control, the deep knowing that what happens to them is a consequence of their own actions.

Definitions – What is Transpersonal Psychology?

Transpersonal Psychology might loosely be called the psychology of spirituality and of those areas of the human mind which search for higher meanings in life, and which move beyond the limited boundaries of the ego to access an enhanced capacity for wisdom, creativity, unconditional love and compassion. It honors the existence of transpersonal experiences, and is concerned with their meaning for the individual and with their effect upon behavior. (British Psychological Society)[1]

Transpersonal psychology is a full-spectrum psychology that studies a continuum of human experience and behavior ranging from severe dysfunction, mental and emotional illness at one end, to what is generally considered "normal", healthy behavior at the other end and various degrees of normal and maladjustment in between – and then goes beyond it by adding a serious scholarly interest in the imminent and transcendent dimensions of human experience: exceptional human functioning, experiences, performances and achievements, true genius, the nature and meaning of deep religious and mystical experiences, non-ordinary states of consciousness, and how we might foster the fulfillment of our highest potentials as human beings. (Institute of Transpersonal Psychology)[2]

Stan Grof, a co-founder of transpersonal psychology, states that "what truly defines the transpersonal orientation is a model of the human psyche that recognizes the importance of the spiritual or cosmic dimensions and the potential for consciousness evolution."[3]

Vitor Rodrigues, European Transpersonal Association, enumerates the transpersonal vision in more detail[4]:
1) accepts that love is healthy, can be developed, and that there are deeper kinds of love, some of them highly impersonal, global and unity-prone;
2) accepts that we do have a body-emotion-mind personal ego that is very important and must be carefully dealt with but also that this personal ego is the instrument and

expression of an underlying reality including a transpersonal Self that is probably the origin of consciousness. Kasprow & Scotton (1999) assert that the idea of human development as being capable of going beyond ego levels is typical of transpersonal theory and does not contradict, but rather extends, other approaches while showing concern for fostering "higher" human development – as was first shown in Carl Jung's and Abraham Maslow's work;

3) usually it accepts the idea that Spirituality is very important for a healthy and happy human life and that within it we find extremely important contributions for personal and collective Peace, both social and ecological well-being, deep Ecology, and even possible ways out of classical and modern political and economic views;

4) deals with cartographies of consciousness states and consciousness development models and also with descriptions of realms accessible through modified states of consciousness (while doing so, it gives the practitioner ways to discriminate among "pre-personal" level, regressive experiences, and truly transpersonal ones where even the loss of ego boundaries can occur in healthy ways);

5) works with notions about subtle energies, the idea that we do possess subtle energy structures that interact with, and influence, our general health, as they also interact with our immune system, nervous central and peripheral systems, endocrine system and so on (such ideas are somehow similar to those we can find in acupuncture underlying theory and graphics with "energy points". And we all know about the success of acupuncture treatments and their acceptance by the World Health Organization);

6) generally it accepts that we have some "anomalous" psychological functions that amount to extra-sensory perception possibilities, anomalous healing and psychokinesis;

7) also of course it emphasizes the importance of consciousness as an utterly relevant object of study for psychology and with it the importance of experience, the development of consciousness and the need for developing ways to deal with our global ego identity. . .;

8) honors creativity and the arts, values and deep meaning structures such as philosophical and religious ones as expressions of humankind at its best. It also asserts that

real social change comes mostly from individual change towards deeper experiences of ourselves, our central and more essential self, our values and, generally speaking, towards a clear expansion of our individual consciousness both inwards and outwards, both quantitatively and qualitatively.

The Study of Human Development to its Full Potential

James Fadiman, co-author of the popular personality theory textbook, *Personality and Personal Growth*[5], once said: "Conventional psychology is at least 150 years old, whereas transpersonal is 45,000 years old."[6]

Hartelius et al.[7] state that "the major subject areas of the field can be summed up in three themes: beyond-ego psychology, integrative/holistic psychology, and psychology of transformation."

The term "beyond-ego psychology" (or "ego-transcended psychology") deals not only with states that are in some measure beyond ego, but also stages of post-conventional development, traits such as compassion and altruism, aspirations for beyond-ego development, and paths such as meditation and mysticism that are designed to cultivate this unfolding. The term "integrative/holistic psychology" (or psychology of the whole person in an interconnected world) covers the beliefs, attitudes, intentions, and the somatic presence of the therapist in relationship to a client; it also refers to the recognition that ego must be seen within the larger fabric of the whole psyche with all its parts, the community, the social history, the environment (including unseen realms), and the transpersonal ultimate. And the term "psychology of transformation" addresses the changes that are possible not only personally but socially, culturally, and spiritually.

Transpersonal psychology is a study of human growth and development to its full potential. The transpersonal perspective is that the continuum of development begins with people who lack ego identity and are consumed with survival issues. As we move toward functionality, people with stronger ego states and abilities to function well in everyday responsibilities are represented as "normal". Moving even further into human development are the mystics and meditators, the humanitarians and visionaries, the saints and heroes who are seen as transcending the conscious ego identity and recognizing an essential interconnectedness with all creation.

Cunningham[8] has offered a succinct summary of the common ground that transpersonal scholars can find, no matter which philosophy or worldview they prefer, in affirming these four key ideas articulated in the Articles of Association for Transpersonal Psychology.[9]

1. Impulses toward an ultimate state are continuous. All people seek fulfillment through actualizing their ideals through a process called "self-actualization", in a way that benefits not only the individual, but also helps the species (Maslow, 1968, p. 25). "Peak experiences" describes those times when the individual suddenly feels at peace, instinctively a part of events from which one usually considers oneself apart, unexpectedly happy and content with one's daily life, or spontaneously experiences an event in which one seems to go beyond one's self, and are evident in the existence of heroic themes and ideals that pervade human cultural life.

2. Full awareness of these impulses is not necessarily present at any given time. Negative expectations and beliefs, fears and doubts can diminish conscious awareness of these transpersonal impulses, leaving the conscious self no longer able to perceive its own greater fulfillment, uniqueness, or integrity. Yet they continue to operate beneath the surface in subliminal realms of consciousness and dreams whether the person is aware of them or not.

3. The realization of an ultimate state is essentially dependent on direct practice and on conditions suitable to the individual. What is often needed to allow impulses toward ideal states of health, expression, and fulfillment to consciously emerge in daily life is not only a belief in their existence and an intense desire and expectation of their occurrence, but also a disciplined openness that permits their emergence, i.e., a spiritual practice.

4. Every individual has the right to choose his or her own path. Transpersonal psychology recognizes the

existential significance of individual differences, free will, choice, and responsibility for one's choices.

And Cunningham concludes "the broad definitional themes of transpersonal psychology – 'highest or ultimate potential,' 'phenomena beyond the ego', 'human transformation and transcendence', 'transcendent states of consciousness', 'psychospiritual development', 'integrative/holistic psychology' – may all sound quite esoteric, but they refer to highly practical experiences and behaviors."[10]

Lucid dreaming, out-of-body experiences, past-life experiences, near-death experiences, spiritual healing experiences, mystical experience, and psi-related experiences (precognition, clairvoyance, psychokinesis) may be considered anomalous phenomena by mainstream psychology because of artificial divisions established within psychology itself between what is common and uncommon, possible and impossible, normal and abnormal, real and unreal.[11] Yet these very experiences have been a part of humanity's existence for as long as history has been recorded, reported and witnessed across virtually all known cultures.[12] And for most of that history, these experiences have remained isolated from society's masses, privy to only a select few mystics, prophets, and renaissance men/women. And so outside of society's conscious scrutiny, deep in the society's collective unconscious psyche. Until recently.

"The cardinal discovery of transpersonal psychology is that the collective psyche, the deepest layer of the unconscious, is the living ground current from which is derived everything to do with a particularized ego possessing consciousness: Upon this it is based, by this it is nourished, and without this it cannot exist."[13]

> Transpersonal psychology views a wide open horizon of potential advancement for all human beings, not just a few extraordinary exemplars. And that advancement is seen as already existing underneath the social conditioning and acquired self-limitations that obscure the true essence, the *trans*personal. Personality is merely a vehicle used to transport our spirit and soul into and through the world in its mission to recover the *Transpersonal Self.*

As a model for the realization of this human potential, transpersonal psychology focuses on developing the positive influences as well as on repairing the diseases and defenses of the human psyche. The transpersonal psychology model integrates the spiritual, social, emotional, intellectual, physical and creative being into one complete element and addresses all of these components equally for the purpose of growth and development, and of therapeutic treatment.

Transpersonal psychology has been influenced by and builds upon a number of fields of psychology: psychoanalytic, Humanistic, Psychosynthesis, Existential, Analytical Psychology, Integral Psychology, shamanic and indigenous traditions, Eastern Orthodox mysticism, Eastern psychology (Hindu and Buddhist), and Energy Psychology. Transpersonal psychology suggests that spiritual and mystical experiences can be examined scientifically for the purpose of healing and advanced adult development. It identifies and studies various non-ordinary states of consciousness, the psychotechnologies available to access them, and the skills needed to navigate back and forth through the different states of consciousness and stages of development.

Chapter Two

Historical Development of Transpersonal Psychology

William James was the first psychologist to use the term "transpersonal". It was in a 1905 lecture, according to *The Textbook of Transpersonal Psychiatry and Psychology[14]*, and he's referred to as the founder of modern transpersonal psychology and psychiatry. As psychologist Eugene Taylor writes in the book:

> He was the first to use the term *transpersonal* in an English-language context and the first to articulate a scientific study of consciousness within a framework of evolutionary biology. He experimented with psychoactive substances to observe their effects on his own consciousness and was a pioneer in founding the field that is now called parapsychology. He helped to cultivate modern interest in dissociated states, multiple personality, and theories of the subconscious. He explored the field of comparative religion and was probably the first American psychologist to establish relationships with or to influence a number of Asian meditation teachers. He also pioneered in writing about the psychology of mystical experience.[15]

By the 1960s in America, psychology was dominated by two major schools—behaviorism and Freudian psychology. American psychologist Abraham Maslow offered an incisive critique of the limitations of behaviorism and psychoanalysis, or the First and the Second Forces in psychology as he called them, and formulated the principles of a new perspective in psychology: humanistic psychology.[16]

This Third Force emphasized the capacity of human beings to be internally directed and motivated to achieve self-realization and fulfill their human potential, and it honored consciousness and introspection as important complements to the objective approach to research. Maslow and Anthony Sutich launched the Association for Humanistic Psychology to incorporate somatic experience, cathartic emotional expression, and Gestalt focus on the here-and-now.

> In spite of the popularity of humanistic psychology, its founders Maslow and Sutich themselves grew dissatisfied with the conceptual framework they had originally created. They became increasingly aware that they had left out an extremely important element—the spiritual dimension of the human psyche (Sutich 1976). The renaissance of interest in Eastern spiritual philosophies, various mystical traditions, meditation, ancient and aboriginal wisdom, as well as the widespread psychedelic experimentation during the stormy 1960s, made it absolutely clear that a comprehensive and cross-culturally valid psychology had to include observations from such areas as mystical states, cosmic consciousness, psychedelic experiences, trance phenomena, creativity, and religious, artistic, and scientific inspiration.[17]

In 1967, Abraham Maslow predicted the emergence of a 'Fourth Force' in American psychology, and by the mid 1970s, a group of psychologists moved to acknowledge that new dimension in the field of psychology, "transhumanistic" psychology, to recognize the importance of the entire spectrum of human experience, including the spiritual and various non-ordinary states of consciousness. The name was soon changed to "transpersonal psychology". Paradoxically, Maslow began to recognize that peak experiences often led the self-actualizing individual to transcend the personal concerns of the very self that was being actualized.

> The goal of identity (self-actualization . . .) seems to be simultaneously an end-goal in itself, and also a transitional goal, a rite of passage, a step along the path to the transcendence of identity. This is like saying its function is to erase itself. Put the other way around, if our goal is the Eastern one of ego-transcendence and obliteration, of leaving behind self-consciousness and self-observation, . . . then it looks as if the best path to this goal for most people is via achieving identity, a strong real self, and via basic-need-gratification.[18]

European psychology had been casting a wider net than behaviorism and Freudian psychology for many decades. Roberto Assagioli[19] explored the spiritual unconscious, Otto Rank[20] researched the dynamic influence of birth on an individual's life patterns, and Carl Jung[21] developed his theories of the collective unconscious, the imaginal realm, and the numinous quality of one's transcendent function.

Transcendence and Immanence, Ascent and Descent

In transpersonal psychology, the term *transcendence* is a dominant concept. As we have seen, the expansion from humanistic psychology, focused on self-actualization, to transpersonal psychology was literally based on Maslow's identifying *transcendence* as the next step in mankind's development. And from the beginning it was clear that this next step was in service to the greater good of all creation; self-serving had a new meaning because "self" had now expanded to include all people, all nature, all creation. "Before enlightenment, chop wood, carry water. After enlightenment, chop wood, carry water." And so everyday life and all of its responsibilities, or immanence, is integral to transpersonal psychology as well.

First, let us establish the "lay of the land" regarding the twin concepts of transcendence and immanence (for a full discussion see Hartman & Zimberoff, 2010).

Immanence and transcendence are reciprocal terms with the former relating to something beyond mere materialism participating within material existence, whereas the latter refers to something that is beyond materialism's limits and outside of material existence (e.g., the immanent quality of a so-called deity would be located within the material world, whereas the transcendent quality of a so-called deity would be radically outside the material world — and, of course, any such deity could be seen as having both qualities).[22]

While here the concepts are placed in the context of spiritual experience, they apply equally well to the field of depth psychology and the relationship of consciousness to the unconscious and the collective unconscious. We could replace the term "material existence" with "consciousness", so that transcendence refers to something outside of consciousness, and immanence to something within consciousness. These categories are never what they initially seem, however, as we know well.

The same distinction is made in the poetic language of *under-the-ground* and *beyond-the-horizon*. The *beyond-the-horizon* is an absence that helps to define one's journey, an unseen but vital realm, the *not-yet-born*. There are many invisible absences of what is *under-the-ground* as well: the other side of a tree, or of the moon, or of my body, the inside of the tree or moon or my body.

> For these would seem to be the two primary dimensions from whence things enter the open presence of the landscape, and into which they depart. Sensible phenomena are continually appearing out of, and continually vanishing into, these two very different realms of concealment or invisibility. One trajectory is a passage out toward, or inward from, a vast openness. The other is a descent into, or a sprouting up from, a packed density.[23]

And so again, applying this terminology to depth psychology, one might say that transcendence refers to something *beyond-the-horizon* (the vast openness of consciousness) and immanence to something *under-the-ground* (the soul realm of the unconscious).

Another culture provides a similar perspective on the interrelatedness of ascent and descent[24]:

> There is a Yu'pik (Alaskan First People) creation tale. The primal wo/man wakes up startled. The celestial heavens are falling down upon her. They fall and fall until they are hovering just above where she lies. In her fright, she starts to sit up and pierces these heavens and finds herself in another world, where the vaults of the heavens are high as they should be. But soon they, too, begin to fall and sit just barely above her head.
>
> Startled even more, she sits up further and finds herself in a third world, where the heavens are held in their rightful place. Then they, too, begin to collapse upon her. She pierces them into yet another world, where she espies the first ceremonial lodge. She enters it and finds ceremonial gear laid

out for her. She takes these sacred animal rattles, masks, and dancing regalia as an inner voice tells her their use. She lies back down, and descends to the first world, where she creates a replica lodge and enacts the first ceremonies in the bottom world. The skies have stayed in place to this day. (My very free paraphrase of Seattle Art Museum Yu'pik installation, 1998.)

The lore of the Yu'piks is full of parallel stories of falling and rising worlds, descending and ascending spirits. The universal pattern of these tales intimates that we are all on esoteric journeys which, while they may begin in the everyday world, soon cross over into the mystical. Jung suggests the same in his language of the *Unus Mundus*—one world of transcendent divinity where personal and transpersonal, sacred and profane, are irrelevant distinctions.[25]

> The New Testament parable of The Prodigal Son tells the same cosmic tale: the involution of spirit into the lower realms of separation and suffering, and then the evolution of return back to source and jubilant reunion.

By *transcendence*, then, we mean extending or expanding the limits of our ordinary consciousness or experience in ways that connect us with a symbolic or phenomenal reality beyond the ordinary. It may mean expanding our ordinary sense of ourselves, who we identify ourselves to be and the nature of our relationships with visible and invisible others. By *immanence* we mean contracting our attention and immersing deep into the phenomenal world and all that lies in and below it, visible and invisible.

Of course, a wonderful irony unites these two seemingly opposite tendencies. For example, Montgomery[26] set out to identify the behaviors of the most successful nurses. In her research, these were defined to be nurses identified by other nurses as being exceptional at their work. The research pointed to the fact that what set them apart from ordinary nurses was, instead of identifiable behaviors, a way of being. She found that the best caregivers expressed a sense of transcendence, the experience of being part of a larger whole, and a spiritual base for their work (usually not stated in the language of specific spiritual or religious approaches).

These nurses were intimately involved with patients on emotional and spiritual levels, and, as a result, they experienced helping as a source of energy rather than of burnout. These exceptional caregivers were the ones most involved with their patients; Montgomery referred to this finding as a "paradoxical aspect of caregiving." Finding a transcendent basis for professional service and being deeply involved with those in our care opens us up to a source of energy and sustenance that reduces burnout. A transpersonal context combines deep immersion (immanence) in the world with a sense of transcendence that gives it profound meaning. And it does matter in the outcomes of caregiving, and, it turns out, in a similar way in the world of teaching as well.[27]

This can be observed in the current cultural focus on environmental psychology and green spirituality, which leads to a conception of transcendence as horizontal rather than vertical; that is, we transcend the mundane through even deeper connection with and responsibility for the life of the earth.

"Naturally, this approach to transcendence and contingency is clearly historical and the product of a particular sort of culture and worldview. But minds nurtured in this tradition find it an almost irresistible way of understanding how meaning becomes Meaning as the deeds of daily life are subsumed under some sort of transcendence. Eliade brilliantly adapted this structure to elucidate the religious meaning of myth and ritual in *The Sacred and the Profane*."[28] "In planting his yams or repairing his canoe in the manner the gods originally performed these tasks, the tribesman is able to live in a space of Ultimate Meaning as he goes through motions that otherwise would fall into the realm of mere contingency and only evanescent meaningfulness."[29]

Chapter 3

Contributing Psychologies – Brief Acknowledgements

Given the eclectic nature of transpersonal psychology and transpersonal psychotherapy, there are a great many influences on its development. It shares many similar values, common assumptions, and practical techniques with Psychosynthesis, humanistic, existential, Jungian, Gestalt, and other approaches to therapy. There are great commonalities between these approaches, and it is useful to recognize them.

We will focus in depth on only a select few. However, the following influences deserve at least to be noted with appreciation:

- William James (1842-1910) –

    William James[30], considered the father of American scientific psychology, set out to divorce his 'natural science' of psychology from 'metaphysical' concepts such as the soul or 'transcendental ego'. Yet he embraced the spiritual as a potential source of data and as a valid object of scientific inquiry. James knew Swami Vivekananda and studied his Vedanta philosophy, and he sponsored one of Vivekananda's talks at Harvard. He separated psychic from psychological science as the proper vehicle for that inquiry, and was among the founders of the American Society for Psychical Research in 1885. This ambivalent attitude toward the place of spirituality, soul, and transcendent experience in psychology continues to this day. Transpersonal psychology has arguably not been integrated into the mainstream of recognized psychology, as indicated by its lack of a Division within the American Psychological Association. James was very clear, however, about the scientific study of the numerous states of consciousness available to human beings.

> Our normal waking consciousness, rational consciousness as we call it, is but one special type of consciousness, whilst all about it, parted from it by the flimsiest of screens, there lie potential forms of consciousness entirely different. We may go through life without suspecting their existence; but apply the requisite stimulus, and at a touch they are there in their completeness, definite types of mentality which probably somewhere have their field of application and adaptation. No account of the universe in its totality can be final which leaves these other forms of consciousness quite disregarded. How to regard them is the question—for they are so discontinuous with ordinary consciousness. Yet they may determine attitudes though they cannot furnish formulas, and open a region though they fail to give a map. At any rate, they forbid a premature closing with our accounts with reality.[31]

- Sigmund Freud (1856-1939) –

Freud, of course, was the progenitor of mapping the terrain of the human conscious and unconscious mind. He postulated the id, which remains completely unconscious along with all the processes that take place in it. However, according to Freud, the id contains more than repressed material such as instinctual drives and painful realities, and is therefore not identical with the unconscious. The id contains the 'archaic heritage' and the 'constitutional factors' of the individual.[32] Separately, Carl Jung expanded and clarified the concept to include two levels or layers of the unconscious: a personal unconscious similar to Freud's id, and a collective or transpersonal unconscious which includes primordial images or archetypes.[33]

Freud deserves great credit, of course, for his intrepid explorations of the human psyche and his keen insights into the labyrinth of defenses that an individual's ego creates to avoid being exposed. Freud's genius attracted many brilliant psychologists and psychiatrists to study with him; many of them eventually left his inner circle of colleagues to found their own 'school' of thought.

- G. I. Gurdjieff (1866-1949) –

A main pillar in transpersonal psychology is the prospect of development of the ego beyond itself, to "erase itself" in Maslow's sense. One example is the Gurdjieff Work, the so-called Fourth Way tradition. "This direct spiritual work is a work on attention."[34] Gurdjieff's Work is to develop our capacity to exercise free will in the way we live life. Ordinarily, we don't really exercise free will because we're moved around unconsciously by interpersonal, psychic, archetypal, and cosmic forces. We're not really paying attention, and thus are in need of *deautomatization, detachment* and *mental freedom* through judicious application of attentional mindfulness by our *observing self*. ". . . the Bible says that a deep sleep fell upon Adam, and nowhere is there a reference to his waking up."[35] Most people are "asleep" in ego illusion, Gurdjieff warned, and his mission was to provide ways to assist people to "wake up" from that unconscious slumber.[36] As we shall see, many of the transpersonal psychologies follow a similar recognition, and dis-identifying from a mistaken belief system is the route toward ego transcendence. One of Gurdjieff's aphorisms is, "Blessed is he who has a soul, blessed is he who has none, but woe and grief to him who has it in embryo."

- Sri Aurobindo (1872-1950) –

Aurobindo, educated at Oxford University and considered a leading spiritual figure in India, offered a clear belief that human beings were more than the sum of their personality, body and consciousness. "It is becoming always clearer that not only does the capacity of our total consciousness far exceed that of our organs, the senses, the nerves, the brain, but that even for our ordinary thought and consciousness these organs are only their habitual instruments and not their generators . . . Our physical organism no more causes or explains thought and consciousness than the construction of an engine causes or explains the motive-power of steam or electricity. The force is anterior, not the physical instrument."[37]

Evolution of consciousness on earth has seen the progressive increase in sentient awareness (intelligence) from inanimate matter through unicellular organisms, plants, lower animals, mammals, and, finally, human beings. Aurobindo argues that evolution is not done; it follows that human intelligence is not the highest possible manifestation of consciousness on earth. Aurobindo coined the term "supermind" to describe the next, higher level of consciousness that he believes will manifest on earth— first and partially, in human beings as far as human nature permits, but later and fully, through a biologically transformed life form that will exceed the human being in the capacity for consciousness as far as human beings currently exceed other animals.

> One of Aurobindo's most useful ideas, both theoretically and practically, is his differentiation of the *psychic being* (the individual soul) from the *subliminal being* (a 'subtle,' or nonmaterial, complex of several layers of consciousness that stand between the soul proper and the outer nexus of mind, life, and body) (Basu, 2000). In Aurobindo's view, the subliminal dimension of human consciousness accounts for most of the reported 'paranormal' phenomena studied in parapsychology, including telepathy, precognition, out-of-body and near-death experiences, lucid dreams, Jungian 'synchronicity' (acausal meaningful coincidences), and the resurgence of Jungian archetypes from the collective unconscious. From the Aurobindonian perspective, Jung's memoirs (Jung, 1961) reveal a richly developed subliminal awareness.[38]

The *psychic being*, the true soul, is an individual portion or delegate of the supreme being/reality that is immortal, but that also evolves through the process of reincarnation as it grows in its capacity to manifest the divine consciousness in the world. Direct connections can be drawn between Aurobindo's spiritual psychology and the work of Carl Jung, Roberto Assagioli, Ken Wilber and other modern transpersonal psychologists.

- Carl Jung (1875-1961) –

Jung was an early colleague of Freud, and eventually broke off his association with Freud's theories of sexual drive being the predominant motivation for psychic behavior. Jung proposed that the human psyche exists in three parts: the ego (the conscious mind), the personal unconscious and the collective unconscious. Jung believed the collective unconscious was a reservoir of the accumulated experience and knowledge of the human species. Jung also believed that it is essential for a person to become whole and fully developed as a human being, integrating the various parts of a person, including the conscious and unconscious. He called the process of an individual becoming his or her "true self" through this integration *individuation*. Jung popularized the concepts of introversion and extraversion, shadows (suppressed behavioral patterns), complexes (splinter personalities) and many other commonly accepted psychological concepts. Jung's work lies at the heart of much of the current transpersonal psychology field.

Singer describes Jung as

> a transitional figure between the dynamic psychiatry of Freud and the ego psychology of his followers and the new field of transpersonal psychology, which deals primarily with those aspects of the person that extend beyond ego consciousness. Jung's psychology involves taking into consideration human yearnings toward a spiritual path in which an individual experiences the self as a whole organism: body, mind, and spirit. Jung's model of the person has been expanded by transpersonal theorists to include at least 4 dimensions: expansion of consciousness, freedom from social conditioning, disidentification from roles, and the focus more on the context of consciousness than on its contents.[39]

Jung stands with Wilhelm Reich, Alexander Lowen, Arthur Janov and other pioneers in the field of the mind-body continuum in establishing the body and somatic experience as a fruitful domain for exploration of the psyche. Jung said: "Of course, it sounds funny, but I start from the conviction that man has also a living body and if something is true for one side, it must be true for the other. For what is the body? The body is merely the visibility of the soul, the psyche; and the soul is the psychological experience of the body. So it is really one and the same thing."[40]

Jung holds that whereas the first half of life is an unconscious, natural process, the second half of life should be a process in which one has to make a conscious effort, the process he called individuation. Jung claims that the transition leading from the first half of life to the second is "a transformation of nature into culture, of instinct into spirit."[41] Nature and culture are, for Jung, respectively biological and spiritual aspects of the human being. The tasks of the second half of life are to integrate the unconscious with consciousness; to face, work on, and resolve the complexes in the unconscious by making them conscious; and to work on realizing the whole personality for the sake of developing one's full potential. These tasks could all be seen as paths to gaining an *objective* view of oneself[42] and together they summarize the basic tenets of today's transpersonal psychology.

- Alfred Adler (1870-1937) –

Adler, founder of Individual Psychology, is not often cited as a contributor to transpersonal psychology, although his notion of the "creative self" was a foundational influence on Abraham Maslow. Adler suggested that there was a power within the human personality that was truly creative in nature – capable of displaying abilities that were record-breaking, that set new standards, and liberated one from normal limitations of mind and body. This creative self at the core of human personality inspired Maslow's emphasis on mental health and human potential, self-actualization and peak experiences. Adler's "creative self" was truly a transpersonal perspective of the human psyche: the active, unifying principle of human life that provides the basic components of one's personality. Personality theorists Hall and Lindzey compare Adler's concept of the "creative self" to the older concept of soul.[43]

- Otto Rank (1884–1939) –

Rank was a close colleague of Freud for twenty years. At the age of forty, Rank wrote *The Trauma of Birth*, emphasizing the mother-child relationship and the profound influence of the birth experience. It was a departure from Freud's father-centered approach to neurosis and the Oedipus complex. In 1926 he moved to Paris, where he met Henry Miller and Anais Nin, who wrote about her therapy with Rank and their subsequent love affair. He is considered by many to be an early humanistic psychologist and feminist. By extending the study of human development back to prenatal and perinatal experience, Rank anticipated the transpersonal work of Stan Grof forty years later.

The theologian Mathew Fox says of Rank: "He died a feminist and deeply committed to social justice, in 1939....His deep understanding of creativity makes him a mentor for all of us living in a postmodern world....I believe that *Art and Artist*, especially chapters 12 to 14, may well emerge as the most valuable psychoanalysis of the spiritual life in our time."[+44]

- Jiddu Krishnamurti (1895-1986) –

Krishnamurti was a well-known speaker and writer in the East and in the West. In his early adolescence, he met prominent theosophist Charles Leadbeater at the Theosophical Society headquarters in Madras. He was subsequently raised under the tutelage of Annie Besant and Leadbeater, leaders of the Society at the time, who believed him to be destined to become a 'World Teacher'. Some years later, he disavowed this idea and dissolved the Order of the Star in the East, an organization that had been established to support the project.

Krishnamurti stressed the importance of learning through self-awareness, achieving a freedom from preconceptions, formulas and authority, all conditioning by family and society, emphasizing the need to "take a leap into the dark".[45] "From his observations Krishnamurti has noted that we cannot arrive at understanding through creeds and dogmas, philosophical inquiry or psychological techniques, but only through an awareness of the content of our mind as it is mirrored in relationship; through an observation and understanding which does not involve intellectual analysis or introspective dissection."[46]

> Thought always cuts up what it observes into fragments within space – as you and me, yours and mine, me and my thoughts and so on. This space, which thought has created between what it observes, has become real; and it is this space that divides. Then thought tries to build a bridge over this division, thus playing a trick upon itself all the time, deceiving itself and hoping for unity.[47]

- Wilhelm Reich (1897-1957) –

Wilhelm Reich was a member of the second generation of psychoanalysts after Freud, with Otto Rank, Carl Jung, Roberto Assagioli, Heinz Hartmann and others. He innovated the inclusion of muscular armoring into analysis; he called it character armor – the expression of the personality in the way the body moves.[48] He incorporated a form of deeper, freer breathing as a part of his therapy to break through emotional inhibition and repressed memories. Reich's work was later developed further as body psychotherapy, Fritz Perls' Gestalt therapy, Alexander Lowen's bioenergetic analysis, and Arthur Janov's primal therapy. Reich's focus was not so much to produce catharsis in therapy, as to reduce the defensiveness that prevents such expression. Lowen said, "only through breathing deeply and fully can one summon the energy for a more spirited and spiritual life."[49]

- Fritz Perls (1893-1970) –

Perls was born in Germany and grew up in the bohemian scene in Berlin, including its artistic avant-garde and revolutionary leftist politics. He joined the German Army during World War I, and spent time on the front lines. In 1927, Perls became a member of Wilhelm Reich's technical seminars in Vienna, where Reich's concept of character analysis influenced Perls to a large extent. In 1930 Reich became Perls' supervising senior analyst in Berlin. Perls fled the rise of Hitler's Nazi anti-semitism in the 1930s, and emigrated to South Africa, where he became a noted psychiatrist and psychotherapist. He eventually settled in New York after World War II, where he and his wife Laura Perls started the first Gestalt Institute in their Manhattan apartment. Perls used the term 'Gestalt therapy' to identify the form of psychotherapy that he developed in the 1940s and 1950s: the core of the Gestalt Therapy process is enhanced awareness of sensation, perception, bodily feelings, emotion, and behavior, in the present moment. Perls spent most of the 1960s living at Esalen, where he collaborated with Ida Rolf, founder of Rolfing Structural Integration, to address the relationship between the mind and the body.

- Heinz Hartmann (1894-1970) –

Hartmann, a respected follower of Freud, a psychiatrist and analyst in Vienna, published an article in 1939 that represents a turning point in the development of modern psychoanalytic theory. Hartmann's ideas have shaped, and become assimilated into, current psychoanalytic thinking to a remarkable degree. In this essay he first introduced the pivotal concepts of the conflict-free ego sphere, conflict-free ego development, and primary and secondary autonomy. His theory foresaw the development of the concepts of ego strength and ego weakness. In the same year, in "Psychoanalysis and the

Concept of Health", he made a unique and important contribution to defining normality and health in psychoanalytic terms, which had focused almost exclusively on psychopathology.

Primary autonomous ego functions, such as the cognitive functions of perception, intelligence, thinking, comprehension, language, learning, and the synthetic function ("the centralization of functional control" or personality integration) are innate, inherited ego characteristics, and are conflict-free. Secondary autonomous ego functions are those functions that were once involved in developmental conflicts, such as oral, anal, or phallic/oedipal and were freed as a result of the resolution of those conflicts through the process of neutralization. In other words, when energies embroiled in conflict are neutralized through resolving the conflict, a transformation occurs so that those energies are freed from contamination with conflict.[50] This concept presages the advent of emphasis on normal psychological health and ego strength later embraced by humanistic and positive psychology, and the more recent concept of archetypal center core phenomena.[51]

- Aldous Huxley (1894-1963) –

Aldous Huxley, one of the great modern thinkers, philosophers, and social commentators of the 20th century, is often hailed as an inspirational figure of the Human Potential Movement and the subsequent development of transpersonal psychology. He wrote the groundbreaking novel *Brave New World* (1932), the non-fiction *The Doors of Perception* (1954) in which he recalls experiences when taking a psychedelic drug, and *The Perennial Philosophy* (1945), a work often credited as one of the early pillars of transpersonal theory. Ken Wilber has built his integral philosophy largely on Huxley's work. Recently, transpersonal scholars have initiated a debate regarding Wilber's acceptance of Huxley's perennial philosophy, noting, instead, the importance of "participatory spiritual pluralism".[52] Huxley died on November 22, 1963 (the same day as the assassination of President John F. Kennedy) just as he had lived: in an experiment of expanding consciousness. As he was dying, Huxley asked his wife Laura to administer LSD to him. She honored his wishes.

- Carl Rogers (1902-1987) –

Rogers was an influential American psychologist and among the founders of the humanistic approach to psychology, which he referred to as a client-centered or person-centered approach. Rogers' theory of the self is considered to be existential. He was strongly influenced in constructing his client-centered approach by the post-Freudian psychotherapeutic practice of Otto Rank. Rogers published sixteen books; his best known was *On Becoming a Person* in 1961. His contributions to the field include the perspective that the best vantage point for understanding behavior is from the internal frame of reference of the individual; recognizing the split between the 'real self' as the aspect of one's being that is founded in the actualizing tendency, and the 'ideal self' which is a self-imposed standard impossible to meet; valuing openness to experience as a trait; and suggesting that people have one basic tendency and striving – to actualize, maintain and enhance their life.

He had a passion for social justice, and was among those who questioned the rise of McCarthyism in the 1950s. Rogers' last years were devoted to applying his theories in situations of political oppression and national social conflict, traveling worldwide to do so. In Belfast, Northern Ireland, he brought together influential Protestants and Catholics; in apartheid South Africa, blacks and whites; in Brazil people emerging from dictatorship to democracy; in the United States, consumers and providers in the health field. His last trip, at age 85, was to the Soviet Union, where he lectured and facilitated intensive experiential workshops fostering communication and creativity.

- Viktor Frankl (1905-1997) –

  Frankl was a Neurologist and psychiatrist, founder of Logotherapy and Existential Analysis, and was a Holocaust survivor. During World War II, Frankl spent 3 years in various concentration camps, including Theresienstadt, Auschwitz, and Dachau. His book, *Man's Search for Meaning*[53] was first published in 1946 under the title *Nevertheless, Say "Yes" to Life: A Psychologist Experiences the Concentration Camp*. Those two book titles convey the essence of his emphasis on the importance of finding meaning in all forms of existence, even the most brutal ones, and his underlying optimism about life and humankind.

  Frankl identified himself as an existentialist, and he once observed[54], "Self-actualization occurs spontaneously; it is contravened when it is made an end in itself." He used this story to convey the message:

  > Generally, one assumes that a boomerang always returns to the hunter; but actually, I have been told in Australia, a boomerang only comes back to the hunter when it has missed its target. Well, man also only returns to himself, to being concerned with his self, after he has missed his mission, has failed to find a meaning in his life.[55]

  Frankl[56] asserted that the core of each person's search for meaning in life involves a process of self-transcendence (other-directed mission or purpose), identifying one of the most basic premises of transpersonal psychology.

- Abraham Maslow (1908-1970) –

  Maslow was a dynamic psychologist. He stressed the importance of focusing on the positive qualities in people, as opposed to treating them as a "bag of symptoms." At Columbia University, Maslow met Alfred Adler, who became a mentor in developing a new and unique psychology emphasizing mental health and human potential, the hierarchy of needs and metamotivation, self-actualization and peak experiences.

Maslow wrote in his book *Toward a Psychology of Being* in 1968, "It is as if Freud supplied us the sick half of psychology and we must now fill it out with the healthy half." In the spring of 1961, Maslow and Tony Sutich founded the *Journal of Humanistic Psychology*, and by 1969 they collaborated to create and publish *The Journal of Transpersonal Psychology*.

Maslow began using the term "peak experiences" for mystical experiences and other experiences of optimal psychological health. Eventually he introduced the term "plateau experiences" for positive experiences that are of longer duration and lower intensity than peak experiences. Meditative states and quiet reverie are examples. He also made mention of "nadir experiences," intensely negative experiences which turn around into positive experiences.

In 1968, Maslow called attention to the limitations of the humanistic model. In exploring the farther reaches of human nature, he found that there were possibilities beyond self-actualization. When peak experiences are especially powerful, the sense of self dissolves into an awareness of a greater unity. The term self-actualization did not seem to fit these experiences, and he began using the term transcending self-actualization. This lead him to the notion of self-transcendence, which became a key part of Maslow's thinking and the roots of transpersonal psychology.

- Rollo May (1909-1994) –

May helped to introduce Existentialism to American psychology in the 1950s. He blended the European existential philosophy of Søren Kierkegaard with a compassionate humanism influence from his close friend Paul Tillich, the philosopher and theologian. May considered Otto Rank to be the most important clinical precursor of existential therapy. One of the driving themes of May's research and work was the debilitating effect that anxiety plays in short circuiting one's living authentically, and the role of will in resolving that deficiency. As May conceived it, anxiety is the experience of a threat to some value which the individual holds essential to his existence as a self, yet that experience of threat can become a defense against authentic living.[57] He quotes Kierkegaard: "Anxiety is the dizziness of freedom."

Another related core theme for May was the internal split in the psyche of modern man: "*Existentialism, in short, is the endeavor to understand man by cutting below the cleavage between subject and object which has bedeviled Western thought and science since shortly after the Renaissance*....[this has been called] the cancer of all psychology up to now... the cancer of the doctrine of subject-object cleavage of the world."[58] This insight presages the focus of later humanistic and transpersonal psychologies on transcending the ego, and on the nondual alternatives offered by Eastern psychologies. "However, this radical thought has proved so foreign to the Western worldview and poses such a profound challenge to our modern idolatry of the self, that it has remained dormant at the edges of psychological thought these many decades, beckoning, but not taken to heart."[59]

- Alan Watts (1915-1973) –

Watts was on the forefront of introducing Eastern spirituality and Buddhism to America, publishing his first popular book, *The Way of Zen*, in 1957. He actually published his first book, *The Spirit of Zen*, in 1936, but later denounced it as unscholarly, out of date and misleading. In *Psychotherapy East and West*[60], he distinguished Buddhism as a psychology rather than a religion, and proposed that it could be used as a form of psychotherapy. In 1956, Alan Watts established the California Institute for Asian Studies, the first formal organization to offer graduate study in Eastern religion, philosophy, and psychology.

- James Bugental (1915-2008) –

Bugental was considered to be the creator, along with Rollo May, of existential-humanistic psychotherapy, and with Abraham Maslow and others, of humanistic psychology. In 1963, he published a landmark article in *American Psychologist* —"Humanistic Psychology: A New Breakthrough" – which presented the fundamental assumptions of humanistic psychology to American psychologists. He elaborated on those fundamentals in his first book, *The Search for Authenticity*:
  - Human beings cannot be reduced to components.
  - Human beings have in them a uniquely human context.
  - Human consciousness includes an awareness of oneself in the context of other people.
  - Human beings have choices and responsibilities.
  - Human beings are intentional, they seek meaning, value and creativity.

- Stan Grof (1931-) –

Grof's[61] contributions to the field of transpersonal psychology are many. One vitally important one is the inclusion of the prenatal and perinatal experiences of a human being as formative in lifelong belief and behavior patterns. These experiences also include karmic influences experienced as past lives. Grof postulates *condensed experiences* (COEX), matrices at crucial moments in intrauterine development, and that these critical moments can be accessed in deep regressive non-ordinary states of consciousness. Death and near-death experiences are another transpersonal realm that Grof has championed in terms of exploration and acknowledgment of the profound impact they have on human development. Grof[62] began working as a psychiatrist with psychedelic drugs, particularly LSD, in the treatment of psychopathology, and in the process discovered the access they provided into the deep recesses of the human mind. He has also expanded the horizons of the transpersonal psychology field of study to incorporate such diverse realms as Archetypal Astrology[63] and the Akashic Field.[64] Grof has been very practical in seeking techniques to open access to the transpersonal realms, from LSD to holotropic breathwork which combines quick breathing, holotropic practices, and evocative music to enter non-ordinary states.

Grof has urged the use of different language for "altered states of consciousness"[65] because of its implied one-sided emphasis on the distortion or impairment of the "correct way" of experiencing oneself and the world. Even the somewhat better term " non-ordinary states of consciousness" is inadequate for transpersonal science, since it could include deliria caused by infectious diseases, tumors, abuse of alcohol, or circulatory and degenerative diseases of the brain. These alterations of consciousness are associated with disorientation and impairment of intellectual functions. Grof has suggested the use of the term *holotropic* for the large subgroup of non-ordinary states of consciousness that are of great importance to transpersonal psychology, spiritual development, shamanic and mystical exploration, and transpersonal therapy. Holotropic refers to "oriented toward wholeness" or "moving toward wholeness", in the same way that *heliotropism* refers to the property of plants to always move in the direction of the sun.

Lenny Gibson[66] summarizes Grof's contribution to the field in this way:

> Contrary to Freud's mechanistic determinism, Grof represents the birth experience as the ontological ground on which the archetypes are sown, an organic ground that is the original instance of human experience. The archetypes manifest in the Shadow with a power that reflects the force and intensity of human birth experience. The development of depth psychology can be presented in three stages, using the classic philosophical theme of universals and particulars:
>   1.   Freud discovers the unconscious and bases individual psychology on it.

2. Jung brings the archetypal universals to light and opens psychology to the transpersonal realm.
3. Grof reveals the ontological process whereby universals become actualized in the particular individual.

- Ken Wilber (1949-) –

In 1973 Wilber completed his first book, *The Spectrum of Consciousness*, in which he sought to integrate knowledge from across disciplines (psychology, anthropology, sociology, mythology, comparative religion, cosmology, evolutionary theory) and across history (ancient to modern). Sri Aurobindo, various Buddhist teachings, and the "perennial philosophy" have been important influences. He was a central theorist in the development of transpersonal psychology as a distinct discipline; he has published more than a dozen articles in the *Journal of Transpersonal Psychology* beginning in 1975 and also helped to launch the journal *ReVision* in 1978. The essence of Wilber's integrative model of Transpersonal Psychology is this: "psychological growth or development in humans is simply a microcosmic reflection of universal growth on the whole and has the same goal: the unfolding of ever higher-order unities and integrations."[67]

The human self develops from "a pre-personal subconscious (characterized by an awareness of nature and body) to self-consciousness (an awareness of mind and psychic realities) and finally to transpersonal superconsciousness (an awareness of subtle, causal and ultimate realities). The evolving self has three components: a basic structure (enduring characteristics such as linguistics, cognition, spatial coordination, etc.); transitional structures (characteristics that develop and dissolve such as world-views, self needs, moral stages, etc.); and the self and its fulcrums (characteristics that unite and integrate the other two components, such as identification, organization, will, defense, and 'digestion of experience') (Wilber, 1997, p. 142-144)."[68] Wilber also identifies the pre-personal level of development as survival oriented, the personal level as concerned with belonging, and the transpersonal level as the ultimate concern of spiritual advancement.

In Wilber's system, a human being develops along at least a dozen quasi-independent *developmental lines* which include the affective, cognitive, moral, spiritual, interpersonal, and object-relations components of the human experience. The *self* juggles these developmental lines, each of which advances at its own pace, sometimes allowing one to become very advanced along one line but developmentally arrested in another. *Translation* is the process of integrating, stabilizing and equilibrating the different developmental lines, considered a function of horizontal development. *Transformation* is the process of transcending one level of consciousness and advancing vertically to the next higher level. *Development* occurs in the tension between the horizontal and vertical dimensions of human maturation.

Wilber has formulated the goal of development into the Integrated Self: *"differentiated* from (or disidentified from, or transcended) an *exclusive* identification with body, persona, ego, and mind, it can now *integrate* them in a unified fashion, in a new and higher holon with each of them as junior partners."[69] This summarizes the emphasis on transcending self-actualization throughout today's transpersonal psychology.

- Perennial Wisdom Teachings –

The Perennial Philosophy has had a powerful influence on many of the transpersonal theorists, especially Ken Wilber. In the early 19th century this idea was popularized by the Transcendentalists. Toward the end of the 19th century the Theosophical Society further promoted the concept under the name of "Ancient Wisdom" through Madame Blavatsky's book *The Key to Theosophy*.[70] In the 20th century it was brought to the attention of many more in the general public by Aldous

Huxley's book *The Perennial Philosophy*.[71] A basic tenet of the Perennial Philosophy is that each world religion is an interpretation of one and the same universal truth regarding the ultimate purpose of human life. Humankind's final end lies in the knowledge of the immanent and transcendent Ground of all being, the presence of divine Reality that can be experienced, and in that experiencing is transformation.

- Transpersonal Feminism

A core concept in feminist psychology is *relationality*, i.e., the theory that we, as human beings, grow and develop through relationship and not in individual vacuums of experience. *Relational-Cultural Theory* is a feminist construct that makes prominent the need for and value of interpersonal relationship in healthy psychological development.[72] Additionally, feminist psychology highlights the necessity of focusing on *subjectivity*, i.e., the actual lived experience of women in order to build theory and practice that will serve diverse populations of women.[73] And so these approaches accentuate a holistic model of identity, recognizing the role of the sociopolitical and environmental milieu in a woman's experience of self. "Contemporary Western feminism and transpersonalism are kaleidoscopic, consisting of interlocking influences, yet the fields have developed in parallel rather than in tandem."[74]

> As a field of study, feminism, in its many forms, centers scholarship around the experiences of women and issues of vital importance to women's lives and well-being, such as economic justice, reproductive freedom, and freedom from harm and discrimination. With regard to areas of focus in much transpersonal scholarship, including states of consciousness, psychospiritual development, extraordinary human experiences, and psychological well-being, considerations of the differences men and women may experience are vastly underrepresented in the literature.[75]

> Michael Daniels (2005) suggested that the field of transpersonal psychology has relied heavily on

aspects of theory and practice historically related to
an *ascending* (transcendent) model of psychospiritual
development rather than a *descending* (immanent)
model. Daniels went on to argue that ascending
models value the masculine while descending models
are often related to aspects traditionally related to
feminine qualities.[76]

This is a very important point for further discussion. We
have already addressed, and will return to the differences
and relatedness of ascending and descending paths,
transcendence and immanence. Being such a
foundational building block in the psychology of the
transpersonal, it is incumbent on all of us to carefully
scrutinize this distinction for gender or cultural bias.

> Feminism is, and has been from its inception, a
> collection of many movements. What is generally
> referred to as second wave feminism developed out
> of four major sub-categories: *liberal feminism* (or
> *equality feminism*), *radical feminism*, *socialist
> feminism* (or *material feminism*), and *cultural
> feminism*. . . . The prominent social and political
> work of radical feminism pursues the elimination of
> violence against women and highlights issues of
> sexuality—most notably the issues of rape and
> pornography—and the effects these two elements
> have on women (Dworkin, 1981; MacKinnon
> 1982/1993). Three major contributions of cultural
> feminism are: (a) the celebration and honoring of
> motherhood; (b) a resurgence of women's
> spirituality, including the resurrection of goddess
> traditions; and (c) re-evaluations and reformations of
> traditional philosophies of knowledge such as strict
> empiricism, materialism, and logical positivism
> (Alpert, 1973; Starhawk, 1979/1999; Wilshire, 1989;
> Lips, 1999).[77]

The feminist as well as the transpersonal approach to
psychology tends to honor the values of egalitarianism,
mutuality, multiple viewpoints, and a respect for
subjective experience. In fact, these are the qualities that
inform two transpersonal research methods which
embrace explicitly feminist epistemologies: intuitive
inquiry and organic inquiry.[78] We discuss these methods

in the chapter on Transpersonal Psychology in Higher Education. Intuitive inquiry is a research process which relies on intuition and empathic identification to analyze the objective and subjective data collected and reflected on.[79] Organic inquiry also stands at the intersection of feminine spirituality and transpersonal psychology, motivated by a desire on the part of the researcher to investigate and share the meaning of her or his own deeply-held experience, and by a desire for social and individual transformation for the researcher, the co-researchers (research subjects), and the readers of the research.[80] Organic inquiry "utilizes nature metaphor such as the cycle of planting, growth, and harvest to highlight non-rational processes available to the researcher as well as synchronistic experiences that may arise while the research is being conducted and reported."[81]

- Afrocentric Psychology

    Recognition of the upper reaches of psychological development supports the investigation of optimal positive well-being and higher states of consciousness. This awareness has always been characteristic of non-Western psychologies: Asian (Buddhist, Hindu, Taoist), indigenous (shamanism), and African (Egyptian, shamanism). However, an exploration of traditional African culture and worldview appears to be conspicuously minimized in the literature of transpersonal psychology.

    > The Afrocentric conceptual system of the paradigm is truly holistic, because ontologically it assumes reality to be both spiritual and material at once. In this regard everything becomes one thing, spirit manifesting. Spirit refers to that permeating essence that is known in an extrasensory fashion (e.g., energy, consciousness, God).[82]

    That the nature of reality is perceived to be both spiritual and material at once, speaks to a type of logic that emphasizes the union of opposites, diunital logic, common to all the paradigms within the purview of transpersonal psychology. Another commonality employing a spiritual/material union is the concept of extended self. Self in the African paradigm includes all of the ancestors, the yet unborn, all of nature, and the entire community.[83] In other words, the holotropic concept of the whole being somehow contained in each of its parts is basic to the African perspective as well as to virtually all transpersonal psychologies. An example of this concept within African thought is Nommo (the power of the word) and the belief that one had not 'died' until the last person who knew him/her by name has 'died'. Then the person was believed to enter the realm of ancestral spirits (universal consciousness).

And so the extended self is a *community within*: "the person should be visualized as a centrifugal force capable of emanating other complex selves that can interpermeate each other as well as other selves generated from other persona-communal centers. The idea of communal interconnection not only promotes the idea of persons within community but also creates a more holistic conception of the person *as* community."[84]

> It is also important to note in this regard that what is being advocated is at this point not exclusively African, nor could or should it be, if the paradigm/theory is valid. The point is that the conceptual system seems to have originated in Africa (Diop, 1974; James, 1954; ben-Jochannon, 1970) and among Black people who would in modern context likely be labeled of African descent. Equally important, however, it is in the process of people of African descent (African-Americans) rediscovering their heritage that this way of viewing life in total is recaptured, and is consequently termed Afrocentric.[85]

What is an Afrocentric perspective? An example of an attempt to define it is the statement of unique experience of transcendence among Africans in the West, based on Sudicism, the spiritual commitment to an ideological view of harmony. Once again we want to recognize a particular perspective on the interconnectedness of ascending and descending paths, transcendence and immanence. In African practices in the West, immersion in somatic rhythms (immanence) drives one toward transcendence.

> The African view is the Sudic Ideal; i.e., the totality of the indigenous African religions; it is the fundamental basis of all African wholism. The African American is to a degree a most Westernized African, yet has retained the Sudic Ideal of harmony, achieved by rhythm, and passed on to other cultures. There is a unique experience of transcendence among Africans in the West, whether they are Cubans, Brazilians, Haitians, Jamaicans, Ecuadorians, or citizens of the United States; they share forms of the same experience in *Samba* the Brazilian dance, *Sango* the Cuban folk religion, *Umbanda* the Brazilian folk religion, *Voodoo* the Haitian folk religion, or *Mya!* a Jamaican religion. At the center of all of these forms of human expression is the same source of energy, the rhythm or polyrhythms that drive the spirit towards transcendence.[86]

Psychology and spirituality influences from the ancient and long standing African worldview are deeply embedded in today's transpersonal psychology. These include holism, i.e., reality is both spiritual and material at once, and therefore everything is spirit manifesting; the concept of extended self, i.e., the individual person incorporates the community in its broadest sense; the holotropic concept of the whole being contained in each of its parts; the recognition of complex selves within, presaging the concepts of ego states and subpersonalities; the understanding of how the community, rhythm and physical movement contribute to harmony for the individual and the community; and the importance and meaning of transcendence.

- Buddhist Psychology –

In 1960, D. T. Suzuki, a Japanese Zen master, collaborated with psychiatrist Erich Fromm to produce the first major synthesis of psychoanalysis and Buddhist thought.[87] They began a dialogue that has greatly influenced the development of transpersonal psychology.

"The essence of agnostic Buddhist psychology, as [Mark Epstein, 1995] explains, lies in using mindfulness (open awareness of the moment) and *vipassana* meditation (focused concentration) to reveal the 'self' as a fluid construct that has no permanent, objective identity. In order to be able to observe one's own psychological processes with such detachment requires, as a foundation, the development of what the analytic tradition calls a well-functioning observing ego. Epstein thus resolves the implicit tension between the Buddhist quest for 'no self' and the psychotherapeutic mission to build a mature ego, by proposing that Buddhist meditation practices do not literally ablate the ego, but rather develop the observing ego in ways that therapy alone does not."[88]

- Hindu Psychology and Kundalini Energy –

The pre-personal and personal stages of identity formation are based primarily on recognized Western psychology and psychoanalytic principles, and transpersonal stages of development are based primarily on spiritual and mystical experiences described by Jung and both Western and Eastern spiritual traditions.[89] Vaughan, Wittine, and Walsh[90], in a chapter in the APA published book *Religion and the Clinical Practice of Psychology*, tend to see the Hindu experience of a transcendent self (*atman*) as being psychologically equivalent to the enlightenment (*satori*, Buddhamind, or original-mind) of Buddhism, and perhaps the optimal Transpersonal Self referenced by Assagioli, Jung, Grof, Wilber and others.

Kundalini is considered to be the developmental force that unfolds humans to their fullest physio-spiritual maturity.[91] The Kundalini energy activates energy centers along the spine when it is raised from its resting position in the first or root chakra at the base of the spine. This usually occurs through specific meditation oriented practices, although it can occur spontaneously and unexpectedly, resulting in a disruption of psychological functioning termed by Grof a *spiritual emergency*.[92]

• Kabbalah and Jewish Mysticism –

According to the traditional understanding, the Kabbalah dates from Eden. It came down from a remote past as a revelation to a select few Tzadikim (righteous people), and, for the most part, was preserved only through oral transmission as an esoteric wisdom by a privileged few. The Kabbalah emerged, after these earlier forms of Jewish mysticism, in 12th- to 13th-century Southern France and Spain, where its concepts were recorded in evocative imagery that evolved into the original Tarot cards. This was to keep the esoteric wisdom contained in the teachings secret, and to disguise the true content from the authorities who were oppressing Jews at the time through the Inquisition.

Throughout the reaches of transpersonal psychology, through many cultural approaches, a consistent conceptualization of advancement involves three stages of refinement. Generically we refer to them as pre-personal, personal, and transpersonal. One way of describing the progression or expansion of an individual's soul is provided in the Kabbalah, with the soul progressing (or not) through five stages: the nefesh, ruach, neshamah, chayyah, and yehidah. The nefesh is the lower or animal part of the soul. It links to instincts and bodily cravings. It is found in all humans, and enters the physical body at conception. It is the source of one's physical and psychological nature. The next two parts of the soul are slowly created over time; their development depends on the actions and beliefs of the individual. They are said to only fully exist in people awakened spiritually. The ruach is the middle soul. It contains the moral virtues and the ability to distinguish between good and evil. It equates to psyche or ego-personality. The neshamah is the higher soul, Higher Self or super-soul. This distinguishes humans from all other life forms. It relates to the intellect, and allows humans to enjoy and benefit from the afterlife. It allows one to have some awareness of the existence and presence of God. After death nefesh disintegrates, ruach is sent to an intermediate zone where it is submitted to purification and enters into "temporary paradise," while neshamah returns to the source where it enjoys "the kiss of the beloved." The chayyah is the part of the soul that allows one to have an awareness of the divine life force itself. And yehidah is the highest plane of the soul, in which one can achieve full union with God.

Jewish mysticism has always incorporated teachings about the transcendent realms available to individuals.[93] For example, a technique of 'mystical weeping' is used to "establish contact with other realms."[94] There is a long history of Jewish mystical practices, known from the thirteenth century up until today. These include trance, meditation, and shamanistic practices conducted within the context of various metaphysical Kabbalistic schools.[95] The Torah provides many examples of mythic and mystical revelations: the prophet Ezekiel's visions, Isaiah's Temple vision, Jacob's vision of the ladder to heaven, Moses' encounters with the burning bush and God on Mount Sinai, and many more. The implication is that first these visions, revelations, and mystical encounters are legitimate sources of knowledge; and second that they are available to anyone given the right circumstances. Both of these premises are basic to our current understanding of transpersonal psychology, and lend to them the authority of ancient wisdom.

- Native American Traditions –

From the Perennial Philosophy and from African, Hindu, Buddhist, and Kabbalistic influences, transpersonal psychology has gained a particular approach to individual mystical experience, recognizing the unique nature of any person's encounter with the ineffable, and discovering the role of tradition and ceremony in accessing those non-ordinary states. Another important aspect of the transpersonal perspective is respect for the intricate interrelatedness of all things, the sacredness of all relationships. *Mitakuye Oyasin* is a Lakota expression meaning "All my relations", and is used in ceremonies to remember just that web of interrelatedness. We can find here a direct connection with the transpersonal phenomena known as "multilocal participatory events"[96] emergences of transpersonal being in which a transpersonal phenomenon can occur in different locations, such as an individual, a relationship, a community, a collective identity, or a place. It is participatory in that all dimensions of one's human nature interact with spiritual powers to co-create spiritual worlds. This mutual participation requires a transformation of the self, and paradoxically it is through that participation that transformation occurs.

> The spiritual traditions and religions of North American Indians are numerous and diverse and defy easy categorization or understanding. . . . However, there is an underlying belief that informs most Indian spiritual practice: 'the belief in the existence of unseen powers. These powers may take the form of *deities* or these powers may be more of a 'feeling' that something exists and is sacred and mysterious' (Beck, Walters, and Francisco 1996, 9). . . . Indian religions, because of their overarching emphasis on individual visionary experiences, are mystical at their cores. Many Indian peoples were and are dreamers, visionaries, and mystics in animated worlds full of spirits. Indians have encouraged the seeking of visions and dreams through various practices and beliefs.[97]

We trace clearly the contributions by North American Native peoples of recognition of the intricate interrelatedness of all things, of the reality of co-creation with the spirit world, and of practices that transform the individual sufficiently to allow mutual participation with the spirit world. In addition, the culture has been able to maintain a stable and traditional approach to community while promoting the primacy of the individual's spiritual experience. "Bound by ineffability, respect, and reverence, American Indian religious ethos provides a central mystery as a middle path between a static theology as dogmatic exclusivism and the potential in visionary plurality for destabilization of tradition."[98]

- Sufism –

Rumi, a celebrated Sufi born Muhammad Jalal al-Din in 1207, was an Islamic scholar who gave up his renown and conventional values to pursue his real self, becoming an ecstatic poet and storyteller.[99] A basic tenet of the Sufis is that one's real self is not what his parents or the environment had developed in him, but what the universe had created in him. Therefore, this real self can henceforth be called the cosmic or universal self, in contrast to the phenomenal self, the product of culture.

Abdol Reza Arasteh, PhD, (1927–1992) was an Islamic scholar and student of Sufi mysticism, a Western trained psychologist (Princeton), and professor at the University of Tehran during the mid-twentieth century. Arasteh[100] formulated a comprehensive theory of personality development organized around Freud's structure of the personality (i.e., the id, ego, and superego), and influenced by Sufism. He proposed three universal stages of human development – natural, cultural, and existential – leading to maturity (i.e., the final stage of human development). The child in the first stage seeks the satisfaction of drives (e.g., hunger, sleep, etc.). The second stage, the cultural state, is characterized by the growth of cultural patterning; this second stage is comparable to Freud's superego, an internalized representation of culture. In this stage, which starts in the second year of life and extends well into adulthood, the individual utilizes culture and reason as a way to control the ego and the natural state. The existential state, or the creative stage, pertains to the ability to rise above culture in order to fully mature. Arasteh developed this third stage based on the model of Sufism, and more specifically Rumi. In this stage, the individual recognizes the limitations of culture in his or her developmental process and seeks a more universal state, i.e., the cosmic self, which provides detachment from a cultural state of being, liberation from rationality, freedom for spontaneity and intuition, and finally taking on the transcendent self.[101]

These three stages reinforce the dominant sequential hierarchy proposed almost universally within transpersonal psychology, usually called the pre-personal, personal, and transpersonal stages. The Sufi perspective recognizes the ultimate need to transcend culture and attain a more fulfilling relationship with spirit. All individuals are innately designed to merge with an object of desire that provides lasting solace, and in that merging to be "born again"[102], transforming into the cosmic self or transpersonal self. It is a path of ecstatic devotion, which nonetheless requires one to first resolve intrapsychic conflicts.

In the Sufi tradition, the fully integrated person in the trans-cultural state finds joy in deeds that benefit others and have no reward, has the ability to endure, can tolerate solitude without boredom, can live in any community, and has allowed any distance between subject and object to disappear.[103]

- Subtle Energy Psychology –

One prominent psychologist in the field of energy psychology, Michael Mayer, has discussed the resonance between that field and transpersonal psychology.

> When I was training therapists at John F. Kennedy University I used this definition: "Transpersonal Psychology, often called the fourth force of psychology, contains an integrative psychotherapy that includes all forms of psychotherapy as well as methods that focus specifically on connecting us with the wider whole of which we're a part. This experience of the wider whole can be accessed through energetic pathways (which can be activated through various altered states of consciousness practices: breathing, acupressure touch techniques, methods of postural initiation such as Qigong, etc.), spiritual practices from East/West/indigenous traditions and symbolic process modes of healing."[104]

Symbolic process modalities might include character armoring[105], "focusing" on the felt sense and energetic felt shift in psychotherapy[106]; dream work[107]; thought field therapy[108]; emotional freedom techniques[109]; therapeutic touch[110]; energy transmission techniques such as Reiki, chakra work[111]; Tai Chi[112], Qigong and Native American medicine[113]; waking dreaming[114]; Jung's active imagination[115]; the practice of yoga[116]; prayer[117]; and shamanism.[118]

The National Institutes of Health (NIH) defines Energy Medicine as:

> … a domain in CAM [complementary and alternative medicine] that deals with energy fields of two types: Veritable, which can be measured [and] Putative, which have yet to be measured … The veritable energies employ mechanical vibrations (such as sound) and electromagnetic forces … In contrast, putative energy fields (also called biofields) have defied measurement to date by reproducible methods. Therapies involving putative energy fields are based on the concept that human beings are infused with a subtle form of energy. This vital energy or life force is known under different names in different cultures, such as qi in traditional Chinese medicine (TCM), ki in the Japanese Kampo system, doshas in Ayurvedic medicine, and elsewhere as prana, etheric energy, fohat, orgone, odic force, mana, and homeopathic resonance.[119]

Mayer[120] calls his bodymind approach *Integral Transpersonal Psychotherapy*, i.e., bringing the body and the healing power of life energy back into psychotherapy, which he maintains has over-emphasized the mind. Mayer has been a pioneer in promoting the incorporation of Tai Chi and Qigong into psychotherapy.

One of the common elements in various forms of current day energy psychology is a muscle testing procedure for accessing deep truth through somatic response to questions or alternative choices. There is an interesting similarity between this procedure and the hypnotic ideomotor signaling utilized in hypnosis and hypnotherapy.[121]

Another intersection of energy psychology and transpersonal therapy is the importance of body posture to inducing specific state-dependent mind sets. We have found this vitally important in assisting a client who is engaged in an altered state therapy session, e.g., hypnotherapy or altered state psychodrama, to discern separate ego states in dream enactment or virtual active imagination. By pairing a specific body position or posture with enactment of an ego state (e.g., my shadow the tyrant, or my fear of rejection) or with an inner resource (e.g., my higher self, or my best possible future self), it reinforces the identification with that state. This clarity provides an easy means of establishing reconnection with that state for purposes of inner dialogue.

The concept of subtle energies and their manipulation is present in all of the following[122]: Judaism[123]; Christianity[124]; Islam/Sufism[125]; Hinduism/Kundalini, Tantra, and Shakta Vedanta[126]; Kashmir Shaivism[127]; Buddhism/Tibetan Tantra and Dream Yoga[128]; Buddhism/ Vajrayana[129]; Taoism/ internal alchemy[130]; Shamanism[131]; Theosophy[132]; Western Esotericism[133]; the Western Mystery Tradition[134]; Western Magic, e.g., the Middle Pillar Exercise[135]; integrative approaches drawing from depth psychology, astrology, and Tarot such as the 'Inner Guide Meditation'[136] and pathworking[137]; Western research based psychotherapies such as Focusing[138]; energy healing[139]; energetic psychotherapies, e.g., Reichian therapy[140]; and systems that teach induction of a 'vibrational state' associated with the out-of-body experience.[141]

- Transpersonal Anthropology –

  The discipline of anthropology has been a major influence on transpersonal psychology. The transpersonal movement has now, in turn, influenced many anthropologists and opened new fields of research.[142]

Anthropologist Lucien Levy-Bruhl's[143] influence can be found in the work of Carl Jung, who borrowed Levy-Bruhl's idea of *representation collective* for his theory of *archetypes* of the *collective unconscious*.[144] Levy-Bruhl formed the *law of participation* to explain, in studying ecstatic states, the necessity for the subject to fuse with the object, to actually participate in the experience in order to fully understand it. This concept is actually a forerunner of *participatory knowing*, which is significant among contemporary transpersonal theorists.[145]

Due to intimidation from the profession, anthropologists have been reluctant to intentionally participate experientially in altered state ceremonies in their field work. Yet "anthropological research involving alternate phases of consciousness has been extensive and has, in fact, provided much of the cross-cultural material upon which transpersonal theoretical work in other disciplines had been grounded."[146] A major thrust of current anthropology is joining science and the sacred.

"The experiences produced within religious traditions were characterized by earlier anthropologists as awe, trance, or ecstasy; now these phenomena are referred to as altered states of consciousness (ASC) or transpersonal consciousness."[147]

- Positive Psychology –

Rather than being an influence on transpersonal psychology, positive psychology has been influenced by transpersonal psychology to explore some of the topics treated by transpersonal psychology since its inception. In general, positive psychology continues to emphasize qualities within the realms of ego and, sometimes, of self-actualization, with less attention to features beyond ego which would include self-transcendence.

Chapter Four

Eight Foundational Psychologies

1. Humanistic Psychology – Self-actualization

Humanistic psychology typically adopts a holistic approach to human existence and pays special attention to such phenomena as man's inherent goodness, his creativity, free will, and the great untapped potential of human development. It encourages viewing ourselves as a "whole person" greater than the sum of our parts. Humanistic psychology prizes spiritual aspiration as an integral part of the human psyche and a prime motivating factor in human behavior.

James Bugental[148] was instrumental in developing and defining the humanistic psychology perspective, and he articulated five core principles of humanistic psychology that were adapted by Tom Greening[149], editor of the *Journal of Humanistic Psychology* from 1970 to 2005. The five basic postulates of humanistic psychology are:

1. Human beings, as human, supersede the sum of their parts. They cannot be reduced to components.
2. Human beings have their existence in a uniquely human context, as well as in a cosmic ecology.
3. Human beings are aware and are aware of being aware - i.e., they are conscious. Human consciousness always includes an awareness of oneself in the context of other people.
4. Human beings have some choice and, with that, responsibility.
5. Human beings are intentional, aim at goals, are aware that they cause future events, and seek meaning, value, and creativity.

One of humanistic psychology's early sources was the work of Carl Rogers, whose focus was to ensure that clinical intervention led to healthier personality functioning through his *person-centered approach*. The term 'actualizing tendency' was

coined by Rogers, and was a concept that eventually led
Abraham Maslow to study self-actualization as one of the basic
needs of humans.

Rogers[150] believed in human beings' optimal development,
in which people continually aim to fulfill their full potential. He
described a fully functioning human being in this way:

1. A growing openness to experience – they move away
    from defensiveness and have no need for subception (a
    perceptual defense that involves unconsciously applying
    strategies to prevent a troubling stimulus from entering
    consciousness).

2. An increasingly existential lifestyle – living each
    moment fully – not distorting the moment to fit
    personality or self-concept but allowing personality and
    self-concept to emanate from the experience. This results
    in excitement, daring, adaptability, tolerance,
    spontaneity, and a lack of rigidity and suggests a
    foundation of trust. To open one's spirit to what is going
    on now, and discover in that present process whatever
    structure it appears to have.

3. Increasing organismic trust – they trust their own
    judgment and their ability to choose behavior that is
    appropriate for each moment. They do not rely on
    existing codes and social norms but trust that as they are
    open to experiences they will be able to trust their own
    sense of right and wrong.

4. Freedom of choice – not being shackled by the
    restrictions that influence an incongruent individual,
    they are able to make a wider range of choices more
    fluently. They believe that they play a role in
    determining their own behavior and so feel responsible
    for their own behavior.

5. Creativity – it follows that they will feel more free to be
    creative. They will also be more creative in the way they
    adapt to their own circumstances without feeling a need
    to conform.

6. Reliability and constructiveness – they can be trusted to
    act constructively. An individual who is open to all their
    needs will be able to maintain a balance between them.

Even aggressive needs will be matched and balanced by intrinsic goodness in congruent individuals.

7. A rich full life – the life of the fully functioning individual is rich, full and exciting and suggests that they experience joy and pain, love and heartbreak, fear and courage more intensely.

Eric Berne's Transactional Analysis was another influence on the humanistic movement. Berne mapped interpersonal relationships to three ego states of the individuals involved: the *Parent, Adult,* and *Child* state. People's interactions and communication were analyzed based on the current activation of each ego state within each person. He called these interpersonal interactions *transactions* and used the label *games* to refer to certain patterns of transactions which popped up repeatedly in everyday life. He published *Transactional Analysis in Psychotherapy* in 1961, and *Games People Play* in 1964. That book uses casual, often humorous phrases such as "See What You Made Me Do," "Why Don't You — Yes But," "Now I've Got You, You Son of a Bitch", and "Ain't It Awful" as a way of briefly describing each game. In reality, the "winner" of a mind game is the person that returns to the Adult ego-state first.

Berne's conception of ego states as relatively discrete subpersonalities, each with its own viewpoint and qualities, laid the groundwork for conceptions of the drama triangle[151], the Victim Triangle[152], the center core phenomena[153], internal family systems therapy[154], and the internal family of selves[155], among many others.

Abraham Maslow[156] was, of course, instrumental in developing humanistic psychology, and then soon recognized the limitation of having omitted a spiritual dimension of the human experience. He called for a new broader approach which he called transpersonal psychology. Rollo May[157] influenced humanistic psychology with his existential approach, and Fritz Perls[158] injected his Gestalt therapy emphasis on here-and-now observations, role playing, and non-verbal cues. Stanislav Grof[159] was instrumental in extending humanistic psychology toward the transpersonal by adding new dimensions of exploration: the prenatal and birth experiences, death, and using psychedelics like LSD for intrapsychic exploration and for therapeutic purposes.

2. Psychosynthesis – the Transpersonal Self

Roberto Assagioli, a student of Freud and a colleague of Jung, founded the psychological theory and methodology of psychosynthesis. He first articulated the principles of psychosynthesis in his doctoral thesis of 1910 and developed them over the 1920's and 1930's. Decades later he published his book *Psychosynthesis* in 1965. "With [William] James and Jung, Assagioli is acknowledged as one of the earlier explorers and practitioners of transpersonal psychology, and psychosynthesis continues to develop as one particular approach in this field."[160]

The concept of synthesis implies a placing together of parts to form an integrated whole; psychosynthesis refers to a process that is directed toward the integration and harmonious expression of all of human nature – physical, emotional, mental, and spiritual.[161]

Assagioli "dealt with the issue of spiritual crises and introduced many active therapeutic techniques for the development of a transcendent center of personality."[162] Psychosynthesis offers a transpersonal orientation, working within a whole person spectrum, including concern with family of origin issues; traumas; current and present centered concerns, such as relationships, work, etc.; and spiritual concerns, including issues of religion, existential questioning, God, and life purpose. He suggested a theoretical structure for the psyche that contained a lower, middle and higher unconscious, and a collective unconscious, acknowledging that the individual is not only connected transpersonally to the larger universe, but collectively and archetypally.[163]

A simple description relates these levels to time. The lower unconscious might include energies and awareness that are associated with primitive instincts and passions, difficult dynamics, or traumas that have not been understood or integrated from the past, and the fears, resistances, and defenses that keep all of this out of sight. The middle unconscious might include energies and awareness that are associated with challenges, motivations, and activities of the present time. The higher unconscious could include energies and awareness that are associated with the talents, abilities, potentials, and resources that can be developed in the future. Psychosynthesis theory suggests that there is a principle of growth within the human psyche, an inner guide – the Higher Self – that can provide the inspiration and wisdom that is necessary to understand more deeply, work more creatively, love more authentically, and meet the challenges of each stage in life successfully.

> The Greeks called it man's inner *daimon*. Current transpersonal psychologists refer to it as an *archetypal center core self.*

According to Assagioli[164], the self is beyond or above the personality and is "unaffected by the flow of the mind-stream or by bodily conditions; and the personal conscious self should be considered merely as its reflection, it's 'projection' in the field of personality." He further differentiates between the little self and the higher, spiritual self by saying that

> the little self is acutely aware of itself as a distinct separate individual, and a sense of solitude or of separation sometimes comes in the existential experience. In contrast, the experience of the spiritual Self is a sense of freedom, of expansion, of communication with other Selves and with reality, and there is a sense of Universality. It feels itself at the same time individual and universal.[165]

By exploring beyond the pathology of the lower unconscious in order to repair damage done, "we shall discover in ourselves hitherto unknown abilities, our true vocations and our higher potentialities which seek to express themselves but which we often repel and repress through lack of understanding, prejudice or fear. We shall also discover the immense reserve of undifferentiated psychic energy latent in every one of us; that is, the plastic part of our unconscious which lies at our disposal, empowering us with an unlimited capacity to learn and to create."[166] Assagioli referred to psychosynthesis as "Realization of One's True Self", the Self being the transcendent center of the personality.

These states of the unconscious point to the wide range of human experience from family of origin wounding (and subsequent splitting, repression, denial, or dysfunctional development), to the life of the personality (both conscious and unconscious) in present time, with real-life concerns, to the arena of meaning, purpose, values, spirituality, and the realm of the transpersonal dimension.[167]

Assagioli conceptualized healthy adult development as consisting of two distinct stages: personal psychosynthesis and spiritual psychosynthesis. Personal psychosynthesis involves exploring the structure of one's own psyche and becoming familiar with the contents of one's personal unconscious, and then improving one's ability to manage them – in short, to integrate the individual around the personal self. Spiritual psychosynthesis consists of the integration of the personality around a deeper center, the spiritual Self, of which the integrated personality becomes an instrument.[168] This deeper center Assagioli called the Transpersonal Self[169], the core point of identity, the center of the whole person.[170] In this he followed Carl Jung's concept of the Self, the central archetype, the union of opposites, especially of consciousness and the unconscious.

> According to Assagioli, however, Jung does not clearly define the collective unconscious; he does not sufficiently distinguish its different discreet levels. Assagioli proposes a lower, middle and higher unconscious, and a distinct level for the spiritual dimension of the unconscious, which he defines as the *transpersonal unconscious*.

Assagioli felt that Jung placed the more primordial and basic levels of the psyche together with archetypes of a spiritual nature into one collective unconscious, "confusing the collective and universal".[171] Importantly, of course, both of these foundational contributors to today's transpersonal psychology emphasized both personal and collective unconscious realms.

Assagioli's distinction of separate collective and universal levels of the unconscious may be germane to the two levels of the transpersonal identified by some current theorists: Subtle and Causal[172]; Transpersonal 1 or Soul, and Transpersonal 2 or Spirit[173]; and Transcendent and Unity.[174] It is the Subtle (the Soul or the Transcendent) level that may be utilized and incorporated into our daily life.

> [The soul] is the part of us that is in touch with the spiritual realm through images and symbols, through concrete representations of the divine. We get in touch with it through ritual and ceremony, or through personal intimations of the

spiritual, or through art or music, or through experiences of nature. It is the realm of the typical peak experience, where we experience ecstasy in some form, or other glimpses of the spiritual order of things.

   . . . the level of the soul is the beginning of the transpersonal, it is not the end. Further on along the path of psychospiritual development, according to Wilber, is the spirit. . . . This is the realm spoken of by the mystics, and not much cultivated in our society. It requires too much effort, too many years of meditation, to reach that stage of development. Yet all of us have the possibility of experiencing it briefly at any time. This kind of ecstasy has no content, unlike the previous level, the level of soul. Soul is full of colours and lights and big experiences – this level has nothing of that kind to demonstrate. But those who have experienced it speak of complete freedom, of a total opening, of an undeniable awakening.[175]

Assagioli defines the *I* as a center of pure awareness and will, independent of any content of consciousness. This *I* is a key to all work in psychosynthesis, for *I* is the resting place of one's experience. It is the "who" that each person is, beyond the specific story of an individual life. The *Self* is the same *I*, anchored at the border of the transpersonal and the universal. *Self* has been said to be distinct, but not separate from *I*.[176]

> One of the key therapeutic principles and active techniques in psychosynthesis is the principle of *disidentification* (or non-attachment).

"We are dominated by everything with which our self becomes identified and we can dominate and control everything from which we disidentify ourselves."[177] Literally the principle is a practice of disidentification, taking individuals through a protocol of disidentifying from their body, their thoughts, their emotions, their social roles, and witnessing being a center of pure consciousness unidentified with any particular contents. This enables one to choose what parts of experience to attend to and act on without being threatened because of identification. The sequence of perspective is:

a. identification (noting one's experience... *I am angry)*,
b. disidentification (stepping back from that experience to an observing place... *I have that anger and I am not that anger*) and
c. Self-identification (anchoring into *I*, the experience of awareness and will... *I am more than this*).

By recognizing and naming subpersonalities, disidentifying from them and dialoguing with them, their underlying unresolved needs and as yet unclaimed higher qualities become apparent. Their distorted behaviors can be transformed and energies released for the benefit of the total person. Thus in a psychosynthesis perspective, the growth process is seen as a series of awakenings.[178]

The most difficult identifications in people's lives are scripted messages from childhood that stick through thick and thin as the way people know themselves. These nearly intractable self-concepts can define a lifetime, eliminating possibilities that inherently exist in that person, by the sheer weight of the limiting experience of *this is who I am*. The power of early identifications is the hardest to step beyond. But when a client has the experience of knowing, *I have that wounded child and I am more than that child*, that person moves one step closer to Self-identification and becomes incrementally more connected to the experience of being *I*. In this moment of disidentification the client is *more*, more than simply personal history, or the residue of traumas, or the sum of strengths and weaknesses.

Appel[179] points out that in many ways disidentification is akin to a choiceless awareness mindfulness meditation[180] sometimes also known as "open monitoring meditation"[181] in which the *experiencer* learns that they may have an experience but *they are not the experience*.

Self-identification, i.e., capital 's' Self, occurs when the ego is able to let go, transcend, and then *I* becomes Self-identified.

> The *Self* looks through the transpersonal or spiritual dimension while *I* looks out at the world through the lens of the personal. Both are *I am*: one at the kitchen sink, one on the mountaintop. A metaphoric description that has often been used is that *I* is the conductor of the orchestra, *Self* the composer of the music, and of course, the musicians are the

subpersonalities, playing a powerful and unique piece of music, in harmony, under direction of *I*, in service of the inspiration of *Self*. This, of course, is on a good day. The orchestra may sound like a group of contentious, angry, confused adolescents given loud musical instruments, while *I* naps and *Self* moans. And so the need for counseling arises. And an assumed goal of psychosynthesis counseling is the process of Self-realization—the orchestra playing harmoniously.[182]

And the parts of oneself that are being disidentified with Assagioli called *subpersonalities*. Other names for these parts could include shadows, inner children, protectors, victim, rescuer, persecutor, etc. "[O]ne of the first people to have started really making use of subpersonalities for therapy and personal growth was Roberto Assagioli."[183] Wannamaker states that "in Psychosynthesis, subpersonalities are thought of as middle unconscious constellations . . . much like the ego states defined by Eric Berne or the complexes described by Freud. They have their roots in the unhappy child of the lower unconscious and constitute a set of behaviors built up by the child in response to early events."[184]

Assagioli drew inspiration from Eastern teachings, especially teachings on energy systems and energetic fields. He attempted to incorporate energy work into the psychosynthesis modality, naming it *psycho-energetics*. He considered it a fifth force of psychology after the fourth (transpersonal), and he explored its potential for future development but did not formulate a completed system.[185] "Assagioli looked to Eastern psychology with the aim of integrating it with Western psychology. In particular, he was influenced by the Yoga and Vedanta-Upanishad philosophies, which he believed made important contributions to the knowledge of human nature and forged important tools for exploring and transforming consciousness."[186]

3. Existential Psychology

The existential approach to therapy, healing and transformation is based on the discrete philosophy of existentialism. Existentialism is a sensibility, a perspective on life, not a set of doctrines. To try to define existentialism is to freeze it, in the words of Jean-Paul Sartre[187], who gave the movement its name and identity.

Robert Solomon[188] traces the sources of existentialist thought in the nineteenth and twentieth centuries primarily through Kierkegaard, Nietzsche, Heidegger, Camus, and Sartre, and identifies three themes that pervade existentialism. First is a strong emphasis on the individual, although that is variously defined and understood. For Neitzsche, the goal in life, to *really exist* as opposed to *so-called living*, is to fully manifest your talents and virtues, thus "becoming the person you really are."[189] Second is the central role of passionate commitment, as opposed to the usual philosophical emphasis on reason and rationality. Existentialism basically urges us to live our lives to the fullest, according to our own individual understanding. For the existentialist, to live is to live passionately. And third is the importance of human freedom to make choices, and the responsibility to do so consciously. "The message of existentialism, unlike many more obscure and academic philosophical movements, is about as simple as it can be. It is that every one of us, as an individual, is responsible – responsible for what we do, responsible for who we are, responsible for the way we face and deal with the world, responsible, ultimately, for the way the world is. It is, in a very short phrase, the philosophy of "no excuses!"[190]

Martin Heidegger[191] dwelt on the concept of authenticity, and encourages us to be authentic, to "take hold of ourselves" and in the engagement with self to make the most appropriate choices in living in the world. Our existence carries possibilities, and offers us the opportunity to make choices among those possibilities. When we fail to face up to our existential condition, we fall back into doing tasks, into mundane inauthenticity, what he calls "fallenness." The primary drive to "take hold of ourselves," to live authentically, is the awareness of our own mortality. Heidegger refers to this as "Being-unto-death." This perspective of life as framed within birth and death, of living with death in mind, forces us to appreciate our limitations and immerse ourselves in our immediate context. Death individuates us.

A very different, but related concept is Nietzsche's "thought of eternal recurrence." Eternal recurrence provides an existential test for how one is living one's life, and what one is doing with one's life. Specifically, if offered the choice to repeat your life as it is, or to change it in some way in a future repetition, which would you choose? If you would choose to make changes in a future repetition, then Nietzsche urges you to choose to make those changes *now*. The alternative is to remain in bondage to the never-ending cycle of satisfying momentary desires at the expense of a more meaningful degree of satisfaction. As Goethe says in *Faust*, "From desire I rush to satisfaction, but from satisfaction I leap to desire."

> The existential approach in psychology is organized around life on earth itself and the social, cultural and spiritual ramifications of it, that is, the "human condition". Existential psychology has a rich history, focusing on certain questions related to existence itself: death, human limitation, and mortality; freedom, responsibility, and agency; isolation and connectedness; and meaning vs. meaninglessness. One of the major distinctions between existential theorists is their view on whether the major questions of our existence can be answered or not.

John Paul Sartre[192] and Irvin Yalom[193] are two primary examples of existential thinkers who believe that there are no ultimate answers to these questions, leading some to assume (incorrectly) that existentialism is inherently atheistic, nihilistic, and pessimistic.

Other existentialists provide a very optimistic viewpoint focusing on the potential for good and growth that is inherent in the human condition, often claiming a spiritual or religious basis for their optimism. Some examples of this perspective include Søren Kierkegaard[194], Paul Tillich[195], Martin Buber[196], and Rollo May.[197]

We have previously identified[198] five themes that pervade existentialism: (1) meaning in life is found in the living of each moment; (2) passionate commitment to a way of life, to one's purpose and one's relationships, is the highest form of expression of one's humanity; (3) all human beings have freedom of choice and responsibility for our choices; (4) openness to experience allows for the greatest possible expansion of personal expression; and (5) in the ever-present face of death itself, we find the deepest commitment to life itself.

Speaking about the connection between existential and transpersonal psychologies, John Rowan says, "The great advantage of using the term 'transpersonal' is that it is quite clear and explicit, referring to a stage of psychospiritual development that is not to be confused with the pre-personal (pre-rational, pre-conventional, etc.) and the personal (everyday life, the 'consensus trance', the 'they', the mental ego, or whatever label we find useful). It includes the authentic (Wade, 1996), and also the further stages postulated in various systems, such as the Soul Path of many mystics and the Impersonal Divine described by others (Cortright, 1997)."[199]

A primary similarity of existential and transpersonal psychology is the values base they share, namely a belief in human potential and a commitment to human dignity. The five themes identified above could probably describe most transpersonal psychologists as well as most existential psychologists. Also, they are both less likely than other therapy approaches to diagnose clients as suffering from a specified psychopathology and more likely to focus on the individual client's subjective experience and inherent potential.

> What difference does it make whether an existentialist writer and thinker accepts the transpersonal argument or not? Either way, he or she may experience being thrown into a world which can be confusing or problematical. But the difference is that the transpersonalist feels wonder at all this, while the person who steers clear of the transpersonal is more likely to feel despair, absurdity or futility. Neither of these responses is true or false – they are just different. And I know which I prefer.[200]

Kirk Schneider[201] has combined the clinical work of existential therapists, including James Bugental[202], Wilson Van Dusen[203] and Eugene Gendlin[204], to develop a set of practices into the Existential-Integrative Model.

Like any transpersonal therapy, this model is "Beyond repairing…wounds".[205] Schneider has identified the key elements of the Existential-Integrative approach as (a) cultivating therapeutic presence, (b) invoking the actual, (c) working through resistance, and (d) the search for meaning.[206] Together these elements bring those involved, client and therapist alike, into greater experience of authenticity, incisive understanding, openness and the rediscovery of awe.

"The emphasis on *being* is the single most defining characteristic of Existential Psychotherapy."[207] Being, or presence, is more than a state of not being distracted or defensive; it is a state of wide-open awareness, keen attentiveness, openness to the moment, and perhaps even awe. As James Bugental[208] puts it, "Presence is the quality of being in a situation in which one intends to be as aware and as participative as one is able to be at that time and in those circumstances….[It] is being there in body, in emotions, in relating, in thoughts, in every way." More specifically, therapeutic presence displays the two aspects of accessibility, which is "having the intention to allow what happens in a situation to matter, to have an effect on one" and "expressiveness…the willingness to put forth some effort…the intent to let oneself be known by [and to dynamically respond to]…the other without distortion or disguise."[209]

Now let's look at presence in its manifestations of nonattachment, the sacredness of each moment, the experience of awakening from the "trance of ordinary life,"[210] and completion with the past (having no unfinished business).

> Nonattachment is the freedom to live with abandon without fear of abandonment. It is living with an attitude of commitment to the path without attachment to the outcome. Nonattachment is learning to pay full attention to one's environment and one's reactions to it, but not to identify with either.

Living in this way results in savoring life, open to the timelessness of each moment, the "fullness of experience," which has been called sacred.[211] Awakening from the "trance of ordinary life" is to disidentify from role, image, or identity. When an individual identifies with an image or an identity, he/she 'takes on' the accoutrements associated with it. Yet,

"[J]ust as it is possible to awaken, to become lucid, in a dream, so it is possible to attain moments or periods of heightened awareness – 'wakefulness' – in waking life."[212]

For most people, the past is alive in the present in the form of unfinished business and uncompleted developmental tasks. As one resolves and completes what was left unfinished, the person opens to the immediacy of the present moment, reducing reactivity and increasing self-esteem. The healthy person asks, "Is there anything that I need to say or do or clear up that I haven't?" and then sets out to establish completion where it is needed, to make amends with the past. Completion allows one to live fully, prepared to meet the uncertainty of each moment without regrets.

Sometimes this open pure presence allows problems to dissolve spontaneously, especially when the therapist neither gives them energy nor takes energy away from them, neither conspires with the client's resistance nor resists it.[213]

See Hartman & Zimberoff (2003) for a more complete discussion of the intersection of existential and transpersonal psychologies.

4. Gestalt Therapy

Gestalt therapy techniques developed by Fritz Perls[214] include *presentness*, making everything very immediate, emphasizing the here and now, and concrete *attention to detail*, rather than abstract conceptualizing, including the importance of somatic and body awareness. Both of these principles lead to heightened emotional intensity of experience, which in turn facilitates greater healing. Gestalt therapists are existentially oriented, framing life as offering exciting choices or opportunities to explore and to discover one's potentials. We have the freedom to choose to be authentic or fraudulent as a human being, and that choice is determined by our actions, in this moment. Years ago there was a popular injunction in Gestalt therapy: *Lose your mind and come to your senses.* Later it was revised to: *Use your mind and come to your senses.* The focus was always on genuinely being in the here and now.

Gestalt therapy is directed toward experiencing, feeling and expressing rather than interpreting; toward what is being done, thought and felt in this moment rather than on what was, might be, could be, or should be; toward understanding that emotional responses to current life events are faulty, habitual residue patterned after original repressed unresolved events.[215] Fritz Perls used several basic premises in his development of Gestalt therapy.[216] One was to make everything very immediate, emphasizing the here and now. His assessment of the importance of *presentness* was influenced by Karen Horney, who supervised Perls in Berlin and emphasized the "Here and Now, the What and How." When people would start telling him about their lives or their problems, he would stop them, saying, "Do you hear the quality of your voice? Can you hear the fear in it?" or "What is your right foot doing? What would it say to you, if it could talk?" He applied the same insistence on present tense experiencing in regards to plans or worries for the future, dreams or fantasies. This orients people out of their familiar mood and ways of engaging or resisting, and forces them to attend to their experience in the present.

The goal of self-exploration is awareness that frees up one's spontaneity. The exploration takes place through repeated observations and inquiry, "experiments" in which a therapist suggests the client attend to a particular somatic sensation, inhibited urge, or other subtle behavior. A Gestalt therapist utilizing this method might say something like, "I notice a slight tension at the corners of your eyes when you say that . . . and I see you folding your arms across your chest." The therapist does not analyze or interpret the observation, but simply brings the client's awareness to it. Then the therapist might suggest, "Okay, I wonder how your body would react if you said it again, but louder."

Emphasis on immediate experience means that awareness is the key to unlock insight and ultimately to bring behavior change. Rather than trying to change something, one might better simply to be aware of it; fully aware, deeply aware. Immediate experience includes whatever a person receives through his senses, i.e., feeling states, proprioceptive (internal) body sensations, movement, and thoughts. Perls referred to this emphasis as the "awareness continuum." Another basic principle of Gestalt therapy is that concrete attention to detail, rather than abstract conceptualizing, facilitates greater awareness. This personal awareness raises the emotional intensity of whatever the individual is saying or thinking about. Used in hypnotherapy, the heightened intensity of experience aides in the depth of the affect or somatic bridge in regressions. Keeping the client's awareness on concrete detail is a constant in hypnotic age regressions, because it promotes *presentness*, emotionally and viscerally.

Generally what obstructs one's ability to be fully present, in the language of Gestalt Therapy, is accumulated unfinished business. Latner refers to unfinished business as "organismic indigestion" that clogs us up, the only-partially digested (and therefore partially *un*digested) resentments, regrets, worries and repressions.[217]

> Every experience strives for closure: everything we have repressed wants expression, and contains "stuck" energy until it is. This need for closure results in obsessive attempts to put it to rest, to find peace, i.e., the repetition compulsion. With a significant part of our energy preoccupied elsewhere ("then and there"), we cannot bring enough of ourselves to new situations ("now and here").

Latner[218] tells a Japanese Zen story to illustrate the need to resolve unfinished business:

> Tanzan and Ekido were once traveling together down a muddy road. A heavy rain was still falling.
>
> Coming around a bend they met a lovely girl in a silk kimono and sash, unable to cross the intersection.
>
> "Come on, girl," said Tanzan at once. Lifting her in his arms, he carried her over the mud.
>
> Ekido did not speak again until that night when they reached a lodging temple. Then he could no longer restrain himself. "We monks don't go near females," he told Tanzan, "especially young and lovely ones. It is dangerous. Why did you do that?"
>
> "I left the girl there," said Tanzan. "Are you still carrying her?"

In Gestalt therapy, there is a recognition that all human experience exists on a continuum with polar opposites, such as passive/ aggressive, sad/ happy or humility/ arrogance. It is often useful to understand psychopathology as an imbalance on one or more of these continuums, with the individual stuck at or near one of the polar extremes. Healthy functioning is seen, then, as access to both polarities and the ability to flexibly experience any place in between as the situation calls for. One of the objectives of Gestalt therapy is for individuals to balance their inner polarities, finding a zero-point within. Such a state may be thought of as a form of nonattachment; Fritz Perls referred to this concept as "creative indifference."

Another principle of Gestalt therapy is the importance of somatic and body awareness. The body's sensations and movements, when paid attention to, can bring into conscious awareness their concomitant but repressed emotions and impulses. This awareness enhances the person's experience of ownership for the feelings, and permits a richer, more genuine expression of them. Perls was influenced by Wilhelm Reich, who was Perls' analyst in the early 1930s, both in relation to presentness and to the function of the body's motor system as an armor. Reich expanded on the classical psychoanalytic focus (called the fundamental rule) on the patient's expression of unconscious tensions and impulses through ideational productions, i.e., associations, fantasies, dreams, memories, slips: "The how of saying things is as important 'material' for interpretation as is what the patient says."[219] Reich's essential therapeutic aim was that of "penetrating to the energy sources of the symptoms and the neurotic character."[220] Allowing physical expression of the psychic energy held in the body intensifies and clarifies the emotions, and ultimately brings release of blockages and resistances. "Perls's basic assumption was that the body and its total processes are somehow anterior to and bigger than the mind. Gestalt conceives of the mind as an interference, as a way of blocking the total momentum of the organism in some way. Not only that, but the mind is not even the noble part of the organism that we always thought it was. For most people the mind and the creations of the mind work against the body. They work against the best interests of the total person."[221]

The Gestalt-oriented therapeutic relationship emphasizes a very real and mutual dialogue between therapist and client, incorporating four primary characteristics[222]:

1. *Inclusion.* This is a high degree of empathy, putting oneself as fully as possible into the experience of the other without judging, analyzing or interpreting while simultaneously retaining a sense of one's separate,

autonomous presence. This is crucial in regression and altered-state modalities, providing validation to the client, and thus safety to explore and greater self-awareness.

2. *Presence.* The Gestalt-oriented therapist acknowledges that the interaction is a dialogue, expressing his/her observations, preferences, feelings, personal experience and thoughts to the client. This develops trust and models the valuing of immediate experience. It is vitally important that the therapist has done his/her own personal work so that their presence is clear and not a projection of the therapist's own issues.

3. *Commitment to dialogue.* The Gestalt-oriented therapist surrenders to the interpersonal process, allowing contact to happen rather than manipulating, making contact, and controlling the outcome.

4. *Dialogue is lived.* Dialogue is 'lived' rather than looked at or talked about. The therapeutic relationship is one of sharing energetic interaction, emphasizing excitement and acceptance of the immediacy of the experience. In hypnotherapy the dialogue is 'lived' also because the client is actually dialoguing with living parts of themselves or internalized others.

The techniques of Gestalt therapy are experimental tasks, intended to expand the client's direct experience. They are not designed to move the client somewhere, to change the client's feelings or behavior, to recondition, or to foster catharsis. Gestalt-oriented therapists use many active techniques to facilitate client *focusing* and directed awareness in order to clarify their experience. All of the techniques are elaborations of the question, "What are you aware of (experiencing) now?" or "What are you feeling?" and the instruction, "Try this experiment, or pay attention to that, and see what you become aware of or learn." *Enactment* is a technique in which the patient is asked to put feelings or thoughts into action. For example, the therapist may encourage the patient to "say it directly to the person" (such as speaking to an empty chair or into a pillow). "Put words to it" or "Give it a voice" is another example when the individual becomes aware of a somatic experience.

Enactment is intended as a way of increasing awareness, *not* as a form of catharsis. *Exaggeration* is a special form of enactment in which a person is asked to exaggerate some feeling, thought, movement, etc., in order to feel it more intensely.

Sometimes a client can bring an experience into the here and now more efficiently by visualizing than by enacting, and the therapist may suggest *guided fantasy*.

Loosening techniques can assist the client who is so fettered by the bonds of the usual ways of thinking that alternative possibilities are not allowed into awareness. One example is just to ask the client to imagine or consider the opposite of whatever is believed to be true.

Integrating techniques bring together processes the client doesn't usually bring together or actively keeps apart (splitting). For example, when the client verbally reports an emotion, she might be asked to locate it in her body. Another example is asking a client to express positive *and* negative feelings about the same person.

Taking back externalizations (projections) is an integrating technique in which the client is able to acknowledge and "own" some personal attribute that has previously been denied and unconsciously projected onto others.

Body awareness techniques include any technique that brings clients' awareness to their body functioning or helps them to be aware of how they can use their body to support excitement, awareness and contact. For example, the therapist might remind the client to take some deep breaths, or to open the mouth wide rather than yelling through clenched teeth.

The Gestalt therapist *balances client frustration and support*. The therapist explores rather than gratifies the client's wishes, even though this is frustrating for the patient, and provides a balance of warmth and firmness. The therapist responds to manipulations by the client without indulging (and thus reinforcing) them, yet without judging and without being purposely frustrating.

See Zimberoff and Hartman (2003) for a more complete discussion of incorporating Gestalt techniques into transpersonal therapy.

5. Jung and Analytical Psychology

In a classic text on transpersonal psychology, *Beyond Ego: Transpersonal Dimensions in Psychology*, Walsh and Vaughan spoke to the connection between Jungian analytical psychology and the transpersonal:

> Of all schools that have developed and departed from Freud's original work, the depth psychology of Carl Jung, also called analytical psychology, has been more concerned with transpersonal levels of experience than any other. The in-depth exploration of the psyche in Jungian work extends beyond both the ego and the existential levels in dealing with archetypes and the collective unconscious. Jung himself was the first Western psychotherapist to affirm the importance of transpersonal experience for mental health. He wrote that the main thrust of his work was not the treatment of neurosis, but the approach to the numinous dimensions of experience. . . . The fact is that the approach to the numinous is the real therapy and inasmuch as you attain to the numinous experience you are released from the curse of pathology. . . . [Analytical] psychology recognizes that the psyche has within it the capacity for self-healing and self-realization, but Jungian work remains predominantly concerned with the contents of consciousness rather than with consciousness itself as the context of all experience. Thus consciousness is experienced only in relation to its objects. It remains at a dualistic level and does not encompass the potential transcendence of subject-object dualism. Analytical psychology values the mythical dimension of experience, such as in the imagery of dreams and active imagination as a powerful therapeutic agent. However, it stops short of valuing the direct imageless awareness attained in the practice of some meditative disciplines.[223]

The Jungian approach offers the advantages of transpersonal psychology, i.e., facility in working with the numinous, it also and importantly addresses the "seamier side" of human experience, i.e., the self-limiting and self-sabotaging aspects of an individual's personality. This "all inclusive" view of the human psyche, with its simultaneous ascent to the heights and descent to the depths, values the "immanent" orientation as well as the "transcendent" potential, and brings a measure of skepticism to the sometimes rather linear, hierarchical view of states being postulated by many transpersonal psychologies such as Wilber's. So here is the flip side to the critique offered by Walsh and Vaughan above, i.e., that Jungian work remains predominantly concerned with the contents of consciousness rather than with consciousness itself. We defocus on the contents of the psyche at our own peril, as Levy articulates, admittedly from a more humanistic than transpersonal perspective[224]:

> One of the major distinguishing features of transpersonal psychology, which differentiates it from other schools, including the Jungian, has to do with attitudes toward the phenomenon of consciousness itself. Transpersonal psychology is fundamentally concerned with the nature and structure of consciousness in its varied forms, and less so with its contents. . . .
>
> The shadow side of transpersonal psychologists' preoccupation with states of consciousness in their own right is their limited understanding of some of the important contents and structural elements of the psyche, particularly the archetypes. Transpersonal psychology to date has seemed too absorbed in the states themselves to explore their inner nature adequately. It's a bit like mapping a territory without bothering to find out who is living there.

Carl Jung spoke of the need to "wake up."

> There are plenty of people who are not yet born. They seem to be all here, they walk about – but as a matter of fact, they are not yet born, because they are behind a glass wall, they are in the womb. They are in the world only on parole and are soon to be returned to the pleroma where they started originally. They have not formed a connection with this world; they are suspended in the air; they are neurotic, living the provisional life. They say, 'I am now living on such-and-such a condition. If my parents behave according to my wishes, I stay. But if it should happen that they do something I don't like, I pop off.' You see, that is the provisional life, a conditioned life, the life of somebody who is sill connected by an umbilical cord as thick as a ship's rope to the pleroma, the archetypal world of splendor. Now, it is most important that you should be born; you ought to come into this world – otherwise you cannot realize the self, and the purpose of this world has been missed.

Then you must simply be thrown back into the melting pot and be born again.[225]

And Jung's work is dedicated to ferreting out the areas in one's life in which he may be 'asleep'. It is necessary to explore the psyche to find all the inhabitants first, in order to know who is ally and who is obstacle in the project of 'waking up'. And for Jung that means to recognize the creations manufactured within the psyche through encounters with traumatic threats to the integrity of the self, with introjection of others' beliefs, as well as with the 'normal' process of enculturation and being socialized.

Jung's paradigm is that a child creates a set of behaviors established to defend against psychic and/or physical assault, and we can call that set of behaviors a *shadow*. As those behavior patterns become more idealized with reference to archetypal power, we can call them a *complex*. The complex, given the job by the child to protect against assault, continues the process of splitting and specializing already underway, calcifies into habitual unconscious autopilot mode, and evolves into an *autonomous complex*.

Jung referred to the ultimate organizing principle of the individual as the Self, or the *Archetypal Self*. The Self is the creator of dreams, the organizer of projections, and the basis of every human being's drive to develop to his/her highest potential.

The locus of identity, or current self-image, is what we may call the *waking ego*. The waking ego represents all the complexes that form the content of the personal sphere of the psyche. All of us have numerous complexes, or sets of conditioned responses to the world. These complexes often center around powerful experiences such as mother, father, competition, authority, the hero, etc. The waking ego is generally aware of all these complexes, although not necessarily in control of all of them.[226]

Complexes are the basic building units of psychological reality, and thus are simply normal parts of the mind. Our complexes allow us to multitask in everyday activities, and to operate on "autopilot" without having to consciously attend to every environmental stimulus. They are formed when a strong emotional experience, or one that is repeated many times, produces a patterning of the mind. The resulting pattern is behavioral (habits), and also consists of beliefs and expectations. A defining characteristic of complexes is that they tend to be bipolar, i.e., consist of two opposite parts.[227] Usually when a complex is activated, one part of the bipolar complex attaches itself to the waking ego, and the other part is split off and rejected. It often gets projected onto someone else. This bipolarity of the complex leads to endless conflict with the illusory other. And an individual may identify at different times with one or the other pole of the spectrum. For instance, in a typical negative father complex, a rebellious son inevitably encounters the authoritarian father in every teacher, cop or boss onto whom he projects his negative father imagery. Yet when he is in the role of the father, or authority, he seems to always encounter the rebellious son onto whom he has projected that role.

> Complexes originate in the immature psyche of a young child, and therefore they carry the simplistic certainty of a black-and-white worldview, in which there are only two possible positions.

When a complex is activated by some event which resonates with it, it steps in to assist or protect the ego self-image, leading to a decrease in the higher functions of consciousness and to a tendency for the complex itself to take over the ego identity. One can be playing innocently with her toddler one moment, and instantly shift into a highly capable adult ego identity when an emergency occurs. Some complexes are not well integrated into waking consciousness, however, and are related to the hidden shadow instead. They may be more demanding when activated, and attempt to invade and usurp the conscious ego identity. They are even capable of "possessing" the individual, in Jung's terminology.[228]

This bipolar split arrangement is referred to within the context of Attachment Theory as a dual and polarized internal working model. "One component contains a set of omnipotent expectations, based on the child's view of the parent's capacities mixed with infantile omnipotence, and the other component is one of total helplessness and enfeeblement, the expectations of an infant facing an unempathic caregiver."[229]

Jung used the term *archetype* to describe a deep tendency to organize experience in certain ways, related to universal human conceptualizations. He likened archetypes to imprinting in animal behavior: there is a critically sensitive time period after birth (or hatching from the egg) that the newborn is innately programmed to follow any available object as its mother. Ducks can imprint on a person or a dog if the mother hen is taken away and not available. The baby ducks now want to follow whatever they have imprinted as "mother", they want to be near it and show anxiety in its absence. Instinct is at work.

In a very similar way, human beings are innately programmed to respond to cute babies and sunsets, to the vastness of the oceans and the fierceness of a wildfire, to the inspirational hero figure and the allure of power. Each of these operates as an archetype in the individual who is touched by it. Archetypes are to the psyche what instinct is to physical existence.

There is an archetypal core to every complex, so that the child's personal experience becomes wrapped around powerful universal imagery. Heroes come to be regarded as superheroes, and villains as supervillains. Authorities may be generalized as protective and loving, or as threatening and dangerous. "Archetypes are like riverbeds which dry up when the water deserts them, but which it can find again at any time. An archetype is like an old watercourse along which the water of life has flowed for centuries, digging a deep channel for itself. The longer it has flowed in this channel the more likely it is that sooner or later the water will return to its old bed."[230] In another analogy, offered by James A. Hall, archetypes are like magnetic fields, having no apparent content in themselves but exerting a strong influence on the arrangement of any magnetizable material within the influence of their fields.[231] Or, in Jung's own words, ". . . the archetypes are, so to speak, like many little appetites in us, and if with the passing of time, they get nothing to eat, they start rumbling and upset everything."[232]

Complexes are dissociated parts of the mind with an archetype at its core, holding clusters of memories together in an unconscious grouping which is dissociated from the rest of mental functioning and serves healthy as well as pathological purposes.[233] Our complexes are created to allow us to multi-function, to operate on autopilot, and to provide cover and deniability to the ego who wishes to appear innocent. "Jung thought that whatever its roots in previous experience, neurosis consists of a refusal - or inability - in the here and now to bear legitimate suffering. Instead this painful feeling or some representation of it is split off from awareness and the initial wholeness - the primordial Self - is broken. . . . This splitting is a normal part of life. Initial wholeness is meant to be broken, and it becomes pathological or diagnosable as illness, only when the splitting off of complexes becomes too wide and deep and the conflict too intense."[234]

> We project the central archetype that is the Center of the Self outward onto an object in the world that represents an image of the ego's potential, and then identify with that projection. We place the projection out there to mirror back to us what we seek to become.

Mirroring is stage-appropriate:

- For a young child, mirroring is provided *unconsciously* by adults and peers – most importantly by parents – to establish ego identity.
- For an adolescent, it is mirrored *unconsciously* by elders and peers – most importantly by peers - to establish ego identity.
- For adults, mirroring is provided *unconsciously* by authorities, celebrities, mentors, spiritual leaders, neighbors, relatives – but most importantly those who trigger one's archetypal complexes – to establish ego identity. Only when the adult matures sufficiently to seek mirroring from a *consciously chosen* other does the mirroring become a proactive request for initiation.

Until adults reach the level of *consciously* seeking initiation, they are *un*consciously attracted for mirroring from people who activate their dominant archetypal complexes. If mother complex is a prevailing force in my life, I am activated to relate to others as either mother (as modeled for me by my mother) or as child (as my experience in relation to my mother dictates). Those that I am attracted to for representing my developmental potential are either a mother and I am the child, or they are the child and I am the mother.

When the "I" is my complex masquerading as my ego

Complexes are inherently bipolar (mother – child, father – child, rival – rival, hero – villain, dominant – submissive, safe – dangerous, etc.), that is, there are at least two adversarial shadows connected with the archetypal core. For example, the child may develop a set of defensive behaviors to deal with the source of trauma, of aggression and arrogance (which becomes a shadow over time – call it the Tyrant). But the child is shamed and punished for exhibiting that shadow, so he introjects the parental judgments and develops another behavior set, that of self-blame and inhibition (which becomes another shadow – call it the Shameful One). Now these two shadows are both intricately connected because each one mutually triggers the other. The child has sought a powerful archetypal ally in the collective that forms the core of an eventual complex around which the implicated shadows constellate. The complex is activated by the conflict between these two shadow tendencies within the complex.

> When the ego is caught up in, or captivated by, a complex, the ego identifies with one pole of the polarity (and its core archetype) and projects the other.

An extreme example of this is domestic abuse: a violent man feels his dignity is being challenged, perhaps by the boss at work or a traffic cop. That experience activates his Shameful One, which is intolerable for him, and so he projects that shadow onto his spouse and he takes up the identity of the Tyrant. Now he strikes out at her; of course, he is really striking out at the boss or the cop, and at a deeper level at the parent who originally disrespected his dignity, and at a deeper level still at the Shameful One within. But his shadow at the other end of that pole, his Shameful One, cannot be ignored through projection forever. Following the carnage wrought by the Tyrant, his Shameful One is activated and vindicated, and he apologizes profusely to his spouse, begging for forgiveness and promising to never do it again. Now his Tyrant is reminded of why he so disdains the Shameful One, and the cycle begins anew. His two shadows, each at opposite poles of the bipolar complex, will continue to irritate and activate each other in an endless loop.

Unfortunately, what I project out there, what my ego has rejected and *dis*identified with, nevertheless remains an inseparable part of me. My complex has created a double bind with no escape: if I identify myself as dominant, then I must project the submissive out onto others (how else can I experience being dominant?), but then I am surrounded by submissive people, or people who challenge me because they refuse to be submissive. The autonomous complex is the embodiment of one's least developed and most conflicted aspect of personality.[235]

The question arises, what is the difference between a complex and an alter personality in an individual diagnosed with Dissociative Identity Disorder (multiple personalities)? The alter personalities in DID are unipolar, that is, there is only one unidimensional shadow which recruits an archetypal ally within each alter. One might be a rageful child, angry at the world for all the mistreatment she experienced. Another might be a careful adaptive child who is hypervigilant, anticipating any potential threat in the immediate environment. Another might be aggressive and arrogant, and another self-blaming and inhibited. Each of these splinter selves has its own archetypal ally, so it exists as one-dimensional. The psyche's conflicts are therefore not *within* each independent personality (as the conflict in an autonomous complex is between component shadows) but rather *between* personalities.

And the healing of DID involves bringing each alter personality from its status as independent to that of being an autonomous complex. Operationally, that means to allow the alter personality to explore its existence and origins enough to develop an awareness of competing shadows. The aggressive and arrogant one becomes aware of the additional dimension of self-blame. The resulting complex has co-consciousness with other splinters within the psyche.

Ultimately, any individual brings all their splinter parts, or subpersonalities, to awareness, and the ego recognizes itself to be a sibling rather than a parent or an overlord. Resolution of lifelong patterns of conflict lies in surrender to the ultimate organizing principle of the individual, the Self, the *Archetypal Self*, the Transpersonal Self, the creator of the grand illusion and the one within most capable of accessing the conflict-free center core resources. We investigate more about that exciting prospect later.

6. Wilber and Integral Psychology

Ken Wilber has been a dynamic force in the creation and evolution of transpersonal psychology. Beginning with the publication of his first book in 1977, *The Spectrum of Consciousness*, he has elucidated some of the basic building blocks of the new branch of psychology. He suggested that human selfhood develops from a *pre-personal* subconscious (survival concerns characterized by an awareness of nature and body) to a *personal* self-consciousness (belonging concerns characterized by an awareness of mind and psychic realities) and finally to *transpersonal* superconsciousness (an awareness of subtle, causal and ultimate realities).[236] The evolving self has three components: a basic structure (enduring characteristics such as linguistics, cognition, spatial coordination, etc.); transitional structures (characteristics that develop and dissolve such as worldviews, self needs, moral stages, etc.); and the self and its fulcrums (characteristics that unite and integrate the other two components, such as identification, organization, will, defense, and 'digestion of experience').[237]

Human beings are hard-wired to develop to higher levels of maturity and functioning in all domains (referred to as "developmental lines"): affective, cognitive, moral, spiritual, and interpersonal. The 'self' juggles these developmental lines as they compete with each other, or eclipse one another, or synergize their growth. Advancing to a higher level is to transcend the previous level, which always means incorporating the accumulated skills and knowledge of that previous level of development. Because awareness has *"differentiated* from (or disidentified from, or transcended) an *exclusive* identification with body, persona, ego, and mind, it can now *integrate* them in a unified fashion, in a new and higher holon with each of them as junior partners."[238]

Introspection is the best source of reliable data for deeper understanding. "The more one can introspect and reflect on one's self, then the more detached from that self one can become, the more one can rise above that self's limited perspective, and so the less narcissistic or less egocentric one becomes (or the more *decentered* one becomes)."[239]

In terms of psychopathology, people operating at the pre-personal level of consciousness identify with only certain acceptable aspects of the 'ego' and project, deny, or repress other aspects. Hence a split occurs and a boundary is drawn between the 'persona' (acceptable aspects) and the 'shadow' (unacceptable aspects), which results in a greatly narrowed self-image. Individuals operating at the personal level of consciousness identify with more of the total organism (known variously as the mind, the ego, the personality, or the psyche), but exclude the body. That is, the split occurs and the boundary is drawn here between the mind and body. "I *am* my mind, and I *have* a body." Therefore, self-identity does not directly encompass the organism-as-a-whole but only an aspect of the organism. The third level of consciousness, and the last in which a split occurs and a boundary line is drawn, is what Wilber calls the 'total organism' level. Individuals at this level of consciousness identify with their whole organism but draw a line between their organism and the environment. This 'skin-boundary' is a fundamental self/not-self distinction. A final stage of development is possible: it is only at the 'unity consciousness' level that all such boundaries are transcended, and a person feels "at one with the universe." Needless to say, few human beings reach this level of consciousness other than as occasional peak experiences.

And Wilber assigns different types of therapies to be most appropriate for people struggling with conflicts related to each of these splits. Those at the pre-personal level struggling to reclaim much of the unconscious psyche so that the 'persona' and 'shadow' are reunited to create a strong and healthy ego would be best served by psychoanalysis and many conventional forms of psychodynamic therapies. At the next level, the personal level, many therapies within the body-mind genre, energy psychology and martial arts, are designed to heal the split between the ego and the body, to reunite the psyche and the soma and, in so doing, liberate the vast potentials of the total organism.

Finally, those at the 'total organism' level, the transpersonal level, struggling to heal the split between the total organism and the environment, can benefit from such disciplines as Buddhism or Vedanta Hinduism, shamanic rituals or various forms of meditation to reveal a supreme identify with the entire universe at the level of unity consciousness.

> But between the level of unity consciousness and the level of the total organism there are what Wilber calls the "transpersonal bands" of the spectrum. It is here then, it seems, that we have found the place on the spectrum for the various transpersonal therapies—psychosynthesis, Jungian analysis, various preliminary yoga practices, certain forms of meditation, for example—that focus on the vision of the transcendent citizenship of the human spirit, the experience of the interconnectedness of all things, a sense of the sublime, and the quest for ultimate meaning.[240]

And it is here in this schema that the difference between humanistic psychology (the Third Force) and transpersonal psychology (the Fourth Force) is most clearly distinguished. Growth for the humanistic approaches is defined as self-actualization and a balanced integration of physical, emotional, and mental aspects of health, whereas the spiritual dimension, which is vital in transpersonal work, may be neglected, ignored, or even invalidated by the humanistic approach. And it is here that ego-transcendence becomes a motivating factor, not as an escape from the rigors of the pursuit of self-actualization but rather as a natural next step of expansion of self identity.

7. Shamanic and Indigenous Traditions

Shamanism may be defined as "a family of traditions whose practitioners focus on voluntarily entering altered states of consciousness in which they experience themselves, or their spirit(s), traveling to other realms at will and interacting with other entities in order to serve their community."[241] Notice that the shaman is presumed to have the ability to enter and exit altered states of consciousness, and to navigate to and through other non-physical realms of reality. The shaman specializes in a trance state of consciousness during which he experiences himself as a disembodied soul or spirit, ascending to the upper realms or descending to the underworld. In these other realms, shamans usually see and interact with 'spirits' from whom they seek power, information, help, or healing.[242]

> Shamanistic healing practices utilize what Dow (1986; also see Winkelman, 2010) referred to as the universal aspects of symbolic healing. The processes of symbolic healing involve placing the patient's personal circumstances within the context of the culture's mythology and cosmology, and then using the drama of ritual to manipulate the patient's emotions, attachments, and relationships. The prior linkages of emotions and cultural symbols permit ritual enactments to produce emotional transformations of the patients. The ritual elicitation and manipulation of unconscious culturally-programmed psychological, emotional, and physiological structures enables shamanistic healers to produce a variety of healing responses, reflected in the psychodynamic differences in the ASCs [altered states of consciousness] of soul journey, possession, and meditation.[243]

One who would journey usually requires some form of preparations, which might range from physical (e.g., fasting, water deprivation, solitude, exposure to temperature extremes, extensive exercise, celibacy, sleep deprivation, or dream incubation) to pharmacological (tobacco or psychedelics), to rhythm (drumming, music or dance), to ritual (group gatherings and involvement or social isolation), to spiritual (purification and prayer).[244]

The entry into the spirit world, in corporeal form or by inhabiting (or transforming into) an animal or spirit ally, is key to many of the shaman's activities. These might include divination, clairvoyance, healing, recovery of lost souls, communication with spirits of the dead, escorting souls of the dead, protection against spirits and sorcerers, and acquiring information about group members or to aid in hunting.[245]

Winkelman[246] has documented a pattern of brain activity common among shamans that he calls the *integrative mode of consciousness*. The integrative mode of consciousness produces an overall slowing of the brain waves, parasympathetic relaxation, and a shift of brain activity towards lower regions. There is greater coherence in the presence of synchronized theta wave patterns reflecting action on serotonergic mechanisms that result in an enhanced integration of information from lower levels of the brain. This integration is manifested in brain wave entrainment in which the frontal cortex is synchronized by highly coherent and synchronized slowwave discharges emanating from the limbic system and related lower-brain structures. These entrainments are characterized by a variety of frequencies of brain waves, but there are two predominant patterns: synchronized slow-wave theta bands (3-6 cycles per second) and the high-frequency gamma oscillations (40+ cps).

> A typical shamanic mechanism to induce the *integrative mode of consciousness* involves the manipulation of the autonomic nervous system through extensive sympathetic activation, produced through entrainment by powerful external stimulation, that eventually leads into a collapse into a parasympathetic dominant state. This collapse phase is accompanied by a slowing of the brain wave discharges into a more synchronized and coherent pattern.

A typical modern day transpersonal psychologist approaches the induction of a similar *integrative mode of consciousness* with different technology. Techniques used for transcendence in more technologically advanced cultures tend to become increasingly subtle, internal, and focused on mental training and control, relying more on meditation, hypnosis and mind control.[247] Meditation and hypnosis yield the same basic systemic physiological patterns underlying the concept of the integrative mode of consciousness—enhanced synchronization of brain wave patterns. "In contrast to the orientation to the external sensory world, hypnosis and other ASC reflect the principles of the integrative mode of consciousness involving an engagement with the imagination that controls the body, including physiological responses, perceptions, emotions, behaviors, and thoughts."[248]

The methods of inducing altered states of consciousness vary in this way, and so do the metaphysical beliefs about the ontological reality of the experiences. "In shamanism, soul journeys are usually viewed literally as a journey across or between worlds. Likewise the inhabitants of these worlds—whether spirits, power animals, or the souls of the dead—are also viewed as real, independent beings who battle or befriend, help or heal. Shamans, in other words, are ontological realists. By contrast most contemporary Westerners would view such journeys, as well as the worlds and beings in them, as imaginal, that is, as products of the shaman's psyche created via processes such as creative imagination or active imagination (Jung, 1961)."[249]

Drumming can induce a hypnotic trance state, and "individuals who report the most unusual or 'visionary' experiences during drumming are probably those individuals who are likely to be most hypnotizable and may be entering an altered state of consciousness similar to that achieved by formal hypnotic induction procedures."[250] Cardena[251] draws some interesting parallels in the experiences of shamanistic "trance states" and deep hypnosis.

> In the self-assessed lighter levels of hypnosis, reports include alterations of the bodily image (e.g., the torso getting increasingly larger) and vivid sensations of sinking (falling without reaching bottom, falling through a shaft, sinking in the sea, etc.) and later becoming separated from the body and floating (or flying through space; being in a plane, etc.). At somewhat deeper levels, there are frequent reports of journeys and adventures of the phenomenal body (e.g., being in a dark world, encountering a limitless sea, etc.) At the deepest level, the experiences reported include hearing beautiful music and seeing unearthly colors, being in a timeless/spaceless realm, becoming light and energetic, losing one's identity, absolute blackness, absolute mental quiet, enormous peace, being one with everything, being in touch with a greater entity, and voidness/blankness.[252]

Not only indigenous shamans experience such disembodied journeys. "Both near-death experiences and dreams can result in journeys that are powerful, informative, transformative, and healing. Of course the specific experiences may be very different from typical shamanic ones. However, the general pattern of entering an altered state of mind, and traveling as a disembodied entity to other realms may occur."[253]

Another example of non-shamans experiencing transpersonal journeys between realms has been chronicled by Kyriacos C. Markides[254], who has studied with and written extensively about Eastern Orthodox mysticism. He insists that "extraordinary phenomena related to shamanism studied by anthropologists in pre-literate societies (Harner, 1982) can also be found within modern societies."[255] He reports on the practices of Orthodox Christian mystics, healers, and psychics who use Christian symbols to explain their experiences and worldview, and whose well-defined tradition of experiential practices lead to mystical illumination and ecstasy.

8. Eastern Orthodox Mysticism

Orthodoxy speaks of three distinct stages that every human soul must traverse in order to reunite with God. First the soul must be purified of egotistical passions and desires, and the mind expanded beyond its exclusive reliance on the senses and rational intellect for understanding reality. For example, fasting is used as a form of spiritual exercise, in order to master the passion of gluttony. Sexual abstinence frees the energy and re-directs it exclusively towards the higher goal of establishing an 'erotic' relationship with God. Poverty and renouncing ownership of material objects or worldly desires and ambitions brings humility.

The last two stages lie beyond the ego. Once the soul has undergone its purification, there is then the stage of the illumination or enlightenment of the soul. This is a gift of grace, and brings with it gifts of the spirit such as divine visions and wisdom, prophetic vision, healing, clairvoyance, and other extraordinary abilities that seem to violate the known laws of the material universe.

Finally, there is the stage of union with God as the final destination and ultimate home of the human soul. This stage is beyond all stages and it defies human understanding. The individual who has attained this level of development by absorbing all the gifts of grace is celebrated by the Divine as was the Prodigal Son on his return to the Father. He does not lose his identity upon his return to the Palace; he carries along with him into his new deified state the accumulated experiences of his worldly sojourn. And with it he becomes an emissary of the Holy Spirit, choosing to live among fellow humans and serving them through word and deed as did the apostles.

[T]he Eastern branch of Christianity, or Eastern Orthodox Christianity, because of its unique historical and theological developments has preserved in its monastic orders a methodology and practice for spiritual transcendence that may parallel those of Eastern religions. Such spiritual methods, once liberated from their archaic cultural context, may be relevant not only to transpersonal theory but also to contemporary western seekers who may feel more at ease with spiritual practices that spring from within their own cultural and religious traditions. In this sense the mystical pathways preserved in Eastern Orthodox Christianity may play a role not only in the enrichment of transpersonal theory but also in making a contribution towards a possible 're-enchantment' of the West.[256]

Orthodoxy has clearly impacted transpersonal psychology through its teaching that people's understanding of God is based on their spiritual maturity, and the level of maturity moves through unique stages of growth toward wholeness. Orthodoxy holds that people fall into three spiritual age-groups: the 'slaves' of God, the 'employees' of God, and the 'lovers' of God.

The 'slaves' hold an infantile understanding of God, viewing God as a punishing overlord who dispenses punishments to those who violate His commandments. The 'employees' are in an exchange relationship with the Divine, doing good and following the commandments because they expect to be rewarded by God. Those who truly understand God are the 'lovers of God', the great saints and mystics of Christianity. These are people who have experienced and tasted the heart of God, who do good and follow the commandments not because of fear or expectation of rewards but because of a passionate love for God.[257]

In transpersonal psychology these three stages are referred to as pre-personal, personal, and transpersonal levels of development or approaches to relationship with creation and creator.[258] These three major phases are also referred to as preconventional, conventional and post-conventional. This applies to the development of cognition, morality, faith, motivation and the self-sense. At the pre-personal level of development the universe revolves around *I, me and mine*, and the determining factor in moment-to-moment experience is pleasure vs. pain, reward vs. punishment. Most people grow into social beings in adolescence, operating at the personal level of development, identifying primarily with a separate, isolated ego and self-concepts determined by social roles. Success in life at this level is defined by the absence of pathology and the ability to achieve a modicum of satisfaction in relationships and work.

Some people are not satisfied with success at that level, and seek ultimate satisfaction or optimum psychological health. Thus is born the search for meaning, the impulse to grow and express oneself creatively, and eventually to transcend oneself and contribute to the common good. These are the transpersonal 'lovers of God'.

> Although each stage of development is replaced by a subsequent stage, the basic structures of consciousness remain intact (Wilber, 2000). The evolutionary process from matter to life to mind to soul to Spirit is reflected in the evolution of self-concepts derived from body, emotions, mind and soul (Vaughan, 2000). The evolution of consciousness offers greater freedom at each stage and an expanded awareness of self and world. For example, when the infant differentiates the body from the environment he or she can act on the environment. When the child learns to control emotions, he or she can interact more effectively in a social environment. When a person learns to control the mind, he or she may begin to attain a sense of inner freedom that is reflected in self-actualization and self-transcendence.[259]

Chapter Five

Transcendence, Self-Transcendence, and Ego Surrender

Non-ordinary States of Consciousness

As has been discussed in the section on Dr. Stan Grof, "non-ordinary states of consciousness" may be a better terminology than "altered states of consciousness" because of the latter's implication of distortion or impairment of the "correct way" of experiencing the world. Grof has suggested the use of the term *holotropic* for the large subgroup of non-ordinary states of consciousness that are of great importance to transpersonal psychology, spiritual development, shamanic and mystical exploration, and transpersonal therapy. Generally we will use the more common "non-ordinary states", and we will explore hypnosis, meditation, shamanistic states, and dreams.

> Spiritual experiences appear in two different forms. The first of these, the experience of the *immanent divine*, is characterized by subtly but profoundly transformed perception of the everyday reality. A person having this form of spiritual experience sees people, animals, plants, and inanimate objects in the environment as radiant manifestations of a unified field of cosmic creative energy. He or she has a direct perception of the immaterial nature of the physical world and realizes that the boundaries between objects are illusory and unreal. The second form of spiritual experience, that of the *transcendent divine*, involves manifestation of archetypal beings and realms of reality that are ordinarily transphenomenal, that is unavailable to perception in the everyday state of consciousness. In this type of spiritual experience, entirely new elements seem to "unfold" or "explicate"—to borrow terms from David Bohm—from another level or order of reality.[260]

To paraphrase Charles Tart, a scholarly approach carried out only in 'normal' Western consciousness, while valuable, is bound to miss some of the most important parts of the spiritual/transpersonal knowledge being studied; for the heart of most, if not all, spiritual/transpersonal systems is state-specific knowledge–knowledge that is only fully accessible in appropriate altered states of consciousness (ASCs). [261]

> We can study accounts and studies and theories of prenatal awareness, or the birth experience, or transcendent peak experiences, but a full immersion in such an experience is required to incorporate the 'knowledge' and make it real.

An example of this general principle is dream work. We have found that analyzing a remembered dream with the resources of the conscious egoic mind is limited by its degree of 'reality-testing' (i.e., implicit assumptions and beliefs about reality), its ability to suspend disbelief, and the extent of stored culturally derived symbolic meanings. On the other hand, entering a dream-like state allows one to virtually re-enter the dream itself and to dialogue with the dream elements or symbols. This creates an opportunity for the same quality of mental processing that *dreamed* the dream to clarify and elucidate the dream. We have found hypnosis to be a viable, reliable, and manageable vehicle for accessing such a dream-like state.

Another example is using hypnosis or ASC-inducing breathing techniques to age-regress to the birth, to the womb, to the moment of conception, or back to the initial entry into the earthly plane, transitioning from what came before. Needless to say, there is a profound difference between intellectually entertaining such an experience and the felt experience of re-entering it through stored body memories facilitated by an ASC.

Archetypal center core energies, e.g., inner resources such as inner strength and inner wisdom referred to by Claire Frederick, are examples of intrapsychic phenomena that "usually require a hypnotic trance state for activation"[262], and that "are transcendent in the specific sense that they promote conscious-unconscious complementarity (Gilligan, 1987; Jung, 1960)."[263] Also, they are liminal; center core activity may initiate long-term change by leading the patient to the threshold of new and transformative realizations, and new behaviors lead to new thoughts and experiences.[264] We will explore archetypal center core phenomena later.

Frederick and McNeal (1999) eventually came to regard inner strength, inner love, inner wisdom—indeed all of the archetypal center core phenomena—as part of the conflict-free sphere of the ego that had been identified and extensively described by Hartmann (1961, 1965). They also thought that they behaved like Jung's archetypes in that they were transpersonal and part of the mental structure.[265]

We do want to note that our use of the terminology 'hypnosis' is a convention in our time in the 20th and 21st centuries and our Western culture. However, many other historical times and diverse cultures have utilized 'hypnosis-like' procedures to induce ASCs in order to access state-specific knowledge for spiritual or other transpersonal explorations.

Krippner[266] asserts that alterations in consciousness are not only sanctioned but are also deliberately fostered by virtually all indigenous groups. He cites Bourguignon and Evascu[267] who read ethnographic descriptions of 488 different societies, finding that 89% were characterized by socially approved alterations of consciousness.

Self-construal and Metapersonal Self

Transpersonal psychology has been differentiated from humanistic psychology largely as affirming and facilitating the potentiality for self-transcendence beyond self-actualization. Therefore it behooves us to explore and define more carefully what is self, and what is self-transcendence.

As we have seen, the concept of self was introduced into psychology as a psychic entity, separate from and supraordinate to ego, by Assagioli, Hartmann, and Jung and accepted by all the existentialist, humanistic, and transpersonal psychologists since them. Freud did not recognize a self that encompassed the ego, id and superego. Actually, the concept of a self was offered by Kierkegaard, an early influence on the existentialists, when he suggested that the self is not, but is always becoming.[268]

Conceptualizing a self is the response to recognizing the presence of both an 'I' and a 'me' in people's internal experience. People develop a sense of self through reflexive consciousness (how one thinks about oneself), through the interpersonal aspects of the self (examining the self in social context, in relation to others), and through the executive function (the decision-maker and action taker).[269] In this way, one consciously looks back toward oneself and constructs a concept of one's self. The Western view of the individual tends to be of an independent, self-contained, autonomous entity. This view reflects the pre-personal and personal levels of development, but not necessarily that of the transpersonal.

In the self-psychology literature, these first two perspectives are called the independent and interdependent self-construals, based on the degree to which people see themselves as separate from others or connected with others.[270] The independent is an individualist, sees himself as a stable set of known and well-defined qualities, and regards others in the same way as characteristics and attributes rather than on how they are related. Another approach to self-construal is dominant in other cultures, for example in most Asian and African societies, and in line with a feminist approach. The interdependent is a flexible and variable self, emphasizing external or public features such as status, roles and relationships, and concerned with belonging and fitting in with others.

There is a less recognized and less common third self-construal type: the transpersonal, or *metapersonal self*.[271] People who cannot be described in terms of the current two definitions of self-construal experience themselves as decentered and free from egocentricity. They may be described as a transcendent self[272], or as self-expansive.[273] The metapersonal self may reflect on others or things and sees them as part of the self, in the sense that when one is hurt we are all hurt, or that there is not a firm boundary between 'me' and the forest. When one construes the self as connected to all things, all of creation, then this reveals the self in social context as metapersonal. When the executive function or the agent of the self, the decision-maker and the one who takes specific action, behaves in a manner that takes into account all things, then the executive function is that of the metapersonal self. This concept has been identified in the transpersonal literature.[274]

> [Metapersonal self] is defined as a sense of one's identity that extends beyond the individual or personal to encompass wider aspects of humankind, life, psyche, or the cosmos (Walsh &

Vaughan, 1993b). The descriptive self-representations of individuals who refer not to individual attributes (as with the independent self), nor to relationships and social groups (as with the interdependent self), but to an essence beyond the individual and others to a universal focus (e.g., I am connected to all of humankind, I am part of a natural order) is that of the metapersonal self-construal.[275]

These three types of self-construal are not mutually exclusive. They may co-occur, depending on how the self is developing.

Research suggests that individuals with an independent self will experience more ego-focused emotions such as vigor, fatigue, anger, frustration, and pride; and individuals with the interdependent self-construal will experience more other-focused emotions such as sympathy and shame.[276] Individuals with metapersonal self will be highly tolerant of ambiguity, and readily forgiving.

The Metapersonal Self Scale[277] is composed of ten questions with self-ratings on a Likert scale.

1. My personal existence is very purposeful and meaningful.
2. I believe that no matter where I am or what I'm doing, I am never separate from others.
3. I feel a real sense of kinship with all living things.
4. My sense of inner peace is one of the most important things to me.
5. I take the time each day to be peaceful and quiet, to empty my mind of everyday thoughts.
6. I believe that intuition comes from a higher part of myself and I never ignore it.
7. I feel a sense of responsibility and belonging to the universe.
8. My sense of identity is based on something that unites me with all other people.
9. I am aware of a connection between myself and all living things.
10. I see myself as being extended into everything else.

Transpersonal Identification and Transpersonal Self

Boyer[278] comments that we are all energetically wired for transcendence.

Self-transcendence refers both to a process of developing beyond one's immediate self-boundaries, beyond one's self-construal, as well as to a quality that emerges as a result of this process, culminating in a broadened worldview.[279]

Of course, one of the treacherous and seductive entrapments in the business of transcendence is to use it as a means of escape from what is being transcended. This can take the form of 'spiritual bypassing', in which the individual focuses on spiritual experience as a short-cut to resolving or avoiding psychological developmental tasks.[280] Wallace Stevens said in his poem *Reply to Papini*[281]

> "The way through the world is more difficult to find than the way beyond it."

Self-transcendence, or transcending the ego, needs to be carefully defined in order to avoid throwing the baby out with the bathwater. Aspiring to more mature stages of adult development does not require abandoning the ego or "killing" it. And yet, as Maslow observed, "its function is to erase itself." Transformational development may be observed as "operating in different ways on many distinctive facets of the ego, promoting change and development *within* the ego, rather than beyond it. This view requires that the ego be understood as a complex and sophisticated matrix of structures, functions and representations, rather than as a single entity that could be readily abandoned. It recognizes the indispensability of the ego while at the same time revealing how meditation practice can uniquely modify it, producing an ego no longer obsessed with its own solidity."[282]

The self-concept "becomes increasingly differentiated, fragmented, elusive and ultimately transparent."[283] The highly developed ego, through its transparency to itself, is able to achieve a "therapeutic split"[284], becoming both subject and object, observer and observed, a witness to the dynamic flow of psychic events. This 'witness consciousness' and the self-transcendence upon which it is based are also foundational ingredients of higher stages of human development, which we will explore shortly.

Another useful definition is, "the extent to which a person identifies the self as . . . an integral part of the universe as a whole."[285] Cloninger et al. devised the Temperament and Character Inventory, which includes a self-transcendence subscale. The developmental theory underlying this body of work suggests that self-transcendence develops in a predictable sequence. Self-forgetfulness leads an individual to more transpersonal identification. Self-forgetful experience is characterized by a state of absorption in external events, and represents the momentary dissolution of self-other boundaries in an experience labeled by Csikszentmihalyi as 'flow'.[286] Increasing occurrence of such a loosening of ego identification lays the groundwork for transpersonal identification, i.e., a relatively steady sense of unity with objects outside the individual self. This is similar to Maslow's distinction between 'peak experiences' (sporadic and occasional) and 'plateau experience' (a relatively stable structure of personality incorporating an expanded state of consciousness).[287]

So, transformation may be temporary or lasting. The temporary transformation we call an "altered state of consciousness" or a "non-ordinary state". It might be a dream state, a hypnotic trance, meditation, absorption in creative activity, or transcendence. Transcendence is traveling beyond, leaving the existing system in place, only to come back to it eventually. These momentary experiences are valuable because they give one a "glimpse" of the possibilities. But the real work of transformation is to extend *peak experiences* into a *plateau experience*, making the extraordinary ordinary, making a transitory altered *state* into an enduring altered *trait*. Or in Cloninger's terminology, self-forgetful experience leads to transpersonal identification.

> Transpersonal identification in turn expands into a stable perspective or worldview toward belief in forces that cannot be rationally comprehended or objectively proven, which Cloninger calls spiritual acceptance, Maslow calls transcending self-actualization, and Wilber calls transpersonal self.

Csikszentmihalyi[288] has compiled a list of eight distinct dimensions of experience common to most people when they are thoroughly enjoying themselves, when they experience the best moments in their lives. Those eight dimensions, the total experience of which he calls *flow*, are:

1. Clear goals: an objective is distinctly defined, and offers immediate feedback – one knows instantly how well one is doing
2. The opportunities for acting decisively are high, and they are matched by one's perceived ability to act, i.e., personal skills
3. Action and awareness merge: one-pointedness of mind
4. Concentration on the task at hand; irrelevant worries and concerns temporarily disappear from consciousness
5. A sense of potential control
6. Loss of self-consciousness, transcendence of ego boundaries, a sense of growth and of being part of something greater than self
7. Altered sense of time, which usually seems to pass faster
8. Experience is autotelic – worth doing for its own sake.

A central key to achieving the state that Csikszentmihalyi calls *flow* seems to be transcendence of ego boundaries, an expansion of one's sense of self that is at the same time *not* self-conscious. It is a merging of the 'I' and the 'Me', it is both transcendent (incorporating the upper realm) and immanent (incorporated into the lower realm). It is, in a very real sense, not conscious but rather unconscious.

Maslow claimed that people are oriented toward either growth or safety in their everyday lives and that a growth orientation more effectively facilitates psychological health and well-being.[289] What is the connection, then, between ego development and Maslow's hierarchy of needs conceptualization of human motivation, where self-actualization "refers to the desire for self-fulfillment, namely, to the tendency for him to become actualized in what he is potentially."[290]

Self-actualization and Transcending Self-actualization

Abraham Maslow originated the notion of self-actualization over 50 years ago to describe the movement, both vertically and horizontally, toward optimal functioning. Maslow[291] specified eight qualities of a self-actualizing moment:

1. "experiencing fully, vividly, selflessly, with full concentration and total absorption";
2. making the progression choice in a given moment rather than the regression choice, the growth choice instead of the fear choice;
3. letting the self emerge by listening to one's inner voice, what Maslow called the "impulse voices," instead of "Mommy's introjected voice or Daddy's voice or to the voice of the Establishment, of the Elders, of authority, or of tradition";
4. being honest rather than not, taking responsibility for one's beliefs and perspectives;
5. being courageous, not afraid, daring to be different, unpopular, nonconformist;
6. using one's intelligence to go through an arduous and demanding period of preparation in order to realize one's possibilities;
7. setting up the conditions so that peak experiences are more likely by, for example, breaking up an illusion, getting rid of a false notion, learning what one is not good at, learning what one's potentialities are *not*;
8. opening oneself up to one's own psychopathology, identifying defenses and finding the courage to give them up.

Maslow[292] goes on to elucidate what happens in moments of peak experience, of here-now immersion and self-forgetfulness, which he also calls "the creative attitude":

1. *Total fascination* with the matter-in-hand, getting lost in the present, detached from time and place;
2. *Giving up the past* to the extent that it is "an inert, undigested foreign body" (p. 61) of platitudes, assumptions, mistaken beliefs, or unresolved conflicts. When I have truly digested past experiences, they are

now integral to my present experience, and live no longer in the past;

3. *Giving up the future* to the extent that it devalues the present. This kind of forgetting about the future or giving up being apprehensive about it is a prerequisite to total involvement with the present;

4. *Innocence,* "being naked in the situation, guileless, without a priori expectations, without 'shoulds' or 'oughts,' without fashions, fads, dogmas, habits, or other pictures-in-the-head of what is proper, normal, 'right,' as being ready to receive whatever happens to be the case without surprise, shock, indignation, or denial" (p. 62);

5. *Narrowing of consciousness,* less distracted by obligations, duties, fears and hopes in relation to others in our life, which in turn means that we become much more ourselves, our authentic selves;

6. *Loss of ego: self-forgetfulness, loss of self-consciousness* due to being totally absorbed in non-self rather than observing oneself like a spectator or a critic; "you become less dissociated than usual into a self-observing ego and an experiencing ego; i.e., you come much closer to being *all* experiencing ego" (p. 63);

7. *Inhibiting Force of Consciousness (of Self).* Consciousness of self can be a locus of doubts and judgments and can inhibit spontaneity when the self-observing ego eclipses the experiencing ego. Yet a functioning self-observing ego is necessary to accomplish anything real.

8. *Fears disappear.* "For the time being, we are courageous and confident, unafraid, unanxious, unneurotic, not sick" (p. 64). Our depressions, conflicts, ambivalence, worries, problems, and even our physical pains disappear.

9. *Lessening of defenses and inhibitions.* Guardedness, Freudian defenses, and controls on impulses tend to disappear.

10. *Strength and courage.* Such courage can take the form of independence and self-sufficiency, sometimes to the extreme of stubbornness, and strength of character or ego-strength, sometimes to the extreme of arrogance.

11. *Acceptance: the positive attitude.* We give up being critical, skeptical and judgmental, instead allowing experience to flow in around us.

12. *Trust vs. trying, controlling, striving.* One rests in a basic trust in the self and in the world, giving up the attempt to control and dominate. Maslow offers some examples of experiences that require a relaxed "letting things happen" approach rather than trying, straining and controlling: giving birth, floating in water, urination, defecation, sleeping, and sexual surrender.

13. *Taoistic receptivity.* An attitude of receptivity and noninterference is evident, of respectful attention and acceptance of things "as they are". This attitude applies to a problem or obstacle, to available resources, to any situation encountered, or to other people. It amounts to an eagerness for things to unfold as they will, according to their innate nature, without being manipulated or forced.

14. *Integration of the B-cognizer (vs. dissociation).* In the act of creating, or experiencing peak moments, one tends to be whole, integrated, all of a piece. "Here-now-allness is less dissociated (split) and more one" (p. 66).

15. *Permission to dip into primary process.* Primary process (poetic, metaphoric, mystic, primitive, archaic, childlike) allows access to recovery of aspects of the unconscious, liberating the person from the limitations of the conscious, analytic, rational intellect.

16. *Aesthetic perceiving rather than abstracting.* This form of perceiving is an attitude of noninterfering savoring, nonintruding appreciation, which keeps one from confusing the map for the territory. "For many confused scientists and philosophers, the equation, the concept, or the blueprint have become more real than the phenomenological reality itself" (p. 67).

17. *Fullest spontaneity.* Our capabilities adapt to the changing situation quickly, effortlessly, and flexibly just as fine dancers mutually adapt to each other, or as water flows into cracks and contours.

18. *Fullest expressiveness (of uniqueness).* Without effortful striving, the only determinant of outcome is the deepest-

level intrinsic nature of the person and the interacting environment together, forming a fusion.

19. *Fusion of the Person with the World.* Maslow quotes Hokusai: "If you want to draw a bird, you must become a bird" (p. 68).

Acknowledging the progression from *pre-personal* and *personal* levels to the *transpersonal*, Maslow eventually began to distinguish *transcending self-actualizing* individuals, described as exhibiting "unitive perception," or the "fusion of the eternal with the temporal, the sacred with the profane"[293] from what he called *nontranscending self-actualizers.*[294] He described such people as "more essentially practical, realistic, mundane, capable, and secular people, living more in the here and now world . . . 'doers' rather than meditators or contemplators, effective and pragmatic rather than aesthetic, reality-testing and cognitive rather than emotional and experiencing."[295] Due to this observation, in his unpublished critique of self-actualization theory, Maslow thought that "self-actualization is not enough" for a full picture of the optimally functioning human being.[296]

> In this progression, the ego's very self-identity changes, elevating beyond itself, beyond personal biographical history. And as that expansion occurs, one begins to see as an object of observation what previously was experienced as the observer. This evolving "subject/object relationship" will be explored further shortly.

Finally, Maslow compiled a set of qualities that distinguish transcending self-actualizers from nontranscending self-actualizers.[297] We present here a summary of characteristics of transcending self-actualizers, or transcenders.

1. For the transcenders, peak experiences and plateau experiences become *the* most important things in their lives, the most precious aspect of life.
2. They speak naturally and unconsciously the language of Being (B-language), the language of poets, of mystics, of seers, of profoundly religious men, of men who live under the aspect of eternity, the language of parable and paradox.

3. They perceive unitively the sacred within the secular, i.e., the sacredness in all things *at the same time* that they also see them at the practical, everyday level. This ability is in *addition* to—not mutually exclusive with—good reality testing.

4. They are much more consciously and deliberately metamotivated by the values of perfection, truth, beauty, goodness, unity, dichotomy-transcendence.

5. They seem somehow to recognize each other, and to come to almost instant intimacy and mutual understanding even upon first meeting.

6. They are *more* responsive to beauty, or rather they tend to beautify all things.

7. They are *more* holistic about the world than are the "healthy" or practical self-actualizers (who are also holistic in this same sense). Mankind is one, and such limiting concepts as the "national interest" or "the religion of my fathers" or "different grades of people or of IQ" either cease to exist or are easily transcended.

8. Overlapping this statement of holistic perceiving is a strengthening of the self-actualizer's natural tendency to synergy—intrapsychic, interpersonal, intracultural.

9. They transcend the ego (the Self, the identity) more often and more easily.

10. Not only are such people lovable, but they are also more awe-inspiring, more "unearthly, more easily revered." They more often produced in Maslow the thought, "This is a great man."

11. Transcenders are far more apt to be innovators, discovers of the new, of what actually *could* be, what exists *in potential*.

12. They can be more ecstatic, more rapturous than the happy and healthy ones, yet maybe more prone to a kind of cosmic-sadness over the stupidity of people, their self-defeat, their blindness, their cruelty to each other, their shortsightedness.

13. Transcenders can more easily live in both the D- and B-realms (Deficit and Being realms) simultaneously than can the merely healthy self-actualizers because they can sacralize everybody so much more easily. The way of

phrasing this paradox that Maslow found useful is this: The factually "superior" transcending self-actualizer acts always to the factually "inferior" person as to a brother, a member of the family who must be loved and cared for no matter what he does because he is after all a member of the family.

14. Peak-experiencers and transcenders in particular, as well as self-actualizers in general, find mystery is *attractive* and challenging rather than frightening. In contrast, most people pursue knowledge to lessen mystery and thereby reduce anxiety. The self-actualizer is apt to be bored by what is well known, however useful this knowledge may be, and encountering new knowledge to be awed before the tremendousness of the universe. At the highest levels of development of humanness, knowledge leads to a sense of mystery, awe, humility, ultimate ignorance, and reverence.

15. Transcenders are less afraid of "nuts" and "kooks" than are other self-actualizers, and are also more able to screen out the apparent nuts and kooks who are *not* creative contributors.

16. Transcenders tend to be more "reconciled with evil" in the sense of understanding its occasional inevitability and necessity in the larger holistic sense. Since this implies a better understanding of apparent evil, it generates *both* a greater compassion with it *and* a less ambivalent and more decisive, more unyielding fight against it.

17. Transcenders are more apt to regard themselves as *carriers* of talent, *instruments* of the transpersonal, temporary custodians so to speak of a greater intelligence or skill or leadership or efficiency. This means a certain particular kind of objectivity or detachment toward themselves that to nontranscenders might sound like arrogance, grandiosity, or even paranoia. Transcendence brings with it a "transpersonal" loss of ego.

18. Transcenders are more apt to be profoundly "religious" or "spiritual" in either the theistic or nontheistic sense,

excluding their historical, conventional, superstitious, institutional meanings.

19. Transcenders find it easier to transcend the ego, the self, the identity, i.e., to go beyond self-actualization. Nontranscending self-actualizers are primarily strong identities, people who know who they are, where they are going, what they want, what they are good for, using themselves well and authentically and in accordance with their own true nature. Transcenders are certainly this; but they are also more than this.

20. Transcenders, because of their easier perception of the B-realm, have more end experiences than their more practical brothers do, more of the fascinations that we see in children who get hypnotized by the colors in a puddle, or by raindrops dripping down a windowpane, or by the smoothness of skin, or the movements of a caterpillar.

21. Transcenders are somewhat more Taoistic; the merely healthy somewhat more pragmatic. B-cognition makes everything look more miraculous, more perfect, just as it *should* be. It therefore breeds less impulse to *do* anything to the object that is fine just as it is, less needing improvement, or intruding upon.

22. "Postambivalence" tends to be more characteristic of all self-actualizers and perhaps a little more so in transcenders. This concept from Freudian theory means total wholehearted and unconflicted love, acceptance, expressiveness, rather than the more usual mixture of love and hate that passes for "love" or friendship or authority.

23. With increasing maturity of character, higher forms of reward and metareward other than money and acknowledgment steadily *increase* in importance, while money is recognized as a symbol for status, success, and self-esteem with which to win love, admiration, and respect.

A major theory of transcendence that has emerged from the standpoint of aging and lifespan development is the nursing theory of self-transcendence formulated by Reed, whose definition of self-transcendence is, "the capacity to expand self-boundaries intrapersonally (toward greater awareness of one's philosophy, values, and dreams), interpersonally (to relate to others and one's environment), temporally (to integrate one's past and future in a way that has meaning for the present), and transpersonally (to connect with dimensions beyond the typically discernible world)."[298] Reed's clinical realm is that of medicine and nursing, focused on sick and elderly populations, and research based on Reed's work has found positive correlations between self-transcendence, hope, purpose in life, and cognitive and emotional well-being.

"Surrendering the ego" is one of the components of developing a transpersonal identification, a transpersonal self. Ego surrender is viewed as an *active* (autonomous) ego making a *passive* behavioral choice (e.g., Gandhi actively chose passive resistance, or one may choose to respond to the incessant demands of another by quietly ignoring them). Here the ego is active in the sense of refraining from being *re*active, i.e., operating with a high degree of internal locus of control. The behavioral choice is passive in the sense of allowing something to unfold without attempting to change, control, coerce or manipulate it. Obstacles to ego surrender are fixations at incomplete developmental stages, and the transpersonal defenses: fear of letting go and trusting. Important to note here is that for the ego to actively make a passive behavioral choice requires a strong ego.

We turn now to the qualities of ego that support surrender and transcendence, and the known ways of actively developing them.

A Quiet Ego

The Quiet Ego provides a central focus on how the individual interprets the self and others; in particular, how the individual might arrive at a less defensive, more integrative stance toward the self and others. This applies especially with forgiveness, gratitude, mutual love, courage, responsibility, altruism, and tolerance. Some may interpret a "quiet ego" as a fragile, squashed, or unwillingly silenced ego. That is not the meaning at all.

To us, the relatively quieter ego listens to others as part of a psychosocial harmony, whereas the noisier ego tunes others out as one would tune out background noise. The quieter ego is attuned to internal rhythms of people's (including the self's) psychological dynamics, whereas the noisier ego is attuned more to the clamoring boom of people's external appearances. The quieter ego, compared with the noisier ego, has more balance and integration of the self and others in one's concept of the self, a balanced recognition of one's strengths and weaknesses that paves the way for personal growth, and a greater compassion for the self and others. The quieter ego is less under the spell or the "curse" of the self's (Leary, 2004) responsibilities and social images. The quieter ego realizes that the self is ultimately a construction or story that not only creates a sense of unity and purpose in life (McAdams, 1985) but also casts illusions, some constructive and some destructive. The noisier ego spends much of its energy identifying and defending the construction of self as if it were not a construction, and then asserting itself into the world. However, quiet is not categorically beneficial; there are risks and benefits associated with both quieter and noisier egos.[299]

> The desirable end result of quieting the ego falls into two main camps, with the primary emphasis on either balance or growth. Research that adopts either of the two perspectives tends to view some ego-quieting as desirable but too much ego-quieting as undesirable. The balance approach is focused primarily on lifting an individual out of the pre-personal level of ego development and enhancing the personal level. The growth perspective is focused on elevating people from the personal level to the transpersonal level.

According to the balance perspective, the objective is "seeking a quiet-enough ego." One problem with a noisy ego is a relative inability to perceive and think about the negative qualities in one's life. Of course, too much thinking about those negatives results in a squashed ego, and research points to an optimal balance of positive and negative self-evaluation.[300] Likewise, too much concern for the self leans toward egotism and narcissism, but too much concern for others leans toward codependent communion, a condition in which one's own ego or identity is lost.[301]

According to the growth perspective, the objective is "seeking an ever-quieter ego." From this perspective, an ego can get quieter and quieter without becoming lost or squashed. This approach generally contends that "the ego quiets as it grows." From the growth perspective, a growing (and thus quieting) ego becomes increasingly aware of the self, less defensive, increasingly interdependent in its construal of self and others, and increasingly more compassionate toward others and the self. The ego's very interpretations of self are progressively transformed in a sequence that proceeds roughly from selfish (pre-personal) to group focused (personal) to interdependent (transpersonal).

There are four prototypical qualities of a quieter ego (i.e., transcending egotism), according to Bauer and Wayment[302]:

a. *detached awareness*, a nondefensive sort of attention, i.e., mindfulness. Detached awareness depends on a certain degree of openness and willingness to accept what one might discover about the self or others.

b. *interdependence*, a balanced or developmentally more integrated interpretation of the self and others, the capacity to understand other people's perspectives in a way that allows one to identify with those other people. This interdependence involves the ability to see past differences to more underlying, unifying aspects of other individuals' humanity.

c. *compassion*, an emotional stance toward the self and/or others that involves acceptance, empathy, and a desire to foster the well-being of the person or group.

d. *growth*, a humanistic or prosocial kind of development over time, where one either is concerned with or actually establishes heightened levels of quiet-ego qualities, things that foster growth—such as openness, humility, self-awareness, acceptance of self and others, genuineness, and self-improvement.

George Kelly's[303] theory of personal constructs advanced the idea that the self is a fiction created by each individual, emphasizing the constructed and malleable nature of the self. In these constructivist approaches, the relatively quieter ego is more aware of the fact that the self is a set of constructs; the noisier ego is less aware of this fact, and this diminished awareness limits the capacity to grasp others' points of view.

From the standpoint of ego development, many qualities of the noisy ego are hallmarks of relative immaturity. On the contrary, many qualities of the quieter ego characterize psychosocial maturity, notably, the increasing capacities to think from others' perspectives and to integrate them with one's own; make meaning of one's inner experience; reason morally in terms of rights, principles, and contexts; control impulses and defenses; relate to others with mutuality and a sense of interdependence; respect the autonomy of both the self and others; address conflict directly instead of with immature defenses; identify with increasingly broader social groups (e.g., from one's ingroup to humanity); and value psychological growth.

An ego prepared to surrender the illusion of its own autonomy is likely to be quiet.

Ego Surrender

"You have to be somebody before you can be nobody."[304]

A long tradition in many cultures has evolved of dividing life into two parts: "It is generally accepted among analytical psychologists that the task of the first half of life involves ego development with progressive separation between ego and Self; whereas the second half of life requires a surrender or at least a relativization of the ego as it experiences and relates to the Self."[305]

> The process of individuation, or ego surrender, requires transcendent experiences, i.e., those based in the collective unconscious, in which the ego discovers its subordinate place to a greater reality, a transpersonal center of which it is only a small part. The mature, individuated ego is capable of surrendering its autonomy to the Self, the totality of conscious and unconscious reality. This surrender of the ego is really giving up the exaggeration of its importance, of the misapprehension of it being absolute, independent, and permanent, the loosening of one's identification with the ego.

It is important to note here the distinction between "dissolution of the ego" and "surrender of the ego." If an individual's ego functioning is too weak to absorb and integrate unconscious archetypal material and primary transpersonal experiences, he/she is *overpowered* by them and may become psychotic. Here the ego has dissolved and been rendered non-operational. Alternatively, the ego can fracture into competing parts and also be rendered non-operational, or psychotic. Here the personality disintegrates into a plurality of autonomous complexes or subpersonalities which take the place of the ego.

Most people do not understand the fleeting nature of the ego identity they have created, that is, that we are a loose confederation of fragments of identity rather than a single permanent and unchangeable 'I'. Every thought, every mood, every desire and sensation, says 'I'. There are hundreds and thousands of small 'I's, usually unknown to each other, and often incompatible. Each moment that we think of saying 'I', the identity of that 'I' is different. We become lost into that identity when it dominates our thoughts, then into the next when it takes over. Just now it was a thought, now it is a desire, now a sensation, now another thought, and so on, endlessly. Anyone who has meditated knows how resurgent the chattering mind can be. Where did all these momentary 'I's come from?

Being a multitude of 'I's is not in itself problematic, and can be highly adaptive. It allows for specialized focus on one area at a time, with the ability to temporarily defocus on others. This is reflected in appropriate boundaries, with one set of behaviors when alone with one's spouse and another in a business meeting. The rigidity of separation between ego states is determined by the degree of dissociation; mild dissociation results in more flexible boundaries and severe dissociation results in rigid, impermeable boundaries.

Recent research indicates that, perhaps paradoxically, an experience of ego surrender tends to *increase* the individual's internal locus of control,[306] and "control is simultaneously enhanced through the process of letting go."[307] Derived from social learning theory, the concept of locus of control defines an individual's belief about who or what is responsible for outcomes in their life. People with an internal locus of control believe that what happens to them is a consequence of their own actions and is within their control. Those with an external locus of control believe that what happens to them is related to external events, powerful others and chance, and thus beyond their control.[308] Research indicates that people with an internal locus of control tend to have more adaptive behaviors, are more proactive in their health care, experience more positive psychological outcomes (are less depressed and anxious), and enjoy better physical health than those with an external locus of control.[309]

With ego maturity, we acquire a clear sense of self. Knowing where the self ends and the 'other' begins, we replace projection with empathy. When the self is contained and secure in its worth, we as individuals, far from being self-invested, accord the same respect to others as we do to ourselves. When the altruism of 'doing for others' is not motivated by a desire for return or secondary gain, who knows - we may well have arrived at ego transcendence.[310]

Surrendering the ego is not the same as abandoning the Freudian ego. That is, it is not becoming free of the observing, analyzing functions of mind. Such would be really an attempted regression to simpler, less capable stages of development, to the magic omnipotent stage of the preschool child.

Surrendering the ego is not elimination of personality, i.e., of the complexities of characteristics that distinguish one individual from another. The mature ego, or individuated person, continues to display to some extent the inherited predispositions, innate abilities and culture that originally influenced personality. Persons who have become that which is not the ego may have modified their undesirable propensities, but they still are subject to them, they are not perfect. Nor are they bland, generic versions of their former selves, devoid of unique qualities. Surrendering the ego is not "diminution of personality," equated by Jung with "loss of soul," a low psychical barometer reading recognized as listlessness, moroseness, and depression.

Surrendering the ego is not enlargement of the personality, experienced as a momentary expansion of personal boundaries through revelation, the idyllic notion of forgetting the self and merging with something greater outside the self. Such a loss of ego boundaries and sense of union could be psychotic or ecstatic, but either way it is not a viable alternative to ego function for maintaining life on earth. This choice seeks, as Freud said, the "restoration of limitless narcissism"[311], that is, the infantile state prior to the development of an ego wherein the infant at its mother's breast makes no distinction between itself and its mother. This is actually ego *expansion*, or *inflation*, rather than ego surrender.

Surrendering the ego is not the interpersonal subjugation of the self to another or to a group. This concept would idealize the loss of ego boundaries wherein a person abandons him/herself in martyrdom to the will of others. Some social sanctions variously advocate this "selflessness" for children, for women, for soldiers, or for spiritual followers. Jung saw this as a case of *possession*, or mass intoxication.[312] Gestalt therapists call it *confluence*, the state in which boundaries between figure and ground, or you and I, flow together indistinguishably.[313] For example, a man stops himself from crying through his confluence with "the authorities" who say, "Big boys don't cry." Confluence is an abdication, and makes for routine and stagnation.

> *Surrendering the ego* is not a developmental stage *beyond* the ego wherein the ego exists and then is abandoned, succeeded by egolessness. Egolessness is not built on the ashes of the destroyed ego. Transcending the ego occurs through letting go of identification with the selective concept of 'I', and fully embracing all aspects of the self, expanding the conception of self beyond the customary limits. In other words, surrendering the ego is not trading in one concretely existing entity (the ego) for another concretely existing entity (egolessness).

Surrendering the ego is not limited to the ultimate state of spiritual perfection described by Buddhists as nirvana, the loss of ego, desire and attachment, but is instead the gradual process known to lead to it. There are four levels of attaining realization of nirvana, all identical in the experience itself, but each resulting in a progressively more permanent loss of ego on emergence from nirvana.[314] (1) The first is "Stream Enterer," having once experienced the state of nirvana. At this level of attainment, the following strata of personality traits fall away: greed for sense desires, and resentments strong enough to produce anxiety; greed for one's own gain, possessions or praise strong enough to cause inability to share with others; failure to perceive the relative and illusive nature of what seems pleasurable or beautiful; the misapprehension of permanence in what is impermanent; and of self in what is devoid of self;

adherence to mere rites and rituals, and the belief that this or that is "the Truth"; doubt or uncertainty in the utility of the spiritual path; lying, stealing, sexual misconduct, physically harming others, or earning a livelihood at the expense of others. Belief is that the final liberation, the total loss of ego and end to the cycle of birth-death-rebirth will occur within seven more lifetimes. (2) The next level of attainment is "Once-Returner," where the elements of ego abandoned with Stream Entry now include gross feelings of desire for sense objects and strong resentment. Attraction and aversion to any phenomena are replaced by an impartial attitude toward all stimuli. Belief is that full liberation will come in this lifetime or the next. (3) The third level of attainment of nirvana is "Nonreturner," where all propensities for greed or resentment drop away, and all aversion to worldly states such as loss, disgrace, pain or blame ceases. Belief is that one is bound to become totally liberated from the wheel of becoming in the present lifetime. (4) The final and full maturity of insight is attained in the state "Fully Realized Being," in which one has permanently overcome the fetters of ego, desire and attachment. This Buddhist paradigm of successive steps toward self-realization is examined in more detail in Chapter 13, The Ox-herder Series.

Surrendering ego can be termed *negation* of ego[315], or *depotentiation* of the ego.[316] It implies limiting the exaggerated importance attributed to ego, and correctly apprehending the ego's relative and dependent position to the total human being. One way to see this perspective is as a process of letting go of possessiveness, where the concept of possession is expanded to include nonmaterial objects such as identity, personality, beliefs, and ideologies.[317] Surrendering ego, then, is letting go of the possessiveness of identity. In the Tibetan Buddhist tradition, the pathway toward mental health is a process of cutting through materialism to uncover a clear, egoless, awakened state of mind. Becoming possession-free does not mean giving up all material objects or renouncing love, intimacy, sex, relationships, pleasure, or comfort; it involves overcoming a neurotic preoccupation with or identification with any of these. Becoming "ego-possession free" doesn't mean giving up the functions of ego, but rather the identification with any one aspect of it.

How do we recognize ego-transcendence when we see it? What does it look like? Following are what we can expect when we make these transformational changes permanent in our lives and in our relationships.[318]

1. *Fully present in every moment, refraining from ego dissociation or distraction.*

   When the ego is no longer fettered by childhood wounds of abuse, shame and abandonment, addictive behavior and dissociation are unneeded. The individual has extinguished the deep underlying fear of nonbeing, and feels existentially complete and chooses to remain present in each moment. This allows the process of reclaiming the real self to unfold. It means that the individual has permission to feel and express the deepest emotions and thus to release the patterns of dissociation. Here we refer to ego *activity*, as contrasted with ego *passivity*.

2. *Daily choices based on intuitive knowledge, wisdom and love rather than on ego-state fear, fabrication and rationalization.*

   When the person's deepest motivation changes from fear or avoiding anticipated pain to an intuitive *inner knowing*, decisions will always serve the highest good of everyone involved.

3. *Identify and manage positive energy and not "take on" negative energy.*

   As the person becomes free of internal ego preoccupation, he/she becomes aware of the impact of subtle energy and the importance of managing it, able to identify healthy and unhealthy energy patterns in every interaction in oneself, individuals as well as in groups.

4. *Live in integrity.*

   Integrity is the natural result of full cooperation between congruent ego states, with the "private self" and the "public self" transparently one in the same: the real self. Living as an integrated person eliminates self-consciousness, anxiety about approval, defensiveness, and secrets, resulting in honesty, keeping commitments and being trustworthy.

5. *Spiritual manifestation of what we say we want.*

   A measure of ego surrender is manifestation of the goals the individual is clear about wanting. He/she has eliminated the causes of any inability to manifest what he/she wants: deep unconscious feelings of unworthiness, or unconscious beliefs that are contrary to what is desired (for example, the person may be asking to manifest money, but the unconscious belief may be that money is evil).

6. *Acceptance of ourselves for who we are, acknowledging the continued growth we desire.*

   The *life path* of transformational work replaces the ego's tendency to judge by performance and conditional love, instead accepting oneself as a "work in progress." Ego surrendering is a continuing lifelong process, not a single event. Here we refer to *internal* locus of control, as contrasted with *external* locus of control, and the importance of *playfulness*. Ego maturity is not a static state; indeed, it is one of constant dynamic growth.

7. *Healing and resolving unhealthy relationships, and attracting healthy ones.*

   Healing any "victim consciousness" pattern imprints in the unconscious mind releases the *repetition compulsion* to repeat those imprinted unhealthy relationships. Every relationship in our lives reflects the deepest belief system in our minds. The surrendering ego is full of compassion.

8. *We freely express our emotions spontaneously through healthy release.*

   In transformational work, people learn to identify emotions through being aware of the bodily sensations that accompany a feeling, and to release these emotions in a way that doesn't hurt another person or property, free from projecting unacknowledged or repressed feelings onto others. Here we refer to *flexibility and spontaneity*, as contrasted with ego *rigidity*.

9. *We are current, not unfinished, in every interaction of every relationship.*

   Ending the repression of feelings or holding on to unexpressed feelings eliminates projection, and thus

unfinished business in relationships. Jungian analyst
Marilyn Nagy says, "Whatever qualities we have that are
unknown to us we experience first of all in
projection."[319]

10. *Prepared for a conscious death, no matter how
    unexpectedly it may come.*

    Socrates said that "true philosophers make dying their
    profession, and to them of all men death is least
    alarming."[320] A conscious death is one that is accepted
    with emotional equanimity and spiritual confidence.
    Being current in relationships is also important when we
    are speaking of a conscious death. Unfinished business
    in this process will be painful. If we are unable to *forgive
    on the Soul level*, then we may karmically attract this
    person back into our next lifetime to replay the
    relationship again in another version.

11. *Recognize the karmic patterns being fulfilled, and stop
    creating new karma (accept that "I am 100%
    responsible for my experience of my life").*

    A powerful way to work through karmic issues is to
    become aware of your individual karmic lessons in this
    lifetime. This gives the very deepest spiritual meaning to
    the concept of "I am 100% responsible for what I create
    and experience in my life." It is only by seeing the
    bigger picture of our lives that we *heal* and *release* the
    old karmic patterns. Once we get the lesson, we no
    longer need to repeat it. We then devote our energies to
    serving the transformation of others helping them to
    transmute their fear, anxiety, negativity, addictions and
    illness into love, power and oneness.

Chapter Six

Transpersonal Techniques of Investigation

Transpersonal psychology is appropriate and useful for psychotherapy, and equally for facilitating growth and development to levels of mastery and optimal performance. And so all the comments regarding transpersonal techniques of investigation apply equally to a therapeutic intention or to an adult development purpose. Therefore the following discussion is germane for therapists, educators, and life or executive coaches.

Hypnosis, Self-hypnosis, and Hypnotherapy

The tradition of transpersonal psychology in particular owes a great debt to the pioneers of hypnosis . . . for providing a Western paradigm that has led to important developments in the fields of clinical psychology, consciousness studies, mind-body medicine, and parapsychology. Historically, the myriad phenomena of hypnosis have provided some of the best illustrations of the core ideas and concepts that one finds today in transpersonal psychology. . . . Hypnosis can help integrate the body, mind, and spirit of human beings in an empirically verifiable manner that has come to satisfy even the most skeptical of former critics. . . . Research in hypnosis continues to be on the leading edge of discoveries that challenge conventional understandings of human nature and human potential. Hypnosis may also be of critical assistance in future studies of the nature of mind using methods of neuroscience and neurophenomenology; from a transpersonal perspective it can be anticipated that such combined efforts might reach similar perspectives as the ancient wisdom teachings of many mystical traditions such as Dzogchen and Tibetan Buddhism.[321]

Rowan[322] describes psychotherapy, at its best, as being about a person opening up to his/her potential. He further describes psychology as "a three-faced Goddess: one face looking back into childhood and the repression and hang-ups of the past, one face looking into the present, i.e. the existential now, and the other face looking forward to spirituality and the divine." Rowan[323] describes the techniques of advanced psychotherapy and spirituality exploration (by which he means transpersonal hypnotherapy, image work, meditation and prayer), as daring to open up to what is inside and going beyond this to explore the sacred, the numinous and the divine.

> One of the ways to define or describe hypnosis is as an 'altered state of consciousness' (Brown and Fromm, 1986). During the hypnotic trance, the individual's more rational style of thinking is pacified, enabling the more imaginative and intuitive style to take over. The conscious mind is calmed, enabling access to the unconscious mind. Maldonado and Spiegel (1998) define this as 'trance logic' – a way of reasoning that does not follow the rules of 'normal' logical processes. . . . The altered state of consciousness in hypnotherapy lessens the activity of those defence mechanisms, enabling more direct access to the unconscious level.[324]

It will be instructive to remember that, although hypnosis can be used as a relaxation procedure, hypnosis is not the same thing as relaxation, and relaxation is not even necessarily a part of hypnosis. Hypnosis can be carried out with the individual being physically active, open-eyed, focusing on the external environment and with no suggestions of relaxation.[325] Bányai and colleagues have reported on a form of active-alert hypnosis which has proven successful in their psychotherapy practice.[326]

Hypnosis and mindfulness generate theta frequency mental activity, the same state as we experience in REM sleep when we are dreaming.

"We know that the neuroscience of mindfulness and hypnosis is parallel, causing changes in brain activation of the same magnitude. Both feature cortical inhibition as revealed by slowed EEG theta waves, and both show higher levels of activity in areas where theta is prominent, such as the frontal cortex and especially the anterior cingulated cortex."[327]

Recall the research on the *integrative mode of consciousness* common to shamanic experience previously discussed. Hypnosis reflects the engagement of the same functions in the brain, activating the imagination to control awareness and the body, including physiological responses, perceptions, emotions, behaviors, and thoughts.[328]

The anterior cingulated cortex (ACC) has been linked to monitoring task performance and the modulation of arousal during cognitively demanding tasks.[329] It is particularly important as an interface switch between executive function and the resting state, and is referred to as the salience network.[330] In other words, this part of the brain decides when to pay attention to the outside world (task-oriented) and when to focus on the internal world (introspection). Both hypnosis and mindfulness meditation states feature higher levels of activity in areas where theta frequency brain waves are prominent, especially the ACC[331] and the hippocampus, source of these theta rhythms.[332] These non-ordinary states of consciousness, then, offer unique access to the mind's higher-order control of awareness and focused attention. Clearly this phenomenon has important implications for exploration of the psyche and also attempts to increase one's self-regulation.

The brain's theta rhythm circuitry is also involved in memory retrieval, survival behavior, navigation including virtual reality tracking, wellbeing, and the integration of emotion and cognition. Hypnosis, which elevates the brain's theta rhythm, assists in memory revivification and the integration of fragmented episodic memories, against a background of anxiety reduction, empowerment and psychic integration.[333]

Another important benefit of the slower frequencies of theta is the brain's opportunity to slow down its task-oriented cognitive processing involving mostly fast-paced beta frequencies. Memory consolidation of one's experience is enhanced when the brain functions at theta frequency, which is increased during hypnosis and occurs in the hippocampus.[334] The brain's theta rhythm circuitry is involved in memory *retrieval* as well as memory *consolidation*. This helps to explain why it is so fortuitous to access and correct old beliefs, release old perseverating memories, and construct new paradigms within the theta-rich hypnotic trance state.

Access to 'Procedural' Implicit Memory

Regarding memory retrieval, the state of hypnosis provides ready access to layers of mental processing that normal everyday consciousness does not. The information that was encoded in memory before language gave names to things is an example. In hypnosis, people frequently "remember" the experience of early childhood or even their birth. Since these source experiences and their embedding in memory were accomplished in an altered state (e.g., trauma or right brain dominated early childhood), they are "state-dependent" and accessing them is accomplished more easily by returning to the source state. We will explore ways in which retrieving core beliefs that are deeply embedded in such memories can be highly appropriate in working with transpersonal phenomena. This is related, of course, to the recognition that certain categories of knowledge are state-specific, i.e., knowledge that is only fully accessible in appropriate altered states of consciousness.[335]

Neural Networks

Hypnosis affects the brain, as well as the thoughts and beliefs processed by the brain, through the process of *neuroplasticity* and *neurogenesis*. The brain is constantly adapting to new information and new circumstances, e.g., modifying patterns of connection between different parts of the brain and reorganizing neural pathways and functions (neuroplasticity), as well as developing new neurons (neurogenesis).

An example of modifying connections is using hypnosis to develop new neural pathways within the *corpus callosum*, the major highway between the two hemispheres of the brain, which is reduced through the effects of stress and trauma.[336] Another example is found with patients who suffer chronic fatigue syndrome, which has the symptoms of persistent fatigue and a decrease in cortical gray matter volume. After successful hypnotherapy which addresses faulty thoughts and beliefs about the condition, patients not only feel better but also show a significant increase in gray matter volume localized in the lateral prefrontal cortex (an area related to the speed of cognitive processing).[337]

Several discreet resting-state networks have been identified. At the highest hierarchical level, there are two opposing systems in charge of intrinsic and extrinsic processing, respectively. They are the *default mode network*, a network of regions that show high metabolic activity and blood flow at rest but which deactivate during goal-directed cognition; and an *attention system* which attends to a specific task at hand but deactivates during periods of rest.[338] A fascinating feature of the hypnotic state is that it configures brain activity to permit both of these normally mutually exclusive states to activate simultaneously.

default mode network	*attention system*
self-referential processes reconstructing the past or simulating the future (such as fantasy, inner rehearsal, and daydreaming) imagination	goal-directed cognition sensory-related tasks motor- related tasks language- related tasks attention-related tasks

Table 1: Features of default mode and   attention networks

Regions included in the attention system network show a synchronized activity in absence of any specific cognitive activity, that is, at rest, while they are known to be engaged during sensory-, motor-, language- or attention-related tasks. As for the default mode network, it includes brain areas associated with multiple high-order functions that are generally stimulus-independent and thus self-referential processes. These can be related to organizing memory such as reconstructing the past; simulating the future such as fantasy, inner rehearsal and daydreaming; and imagination such as free association, stream of consciousness, and taking other people's perspective.

Insight into the default mode network shows us what advantages the hypnotic trance state or a mindfulness meditative state offers one to facilitate just these activities related to past, future, and other people's perspective. In short, the default network is responsible for self-projection—mentally transporting oneself into alternate times, locations, or perspectives—as manifested in episodic memory, navigation, prospection (i.e., anticipating future events), and theory of mind (taking another's perspective).[339] Self-projection into alternative pasts and futures actually offers vitally important applications to our work in transpersonal psychology. One is that understanding the default mode network can help to identify and explain, and potentially access, preconscious and unconscious mental activity such as moodiness, prejudice, irrational fears, or uncontrollable anger. Another is that some default mode functions may be brought under conscious control and direction, potentially through hypnotic trance states. Thus, a facilitator may be able to guide a client to reframe a past failure as a valuable learning experience, to gain a new perspective on the perplexing behavior patterns of a colleague, or to vividly envision a desired future that is outside the client's current capacity to imagine.

> This is the case because mindfulness meditative states or hypnotic trance states allow access to both the focused attention of executive function and the relaxed openness of default mode *at the same time*.

Most states of consciousness carry an anticorrelation between 'rest' and goal-directed behavior, between self- and external-awareness networks, between openness and focused attention. The more awareness is focused on internal processing (introspection, or self-awareness), the less it is available for attention to sensory input (external awareness) and goal-directed focus, and vice-versa. The hypnotic trance state is an exception; parts of the brain that are normally activated with an opposite on/off switch can be dissociated from each other to allow both to activate at the same time. Under hypnosis, the anterior cingulated cortex (ACC) is activated which narrows attention. But, unlike in the waking state of narrowed attention, the posterior attentional system which stimulates vigilance is *de*activated during hypnosis.[340] Thus hypnosis creates a state of dual effect: relaxation yet responsiveness. The conscious mind is calmed, enabling access to the unconscious mind. Through this mechanism, an individual may have experiences and interpret them in ways that are not in accordance with the person's conscious rational belief system.[341]

In a similar dual effect, meditation has been shown through fMRI and EEG studies to activate both the sympathetic and parasympathetic nervous systems simultaneously, creating a calm state with enhanced alertness.[342] There is, in addition, increased activity in the reward pathway, particularly the hippocampus and the amygdala during meditation,[343] with increased levels of dopamine,[344] as there is under hypnosis. However, there is a marked neural difference between hypnosis and meditation. In hypnosis, a decrease occurs in functional connectivity across the hemispheres, measured by EEG gamma band coherence,[345] while in meditation there is an increase in this coherence between and within hemispheres.[346] EEG coherence normally means more of the brain is being used, with an associated improvement in quality of attention. In the case of hypnosis, the decrease in coherence indicates a dissociation, or decoupling, of attention to more than one thing rather than a decrease in mental processing. This dissociation allows one to attend to apparently incongruous thoughts; for example, a person can experience being a child of seven in age regression and at the same time experience being a healthy adult available to nurture that child ego state.

Dream Work and Dream Journeying

An important part of the therapist's or coach's role is to help clients with their journeys into self-awareness. First we will address dream work by coaches in the venue of adult development in order to emphasize that it need not be limited to a therapeutic context. Manfred F. R. Kets de Vries[347] suggests that, to help coachees with their journey into their own interior, coaches can also pay attention to their clients' dreams. Clients' dreams can offer useful clues about their main out-of-awareness preoccupations and concerns, their internal struggles and challenges. Making sense of dreams can be a very powerful problem-solving and inspirational tool as well – the theta-rich dream environment is highly creative and free of many of the mental limitations that dominate our everyday thought processing.[348]

Dreaming is a state in which we can access our inner selves, find inner resources to discover new solutions not available in our waking state. Dreams can open our perspective on what is possible, beyond our self-limiting everyday beliefs and behaviors.

Of course, revealing their dreams to a coach may be personally challenging for many clients, fearing that their dreams may unmask parts of themselves unknown even to themselves. That may be a degree of vulnerability too far for some. Even the idea of incorporating dream work into life coaching may strike some as outlandish, "new age", or a waste of time. Working with their coach over time will hopefully nurture a growing sense of trust in the coach and his expertise (even if it includes dream work).

Clearly, the dream belongs to the dreamer, and the interpretation of it also belongs to the dreamer. A qualified coach will not offer interpretations of dreams, but only listen intently, ask probing questions, and suggest possible correlations to other material the client has brought to the coaching relationship.

Coaches may ask the client to reflect on their dream imagery to encourage uncovering the meaning of the dream. For example, what emotions did they experience? Were they scared, angry, embarrassed, joyful, jealous, disgusted? Did they still have those feelings when awake? How comfortable were they with those feelings? Can they identify any recurring thoughts associated with their dreams? If so, in what other situations have they had them?

An even more kinesthetic method for helping the client to realize the messages in the dream is to ask the client to have a dialogue with certain dream elements, those that hold the most fascination or disturbance. "John, now that you've identified how intensely you react to the policeman in your dream, I suggest that you *become* the policeman for a moment and speak to John, the dreamer. Tell him why you have acted the way you did in this dream, why you said what you did, and what message are you in the dream to deliver to John?" Then allow John to address the policeman dream element, and for a dialogue to develop between the two. You can proceed to do a similar process with other symbols in the dream that are particularly engrossing to the client.

I do realize that this kind of work is not for every executive coach. Dreams are full of discontinuities, ambiguities, and inconsistencies that can be downright bizarre, necessitating nonconformist thinking, acceptance of ambiguity, and flexibility of thought. In dreams, content and organization are illogical; the conventional notions of time, place, and person do not apply; and natural laws are disobeyed. Sense-making becomes a kind of detective work, for both client and coach. . . .

Executive coaches should view dreams as stories or puzzles that clients must solve to be free.[349]

Another way of working with dreams is to approximate them in the waking state so that the coach is available to participate directly. The **waking dream technique**[350], developed by Dr. Paul Schenk, is similar to a daydream, and consists of having the client go into a relaxed state, after which the coach might advise the subject that he or she relax and go within even more deeply. The subject might then find himself or herself beginning to imagine being someone in a movie: a person whose story will contain experiences that will be timely, useful, and constructive for them in their own life. A client who has unfettered access to her imagination and who is willing to share it with the coach without inhibition will produce valuable dreamlike imagery and storylines.

Coaches are well-advised to incorporate their clients' imaginal capacities through engagement of evocative metaphors, images, and creative modalities within the trance state or otherwise. Encourage free-flow thinking, right-brain thinking, intuition, and storytelling. These are ways of accessing the client's unconscious processing that often uncovers aspects of herself and her interpersonal relationships that are known neither to her nor to others.

Dream Journeying

Dream journeying is a ritual developed by Hartman and Zimberoff as a way for individuals to share their dreams with a community, all members of which are in a non-ordinary state of consciousness during the ritual.[351] Our nightly descent into dreaming is an initiation that can enhance our expansion, create new possibilities, open the mind and the heart, and reintroduce us to our soul. Inviting others into the felt experience of the dream enhances its meaning for the dreamer and catalyzes healthy intimacy within the community. Because dreams are a portal into the underworld, the land of soul, each participating member in the ritual must be capable of such a descent, without fear and without ego. We dissolve and release our attachments through dreams, and the ritual calls on each participant to do the same.

Martin Prechtel is a Mayan shaman from Guatemala, and he explains the deeper transpersonal significance of dreams in the following excerpt of an interview:

> *Martin Prechtel*: If this world were a tree, then the other world would be the roots — the part of the plant we can't see, but that puts the sap into the tree's veins. . . .
>
> The Mayans say that the other world sings us into being. We are its song. We're made of sound, and as the sound passes through the sieve between this world and the other world, it takes the shape of birds, grass, tables — all these things are made of sound. Human beings, with our own sounds, can feed the other world in return, to fatten those in the other world up, so they can continue to sing. . . .
>
> *Derrick Jensen*: There's an old Aztec saying I read years ago: "That we come to this earth to live is untrue. We come to sleep and to dream." I wonder if you can help me understand it.
>
> *Martin Prechtel*: When you dream, you remember the other world, just as you did when you were a newborn baby. When you're awake, you're part of the dream of the other world. In the "waking" state, I am supposed to dedicate a certain amount of time to feeding the world I've come from. Similarly, when I die and leave this world and go on to the next, I'm supposed to feed this present dream with what I do in that one.
>
> Dreaming is not about healing the person who's sleeping: it's about the person feeding the whole, remembering the other world, so that it can continue. The New Age falls pretty flat with the Mayans, because, to them, self-discovery is good only if it helps you to feed the whole. . . .
>
> A new culture will have to develop, in which neither humans and their inventions nor God is at the center of the universe. What should be at the center is a hollow place, an empty place where both God and humans can sing and weep together.[352]

Dreams allow access to that hollow place, and technologies exist for exploring it and growing closer to the empty place where both God and humans can sing and weep together. And dream journeying allows people to share in exploring that portal. A central key to the participants' state of consciousness that allows this ritual to work is transcendence of ego boundaries, an expansion of one's sense of self that is at the same time *not* self-conscious. The state depends on the willingness and capacity to detach from the external world and one's self in it, according to Bartocci and Dein.[353]

> These authors suggest that the peek-a-boo game in which the baby covers his or her face to make the external world disappear and then uncovers the eyes to make it reappear, and similar 'being gone' fantasies of children, represent a primitive way to detach from perception of external reality. Trance states represent the capacity to voluntarily make use of detachment as a technique to gain a 'suspended state of consciousness' rooted in a momentary dissociation.

Transcending ego boundaries in working with dreams means allowing the dream to speak for itself without turning it over to one's ego for interpretation. However, that is what most psychological methods of working with dreams do, including such transpersonal methods as Jungian or Gestalt approaches to dreams. Each "finally returns the dream to the waking ego, who romantically absorbs the dream through his feelings. This engorges the ego, who swallows his own dream by becoming its images, instead of working on his reactions within them."[354] Such an approach to understanding dreams leads to insight and growth, "but what grows is the ego, whose personality enlarges at the expense of the dream persons that it has become. In this subtle way, Gestalt dream-work, following from Jung's subjective level of interpretation, can expand my person to take in the persons of the dream and eventually the Gods, who are in those dream persons."[355]

How, then, do we work with dream material without sanitizing it of darkness or usurping its light? First the exploring individual must overcome the barriers to the repressed Lower Unconscious, the guardians to the underworld (shame, fear, addictions, unworthiness), integrate aspects of it, and develop personal power. It is the work that Maslow called *self-actualizing*, and Assagioli called *personal psychosynthesis*, the increasing ability to express a sense of unique, well-articulated individuality. A further step in that growth process is achieved by overcoming the barriers to the repressed Higher Unconscious - fear of letting go and ego surrender, or "spiritual agoraphobia" as Larry Dossey[356] calls it - and embracing it. This is Assagioli's *transpersonal psychosynthesis* and Maslow's *transcending self-actualization*. This represents an increasing experience of higher, mystical, and spiritual states of consciousness. Expanding into the lower but not the higher leads one to become psychologically healthy but not spiritually fulfilled, and expanding into the higher but not the lower leads one to become a psychologically unhealthy spiritual seeker (the spiritual by-pass).

Mario Jacoby warns that it is self-delusion to believe that "one need only plunge into the mythic depths and existence would be transfigured into a kind of Paradise – psychic deep-sea diving, as it were."[357]

When we are successful in allowing the dream to have its own existence, and in learning dream-language instead of translating it into the language of ego, then the images and content of the dream stand boldly, independent of the dayworld ego. The dream-mother and dream-enemy and menacing neighbor and woman in the revealing dress become Mother, Enemy, Menacing Neighbor and Woman in the Revealing Dress. They are seen for what they are: archetypal images, collective memories, the lexicon of ancient myth and species' instinct. The dream images do not belong to the dayworld ego, and they cannot be domesticated for the ego's amusement or enlightenment.

Then individuals are ready and capable of entering the liminal ground of dream journeying together.

Dreams can be personal, and they can be interpersonal. For example, in Native American cultures the dream is both a personal entity and an interactive social process.[358] Within this tradition, dreams exist in a magical space that is created during the process of dialoguing with the imaginal world, the world of spiritual beings, in the presence of elders. In such a setting, through the mechanism of telling the dream to trusted others, a power dream changes from a personal experience into something much more.[359]

Utilizing a similar tradition of dialoguing with the imaginal world in the presence of elders, the Senoi people of Malaysia share their dreams openly and daily with each other. According to Senoi Dream Theory, dreams can be shared and shaped in groups in a positive and supportive fashion for the benefit of everyone, not just specific individuals.[360] Sharing their dreams creates an opportunity for feedback from others who may have more or different knowledge to illuminate the meaning of the dream. Yet there is another, more subtle but more far-reaching implication in the Senoi paradigm: open sharing of dreams on a daily basis actually begins to *shape* the dreamer's pattern of dreaming.

Spontaneous group responses to dream-telling can often be judgmental, defensive and rejecting. Group participants often evade linking the related dream to their own emotions and life, defensively projecting their identifications onto the dreamer.[361] Therefore, it is necessary to prepare the group (the 'container') for dream-telling, helping them to establish a setting that enables the group members to 'receive' it as a midwife receives a baby.[362] Creating a healthy processing partnership in the group requires a non-interpretative approach to dreams. Preventing participants from 'interpreting' the dream told, as much as possible, is an important first step in avoiding harm to the dream-teller.[363] At the same time, we want to encourage members to share their authentic emotional resonance to the dream, their 'echoes' of the dreamer's experience, as long as they are freely generated *primordial* associations and not projective or transferential ones.[364]

> When we learn how, i.e., have been initiated into how to relive dreamtime through ceremony, the bridge between this world and the underworld of dream and archetype and soul has become a two-way bridge. Before initiation it was one-way only: the inhabitants of that realm have full access to this world, to all that occurs here. In fact their substance and nourishment must come from those in this world. But their lessons, indeed their very existence, remain a secret to the everyday ego mind.

Opening the sacred circle. In all the Heart-Centered transformational modalities we acknowledge the presence and contribution of the Divine. Within the shamanic setting it is no less important to do so, and the form that tradition brings to us is the sacred circle. We open that gathering by acknowledging the four directions (East, South, West, North), Father Sky and Mother Earth. We honor those group members who sit in each of the four directions for protecting the circle, and for welcoming the spirits to enter from that direction.

The Mask makes the invisible visible. Each person in the circle has a plain white ceramic mask to hold up in front of their face when telling their dream, or when sharing an intuitive association to another's dream. The mask serves several purposes. One is to remind the speaker that he/ she is speaking not from a personal, individual outlook, but rather from a collective, archaic perspective. It is not the triumvirate of my ego, persona, and shadow that speaks to the others; this protects everyone from likely judgments, projections, or analytic interpretations. It is the deeper voice within me, the anima/ animus who speaks for the invisible and voiceless archetypes. The mask also, of course reminds the listeners in the group of the same thing. The mask helps to make the invisible visible.

At night, in the dark, outdoors. To enter the state of consciousness that grants access to the underworld, it is auspicious to gather at night, in the dark, outdoors in nature, just as we dream at night, in the dark. We gather in our sacred circle in a special ceremonial site, bundled up against the cold, sitting with raingear to keep the rain from soaking through, burning citronella candles to warn away the mosquitoes when necessary. We avoid lights, unless the moon is serendipitously overhead.

Closing the sacred circle. Every ceremony that invokes sacred presence must acknowledge that presence and bring its summoning to completion. When you invite a guest for dinner, the time comes to end the visit and bid them safe journey home.

And so one final purpose becomes clear for exploring the dreamworld and pursuing a synthesis between the conscious and unconscious, the ego and anima. A group of like-minded conscious people, using the dream journey ceremony, can not only shape their patterns of dreaming and otherwise affect their own unconscious, but also affect the unconscious-at-large, the collective.

Meditation and Contemplative Psychotherapy: The Royal Road to the Transpersonal

"A core practice for transpersonal psychology includes meditation, mindfulness, contemplation, and phenomenological inquiry. Comparing the role of meditation in transpersonal psychology to the role of dreams in psychoanalysis, Walsh and Vaughan (1993a) referred to meditation as 'the royal road to the transpersonal'."[365]

There is a path to mindfulness, or rather many paths, and they seem to be very consistently prescribed by wisdom traditions across cultures and history. The three basic elements needed for transformational work are summarized by Sanchez and Vieira[366]:

- presence (awareness, mindfulness)
- the practice of self-observation, gained from self-knowledge
- understanding what one's experiences mean (an accurate interpretation provided by a larger context such as a community, a teacher, or a spiritual system).

Mindfulness is a term that has come into general use, often without precise definition. The concept has historical roots in several related mental processes, as discussed by Martin[367]: *deautomatization* and the *observing self*[368], *decentering*[369], *mindfulness as a creative cognitive process*[370], *detachment*[371], and *mental freedom*[372]. Each of these interrelated and overlapping concepts contribute to a fuller understanding of mindfulness, which Martin defines as "a state of psychological freedom that occurs when attention remains quiet and limber, without attachment to any particular point of view."

Hick[373] utilizes the following working definition of mindfulness, collated from definitions by Kabat-Zinn[374], Shapiro[375], and Segal[376]: "a nonelaborative, nonjudgmental, present-centered awareness in which each thought, feeling or sensation that arises in the attentional field is acknowledged and accepted as it is." There are three primary components to mindfulness: paying attention, purposefully or with intention, and with an attitude of openness and nonjudgmentalness. Attention involves observing, noticing, bringing awareness in the present moment, with beginner's mind. Intention involves a personal commitment to participate in one's present-moment experience with the specific purpose of heightened receptivity to the internal and external environment. Openness to experience may be operationalized as non-defensiveness, willingness to share experiences, openness to the unknown and unknowable, to emotions, ideas and spirituality, and to seeming incompatibilities.

Cassandra Vieten and her co-authors[377] identify predictors, mediators, outcomes, and developmental milestones that appear to be common to the process of spiritual transformation. They define transformation as a "profound shift in our human experience of consciousness that results in long-lasting shifts in worldview or ways of being and changes in the general pattern of the way one experiences and relates to oneself, others, and the world. Spiritual transformation is transformation that occurs through spiritual experience or practice." Schwartz defines spiritual transformation as a "radical reorganization of one's identity, meaning, and purpose in life".[378]

Vieten et al. speak of transformation as a turning of attention and a redirecting of intention that shifts the entire landscape and one's trajectory through it. Common words used by research subjects to describe this shift in perspective are "opening," "a larger, wider, more inclusive and expanded depth perception," "a shift in worldview, assumptions, values, and beliefs," "a perception of vastness and being in touch with a larger consciousness," and "an expanded awareness."

Vieten's respondents reported an expanded worldview and an alteration of one's sense of self, often described as radical widening and deepening of one's personal identity. Many respondents described spiritual experiences of awakening to a witnessing self fundamentally distinct from particular thoughts, impulses, feelings, or sensations, accompanied by a feeling of being more real, more genuine, more authentically themselves. A part of many spiritual experiences involved less sense of a personal identity and a greater sense of connection to others, leading to less reactivity and judgmentalness, and a greater sense of compassion for one's own and others' failings.

Other words used to describe this shift in sense of self from a self-centered perspective to a more communal sense of self: "a deep connection with all of life," "feeling aligned with a greater force," "a deepening into the self," "less feeling of fragmentation and isolation," "a feeling of not being separate, of being interconnected," "a realization that 'I am part of a consciousness that is so much bigger'."

The most common indicator across traditions of a "transformed" person was a consistent sense of presence, an authenticity, and a lightness or ease of being, across situations. Other words commonly used to describe a transformed person were: childlike, simple, transparent, loving, wise, compassionate, patient, tolerant, forgiving, collaborative, mindful, solid, real, whole and possessing the qualities of equanimity, integrity, peace of mind, generosity and a deep acceptance of self and others as they are. Others characterized this state of being by what was *not* present – i.e., not ego-driven, ostentatious, achievement-oriented, narcissistic, not hiding anything, and not necessarily perfect or having everything worked out, but bearing difficulties and failings with grace and humor.

One enduring outcome commonly reported was the presence of an observing or witnessing self, described as a heightened awareness, detachment, or mindfulness, of one's experience, regardless of the content. Another commonly reported outcome that remained present in times of difficulty was an increased ability to stay open, to allow, to not attempt to avoid, contract, resist or harden in response to painful experience. An increased capacity for acceptance and compassion toward self and others in times of conflict was also a theme. An overarching theme was less reactivity to painful experience and a greater self-efficacy for coping.

Peak experiences such as moments of insight or epiphany are often followed by plateaus. Such insights can fade quickly without the presence of a "scaffolding" for the learning process to assist with making meaning of the unfamiliar experience, such as: (1) having a language and cultural context for the experience, bringing it from unconsciousness to conscious awareness; (2) having supportive like-minded community, including contact with more experienced practitioners (also necessary for ego development); (3) encountering or intentionally placing daily reminders of the experience in one's environment, which in NLP terms are called *anchors*; (4) continuing to access similar teachings; or (5) expressing the insight through art, writing or other action (using the sensual alpha brain wave state as a bridge from deep subliminal theta experience to everyday mind beta experience). The process is inhibited by lack of quiet solitude, not enough time in nature, staying too busy, and too quickly returning to contexts apathetic or inimical to transformation.

The task of awakening can be viewed from one perspective as a progressive disidentification from mental content in general and thoughts in particular. This is clearly evident in practices such as insight meditation where the individual is trained to observe and recognize all mental contents without identifying with any of it.

> We have examined the research on meditation, particularly mindfulness meditation, where the neural response coincides with that in the hypnotic trance state. As observed, there is one particularly cogent difference between the two: in meditation there is an increase in coherence between and within hemispheres rather than a decrease. Coherence signifies that more of the brain is being used, with an improvement in left-brain right-brain interface.

Now let's review the research on the neuropsychology of aesthetic, spiritual, and mystical states by Eugene G. d'Aquili and Andrew B. Newberg.[379] Spiritual-mystical states can be recognized by four particular defining characteristics: (1) an experienced sense of greater unity over diversity; (2) the sense of transcendence, or otherworldliness; (3) the progressive incorporation of the sense of the observing self in each successive experience or state; and (4) the intense and progressive certainty in the objective existence of what was experienced in the spiritual-mystical state.[380] A good example of this is the relatively common near-death experience.

The incorporation of the sense of the observing self, to one degree or another, is essential to spiritual-mystical states. The whole point of most spiritual-mystical experiences is for the self to have a sense of being fundamentally and essentially related to some aspect of whatever ultimate reality might be. 'Peak experiences' and deeply moving aesthetic experiences are on a continuum with spiritual-mystical states, but it is by no means necessary in these to have the sense of being essentially related to an aspect of an ultimate reality. Nor in these non-spiritual-mystical states is the sense of an observing self necessary, but when there is an incorporation of the observing self to some extent in an aesthetic experience, it is experienced as much more powerful.

A somewhat different set of characteristics of mystical experience is proposed by Gimello[381] to be core manifestations. A mystical experience is a state of mind, achieved commonly through some sort of self-cultivation, of which the following are usually or often the salient, but not necessarily the only, features:

- A feeling of oneness or unity, variously defined.
- A strong confidence in the "reality" or "objectivity" of the experience, i.e. a conviction that it is somehow revelatory of "the truth."
- A sense of the final inapplicability to the experience of conventional language, i.e. a sense that the experience is ineffable.
- A cessation of normal intellectual operations (e.g. deduction, discrimination, ratiocination, speculation, etc.) or the substitution for them of some "higher" or qualitatively different mode of intellect (e.g. intuition).
- A sense of the coincidence of opposites, of various kinds (paradoxically).
- An extraordinarily strong affective tone, again of various kinds (e.g. sublime joy, utter serenity, great fear, incomparable pleasure, etc.—often an unusual combination of such as these).

> As mentioned previously, meditation has been shown to activate both the sympathetic and parasympathetic nervous systems simultaneously, creating a calm alertness. The deeper the meditative state, i.e., the closer to the mystical experience end of the spectrum, the more dramatic is this effect.

Rhythm in the environment, be it visual, auditory, tactile, or proprioceptive, entrains brainwaves and when it drives the sympathetic system to maximum capacity, intermittent spillover can occur which simultaneously activates the parasympathetic system. This creates non-ordinary subjective states with an increasing sense of wholeness, ecstasy and bliss. A shaman's drumming and a Sufi's whirling dervish dance are examples of this process in action.

Such a progressive activation of the 'holistic operator' (the name given by d'Aquili and Newberg to certain parts of the nondominant parieto-occipital region of the brain) can be achieved through other means than ritual rhythmic activity. Certain types of quiet meditation drive the parasympathetic system to saturation and spillover, causing simultaneous activation of the sympathetic system. The end result is the same in both cases.[382] So, functioning of the holistic operator may be increased through rhythmicity and entrainment of brainwaves; profound meditation; olfactory stimulation such as incense, perfumes, sage or sweet grass; extreme fasting; or electrolyte imbalance.

The far end of the spectrum of spiritual-mystical states is a state described in the mystical literature of all the world's great religions and spiritual paths. d'Aquili and Newberg name this ultimate mystical state *Absolute Unitary Being*. In that state people lose all sense of discrete being, and the difference between self and other is obliterated. There is no sense of the passing of time, and all that remains is a perfect timeless undifferentiated consciousness. However, because both branches of the nervous system are firing maximally, the experience of Absolute Unitary Being is not a vague sense of undifferentiated wholeness but a sense of intense conscious awareness.

When such a state is suffused with positive affect, it is usually described, after the fact, as personal, i.e., as a perfect union with God or the perfect manifestation of God. When such experiences are accompanied by neutral affect, they tend to be described, after the fact, as impersonal, i.e., as the abyss, the Void, Nirvana, or the Absolute. "There is no question that whether the experience is interpreted personally as God or impersonally as the Absolute, it possesses a quality of transcendent wholeness without any temporal or spatial division whatsoever."[383]

> It is clear that all these experiences in one way or another involve self-transcendence. . . . It is not so clear why one would wish to transcend the self. The answer is obvious to those who have had mystical experiences. It seems that such experiences are characterized, at the lower end of the aesthetic-religious spectrum, by a sense of insight into the world of the mysterious bordering on the supernatural, and at

the extreme end of the spectrum, by a sense of attaining absolute reality, union with God or the Absolute, a sense of either bliss or utter tranquility, and perhaps most important of all, a lack of fear of death. . . . This is not necessarily because they believe in an afterlife. They may or may not, depending on the general structure of the religious belief which they hold separate from their mystical experiences. Even if they do not believe in a specific afterlife, mystical experiences tend to generate a sense of the ultimate goodness and appropriateness of reality, and death is perceived as simply an ordinary part of that reality, something which is not feared.[384]

Meditation is a valid technique for investigating transpersonal states of consciousness, especially the phenomenon of self-transcendence. Clearly, the states and the knowledge to be gained from exploring them are highly state-specific.[385] That is, they are accessible only through first-person personal experience. It is reassuring to know that the experience of such non-ordinary states can be attained through numerous approaches: Orthodox mysticism, Buddhist or Hindu or Taoist practices, and including hypnosis and shamanic journeying.

Guided Meditation or Guided Imagery

Guided meditation or guided imagery is very helpful for mindfulness, relaxation, and de-stressing. Coaches and therapists can bring guided meditation or guided imagery to the attention of their clients to help them enhance performance as well as to reduce stress.[386] The technique is also sometimes referred to as *imagery rescripting*.

A variation of these techniques is *anticipated memory* – visualizing future thoughts that help to frame hopes and dreams and make them become real.[387]

A specific example of guided imagery is presented by Alcid M. Pelletier as an excellent technique for establishing goals. Although she writes the instructions for use by a psychotherapist, the technique is equally useful in a coaching context.

A Creative Thematic Apperception Test

The psychotherapist lightly relaxes the patient by verbal suggestions while the patient faces a painting on the counseling room wall. A plethora of paintings which are colorful with an abundance of recognizable and natural detail may be used.

Once the patient is relaxed the therapist gives instructions much as one does in administering the Thematic Apperception Test. "Please look *into* the painting *there.* Let your *imagination* become *very active* until *your* activity seems *very real* and enjoyable. *Be aware* of *every* detail of your *activity there.* (Italicized words are emphasized for deeper suggestion).

The patients have been instructed in ideomotor responses to signal the therapist whenever they are actively involved in the scene. "Now please tell me *your* story. How did it *begin?* Then tell me *exactly* what's *happening* in your *present* involvement. Then, follow *the story* on to its conclusion so *we will know* the *ending.* As soon as the story ends you will remain relaxed and everything will be like it was before the involvement in the story." Bring the patient out of trance.[388]

Stories dealing with past or present events in the client's life are helpful in diagnostic procedures and indicating the need for the use of psychodynamic work. Stories which are future oriented can be helpful to assist in determining previously unacknowledged possibilities and the establishment of goals.

Shamanic Journeying

Shamanic journeying is a specific technique for accessing the transpersonal realms, one known to indigenous peoples throughout history and across cultures. It can be experienced by an initiated individual or within the context of a community ceremony. Shamanism is defined as a family of traditions whose practitioners focus on voluntarily entering altered states of consciousness in which they experience themselves, or their spirits, traveling to other realms at will and interacting with other entities in order to serve their community.[389]

Shamanic experiences cannot be divorced from the spirit-centered worldview of their indigenous community. The indigenous worldview, exemplified by the Lakota people of North America, sees the entire universe imbued with and intimately related to spirits and spiritual forces that have real power to influence outcomes. The notion of a separate, independent, individual ego is foreign to the Lakota cosmology. Each person is a living testament as well as a collectivity or legacy of his or her ancestral spirits and the spirits of creation.

Amiotte[390] describes the four dimensions of self according to Lakota understanding. The concepts include the woniya, nagi, nagila, and sicun. The woniya or niya is the self of the physical body, it anchors the self of the spiritual body. The niya is the "vital breath," which gives life to the body and is responsible for the circulation of the blood. The nagi comprises all that one knows. It is the capacity to understand. It carries all the personalities that one knows and does not know who influence the self (for example, the personalities of our parents, relatives, and ancestors). It is the legacy of one's stored memories. The nagi is the idea of who one is, the self-concept; it encompasses one's total personality of self and others.

> Not unlike Jung's concept of the personal unconscious, inclusive of the personal as well as the deeper transpersonal psychological structures of the collective (tribal) unconscious (1931/1960), the nagi encompasses the personal conscious and unconscious. It is the conscious and unconscious collection of personalities across generations that constitutes who one is. . . . From a cognitive–behavioral perspective, the nagi is composed both of one's false and of one's true selves; it can illuminate one's understanding of oneself and one's world, and it can distort or play tricks on one's understanding of the way things are. Encountering one's nagi can be terrifying or heartening or expansive, depending on one's family or collective legacy. . . . The nagi also includes what Jung identified as the 'shadow' and the 'autonomous complexes,' which are powerful unconscious influences on the individual and can actually function as if they were foreign or not part of the self (Jung, 1971).[391]

> The nagila is the divine spirit immanent in each human being (Goodman, 1992). Amiotte (1992) explained this dimension as the aspect that participates in paranormal phenomena; it is the "other" realm of knowing, the shamanic or spirit realm. The nagila is "something of the sacred" in the human being. It has also been translated as the "little ghost" (Amiotte, 1992). The nagila can be distinguished from the nagi in that it is similar to Jung's notion of the 'collective unconscious,' which is totally unconscious and is not a personal acquisition. The nagila is not based on one's personal experiences, but is similar to an impersonal aspect of a 'collective self' or a 'transpersonal self.' The nagila is paradoxical: It is the "self-not-self," "part-

of-me-but-not-part-of-me" part of who one is. This collective, unconscious self is influenced by archetypes, just as the personal unconscious (similar to the nagi) is influenced by the personal 'complexes'. . . . The nagila is the part of one's collective unconsciousness that participates in the dream or spirit world. How is it that one can dream of flying or of defying gravity? How is it that one can dream of snakes even when one has never seen a snake before? How does the mother of a three-year-old know that her child is in danger, run back to where she left the child, and see the child at the bottom of the pool just in time to revive the child? The nagila constitutes this other kind of knowing, perhaps similar to intuition, extrasensory perception, paranormal phenomena, or nonlocal consciousness. Often a person appeals to his or her nagila for assistance. The nagila is a power within each person that can help him or her overcome obstacles in life.[392]

The *sicun* is the integrated and energetic 'self,' which comprises all aspects—somatic and dynamic (*niya*), ancestral and personal (nagi), collective and impersonal (nagila), and conscious and unconscious (nagi and nagila).[393]

"Archetypal reconnection can be accomplished in a number of ways. Among them, active imagination and dreamwork are perhaps the most well-known modalities. The original route, however, is the shamanic path. The psychotherapeutic incorporation of shamanic ideas and images - which Jung cited as 'illuminating' examples of natural archetypal motifs - links us with a healing power traceable to our ancient roots (Jung, 1980, p. 253)."[394]

Later we will discuss two Native American ceremonies which call on shamanistic traditions to help loosen the ego's grip on identification and promote self-transcendence: inipi (sweat lodge) and hamblecha (vision quest).

Active Imagination

Carl Jung's favorite and best access to the unconscious and its inhabitants was *active imagination*. It is a method for exploring the meaning of dreams, but is also a way to explore the unconscious through non-dream imagination. Dreams and active imagination are dialogues that you enter into with the different parts of yourself that live in the unconscious. Active imagination, along with dream work, provides access to the transpersonal within. It is the process developed by Jung to replace Freud's technique of free association.

Robert Johnson, a Jungian analyst, explains, "dreams are the first of the two great channels of communication from the unconscious; the second is the imagination. . . . Dreaming and imagination have one special quality in common: their power to convert the invisible forms of the unconscious into images that are perceptible to the conscious mind. This is why we sometimes feel as though dreaming is the imagination at work during sleep and the imagination is the dream world flowing through us while we are awake."[395]

> Active imagination and dreaming provide an opportunity to work out some immediate problem or conflict at the personal level, *and* they make a space in one's life where we observe the great archetypal themes living themselves out through us as individuals.

"In the deepest sense, this symbolic interaction with the archetypes puts us in the remarkable position of playing a role in the working out of fate. . . . It becomes possible to consciously and voluntarily enter into the life of the archetypes that surround us, rather than sit helpless and mute, determined by powers that we can neither see nor understand."[396]

It is important to distinguish between active imagination, which is intentional, and fantasy, daydreaming, anticipation or worry. Active imagination and meditation lead to consciousness of the self; the others to enhancement of the ego. Fantasy and daydreaming create illusion and distract us from reality; active imagination or meditation create illumination and clarify reality. Fantasy deals with the ego's needs and desires, while imagination transcends the ego to provide insight into the nature of the self.[397] Imagination leads to new, unexpected information.

The actual process of active imagination is deceptively simple, yet profoundly challenging to the ego of everyday mind: imagination transcends the ego.

Contemplate and carefully observe how the picture [an image or figure that has already been dreamed] begins to unfold or to change. Don't try to make it into something, just do nothing but observe what its spontaneous changes are. Any mental picture you contemplate in this way will sooner or later change through a spontaneous association that causes a slight alteration of the picture. You must carefully avoid impatient jumping from one subject to another. Hold fast to the one image you have chosen and wait until it changes by itself. Note all those changes and eventually step into the picture yourself, and if it is a speaking figure at all then say what you have to say to that figure and listen to what he or she has to say.[398]

Active imagination naturally falls into four basic sequential stages. Marie-Louise von Franz, one of Jung's closest colleagues, suggests conceptualizing these four stages[399]: (1) empty the ego-mind; (2) let the unconscious flow into the vacuum; (3) add the ethical element; and (4) integrate the imagination back into daily life.

Robert Johnson, in his book *Inner Work: Using Dreams and Active Imagination for Personal Growth*[400], describes these four stages as follows:

1. **Invite the unconscious**. Take your mind off the external world, focus on the imagination, and wait to see who will show up. We empty the ego-mind, and refrain from the temptation of the ego to select who or what enters the scene, to orchestrate the situation, to control what happens, or even to interpret the meaning of any interactions.

2. **Dialogue and experience**. Once inner figures appear, let them have a life of their own, because in reality they do. Show a willingness to listen. Ask questions. Who are you? What do you want? What do you want to tell me? The dialogue may involve words, or it may be conducted through actions without words. If the inner figure tries to draw you into an activity, or lead you on a journey or down a path, follow. Of course, you can refuse if you wish, and enter into a discussion about what they want and what your reasons are for not doing it. This may illuminate an important conflict between this figure (a part of you) and what you think you want, or don't want, or don't approve of, or are afraid of. Let your feelings out, and invite your inner person to do the same.

   "It is awesome and frightening to take your sense of inferiority, guilt, or remorse, put that part of you in the witness box, and say: 'You have every privilege. You are the one who bears witness to that which I neither know nor understand. You may say whatever you wish, at whatever length. You will be respected and honored. And what you say will be recorded.' But it is from this that the true power of Active Imagination rises: We learn to listen to the ones whom we have kept mute. We learn to honor those whom we have dishonored."[401] And if you really listen to your unconscious, it will listen to you, the conscious.

The interaction with an inner figure has a beginning, middle, and ends in resolution or new knowledge. Stick with the image or figure you start with; don't be distracted by all the other competing colorful images and figures unless they are part of a continuous, coherent narrative with the original figure.

3. **Add the ethical element of values**. Jung said that the ego's relationship to the huge unconscious is like that of a tiny cork that is being tossed about in the ocean of life, completely at the mercy of the waves and storms that push and pull us. Yet the cork is morally equal to the ocean, because it has the power of consciousness, which gives the ego a position that is as necessary, strong and valuable as the vast richness of the unconscious. The conscious self must set limits on the personified primordial, instinctual forces of nature that accept our invitation to come up to the surface and be heard. If an inner figure is in need of help, the conscious and ethical human being will provide assistance. If an inner figure is destructive or violent, the conscious and moral human being will intervene to stop or limit the damage. In either case, after all, it is the health and well-being of our own inner selves that is at stake.

4. **Make it concrete with physical ritual**. We want to avoid *acting out* the inner, subjective conflicts and urges that surface in our interactions with the unconscious in the external world. We need to be alert to the possible tendency of taking an argument with an inner shadow or anima or personified archetype in Active Imagination, and starting up the same argument with those in our life

onto whom we have projected them. Quite the opposite, we want to bring the distilled insight and wisdom from our inner encounters back into our everyday life and integrate the two. Find a way to "make it real" in your life, to physically represent the new inner attitude. Ritual transforms a physical act into a conscious symbolic expression of one's relationship to the inner world of the unconscious. Post the affirmation on your bathroom mirror; enact a symbolic funeral and burial for the cigarette smoking habit you are resolved to quit; write a letter to the part of yourself you have interacted with about your emotional reaction to him/her. The best rituals, those that resonate most deeply with the unconscious, are physical, solitary, and silent.

First, you create the space for an inner dialogue. Then you recognize a feeling, or belief, or quality within you; perhaps you are feeling jealous of someone else, or believe that you cannot pass a test you are scheduled to take, or experience an arrogance related to a special skill or talent you have. Invite it to personify itself, to clothe itself in an image so that you can interact and dialogue with it. When that personification appears, ask questions and expect answers, be curious and allow yourself to learn from it. This technique, once mastered through practice, is a highly effective way to transcend the ego, and to access and interact with the deep unconscious.

Chapter Seven

Transpersonal Therapy

.   .   .   transpersonal psychotherapy may focus on disidentification from roles and labels, rather than on improving personal performance. William James (1890), who suggested that self-esteem could be measured as success divided by pretensions, pointed out that giving up pretensions is as much of a relief as gratifying them. The psychotherapist may readily affirm the validity of this statement with respect to clients, but being socially immersed in the western ethic of achievement, he/she can easily lose sight of his/her own pretensions as a factor in determining the success of therapy. The effectiveness of therapy cannot be evaluated apart from the psychotherapist's values and concepts of what constitutes psychological health.[402]

The Goals of Transpersonal Therapy

The transpersonal therapist is guide and companion to his/her client on their healing journey. It is, in fact, "their" journey, client and therapist, because each one's deeply held beliefs can either limit or liberate their common course. It is the client's responsibility to determine the direction, extent, and pace of his/her own healing and growth. It is the therapist's responsibility to encourage without bias, to participate fully without attachment to outcome, and to be meticulously free of contaminating metaphysical beliefs. This can often involve exploring inner voices sufficiently to find and trust the highest, most mature aspect within, the transpersonal self. The growing awareness of this transcending resource within begins to shape the individual's self-image, self-concept, and to loosen the ego's grasping onto an idealized construal of itself. This expansion and elevation of self-perception affects one not only at the psychological layer (pre-personal and personal) but also at the spiritual layer of being (transpersonal).

In the therapeutic relationship consciousness itself is both the object and the instrument of change. The state of consciousness of the therapist is therefore of crucial importance in determining the outcome of the work. . . . An important assumption here is that *who* one is is more important in the process of psychotherapy than *what* one does or what one says.[403]

The goals of transpersonal therapy include both traditional ones such as symptom relief and behavior change, and where appropriate, optimal work at the transpersonal level. This may include the provision of an adequate conceptual framework for handling transpersonal experiences; information on psychological potential; and the importance of assuming responsibility, not only for one's behavior, but also for one's experience. In addition to working through psychodynamic processes the therapist aims to assist the client in disidentifying from and transcending psychodynamic models and expectations. The therapist may also intend that the therapeutic encounter be used as a karma yoga [the yoga of service to others] to optimize growth of both participants in a mutually facilitating manner. These goals in turn facilitate the aim of enabling the client to extract awareness from the tyranny of conditioning.[404]

Several key concepts are identified here that deserve closer scrutiny: ultimate human potential, responsibility, disidentifying from and transcending ego states, and karma yoga. We have contemplated the characteristics of a self-transcending individual, and we will assess the horizons available for human development in the chapter on optimal functioning, eudaimonic growth and self-authorship. One of the legacies of the existential influence on transpersonal psychology, of course, is the demand for personal responsibility and accountability: "No excuses!" Disidentifying from and transcending ego states is implicit in the lineage of influences from William James and Gurdjieff to Hartmann and Assagioli. It provides the foundation for all that transpersonal approaches offer, and we will examine more closely some of the means to accomplish it in the section on the role of ego development in transcendence. Karma yoga suggests an apt analogy for the process and the outcome of this work. Walsh summarizes what the classic texts on karma yoga emphasize as its three main components:

- At the beginning of any activity offer or dedicate the
  activity to Brahman (God).
- Do your *dharma* (work) as impeccably as possible.
- Simultaneously release attachment to the outcome. As the
  Bhagavad Gita puts it (Prabhavananda and Isherwood,
  1972, p. 45):

> Perform every action sacramentally,
> And be free from all attachment to results.

This three-fold practice is profound. It combines a
transpersonal motive which undercuts egocentric motives, a
commitment to impeccability which requires cutting through
personal blocks and barriers, and a relinquishment of
egocentric attachment to having things turn out as we want
them to rather than the way they actually do. This last step of
relinquishing attachment to outcome can also be seen as the
practice of acceptance which is a powerful practice in its own
right.[405]

Note the similarity of Walsh's last step in karma yoga,
acceptance, and the transcendent state identified by Cloninger[406]
as that which results from transpersonal identification: spiritual
acceptance. Also, this 'flow chart' of the process of karma yoga
tracks very closely with that defined by Assagioli in
Psychosynthesis.[407] Remember that Assagioli was deeply
influenced by the Yoga and Vedanta-Upanishad philosophies.

"The end state of psychotherapy is the daily experience of a
state known in different traditions as certainty, liberation,
enlightenment, or gnosis."[408]

Transpersonal therapy is not identified with specific
techniques, but three distinct stages of therapy are usually
recognized.[409] The first stage of identification develops self-
awareness, and is concerned with taking responsibility for
oneself and owning one's body, emotions, and thoughts. This
new level of insight can focus on self-acceptance, and awaken an
expanded vision of oneself and one's potential. The second
stage, paradoxically, is one of disidentification, in which
consciousness is differentiated from its contents. The newly
expanded sense of self undermines the ego's tendency to define
itself based on roles, activities, relationships, possessions, status,
physical abilities, and external validation. The individual learns
to disidentify from the ego and identify more with the observing

self, identified with more than the egoic personal, with deeper layers of the internal unconscious and with a broader expanse of outward connections. The third stage is described as self-transcendence, in which self-absorption and concern with self-improvement is replaced by concern with service and the quality of life. The emergence of meaning on a new level of consciousness means actually moving beyond the concept of a transpersonal self, living at ease without being self-conscious because self is experienced as awareness flowing with the unity of earthly existence, without judgment or attachment. This flowing sense of self aligns with reality as it is, working with the forces of nature rather than seeking to dominate or control them.

One of the elements that contributes to a therapeutic intervention being transpersonal is establishing a *spiritual or transpersonal context* for the client. Conveying to a client that you see him or her as being a spark of the Divine is to begin to counter his/her life-long identification with personality. Asking if what they are doing or want to do is honoring the Divinity within them may inspire a new and higher self-image. Another element is some form of *mindfulness meditation* or other introspective practice. Other tools, or *psychotechnologies*[410], to help with transpersonal exploration and transformative restructuring include breathwork, regression hypnotherapy (including the potential for past-life regression), Kundalini yoga, visualizations, shamanistic journeying, dream work, immersion in myth and symbols, and altered state psychodrama, among others.

> The single most noteworthy feature of a psychotherapy that distinguishes it to be transpersonal is the inclusion of modified states of consciousness as a way to deeply understand and manage the client's identity structure.

This clarity allows him/her to find the core woundings[411] that gave rise to his suffering, avoidant behavior, disturbance and other correlates of an unhealthy personal identity, and then change it into something new. The transpersonal therapist is skilled at conventional assessment and treatment methods, but brings the added benefit of techniques of modifying consciousness. We expand our client's consciousness in breadth and depth. We help to broaden the perspective out to incorporate other points of view, a wider time frame into the past and the future, and an appreciation for unseen influences in our environment; to recognize projections and recollect them; and to integrate our interconnectedness with the natural world. We help to deepen the perspective inward to reveal unacknowledged subpersonalities within; to liberate inner resources that have been trapped in arrested development; and to open portals to allow access for energies to enter conscious awareness from the unconscious. Peres, Simão and Nasello found that the use of modified states of consciousness in therapy is highly relevant as it promotes both voluntary and spontaneous recall of traumatic memories, but can also help reframe them in more positive ways.[412]

Saldanha[413] describes seven phases that usually unfold during a therapeutic session resorting to "transpersonal" techniques (quoted by Rodrigues[414]):

1. *Acknowledgement.* The client gets in touch with his symptoms or troubles with the help of the therapist. This can happen at any, or several, levels of the client's personal or even subtle structure;
2. *Identification.* The client focuses on the symptom or suffering, gets into it, expresses it with the greatest possible intensity. The role it has on the full psychological structure is clarified;
3. *De-identification.* The client allows a distance from the contents of the experiential work, de-identifies after a previous catharsis, and starts opening for new possibilities;
4. *Transmutation.* The client gets insights, elaborates, as superconscious levels or energies get more clearly into the picture and help finding new meanings, creative solutions and postures;
5. *Transformation.* The client feels differently about his previous conflicts, finds a new perspective, as he feels that his previous situation has changed;
6. *Elaboration.* A global vision of the situation the client has been going through emerges and he is now fully getting into a different mindset;
7. *Integration.* The client integrates the therapeutic gains into his personal life and his worldviews and even changes his values.

This depth approach to psychotherapy encourages the client to deeply understand and manage his/her identity structure, which has developed over time into what *is experienced as* a fixed personality. The subpersonalities (ego states, inner children, autonomous complexes) too often operate under the radar of conscious awareness like unruly small children running wild. The unchallenged beliefs about worthiness, safety, identity, authority, or power wield their influence silently, undetected because of being with the individual perhaps since conception, or before, and reinforced in prenatal or perinatal moments in the developmental history of our biographical identity. Early introjects from influential caregivers and behavioral decisions burned deeply into the unconscious through traumatic shame, fear, rejection or abuse all coalesce into the individual's current identity structure.

> Broadening and deepening one's awareness of these components of the structure, bringing to consciousness what has been unconscious, establishes the opportunity for choice. And here we speak not only of the limiting and unhealthy aspects of that structure, but also of the untapped potential.

The restructuring of identity opens one to experience "a *non-linear time* (instead of our normative arrow of measurable time running from past to present to future), a *'space' that can imply more than three dimensions,* a *subject that can merge with objects,* a *causality that can be non-local* and *an 'I' that does not have to be the typical, biographical, subject of normal experiences within normal time and space.* This 'I' or ego is not necessarily constrained by the need for stability and is not necessarily environment-dependent."[415]

There is some closeness between the views of transpersonal psychotherapy about human beings and those we can find in humanistic and existential approaches. We emphasize the importance of self-acceptance and free expression from the patient but also of the therapists ability to stay in the relationship with an unconditionally loving attitude, a positive esteem towards the patient and a tendency to help him find his ways and express his feelings more than giving him interpretations, solutions or methods. On the other hand, we believe that 'normal' behaviour is not at all something we can infer from statistics but rather we prefer to talk about healthy behaviour and also health promoting procedures. We would say that a healthy human being is mature, open to change, accepts that others can behave differently and have different views, is self reliant, focused, socially constructive, loving, resilient, has a sense of purpose in life, has a good sense of his many dimensions and can consciously navigate them, is integrated and lives some degree of conscious unity he calls himself, and is able to somehow resort to humour and distancing from himself and life situations. He can stay in the present, enjoy life experiences, and has a tendency to got [sic] through moments of consciousness expansion during ethical, aesthetic, and generally pleasurable experiences. On the contrary, problematic human behaviour tends to be on the side of dissociation, disintegration, lack of resonance to others, identification with pathology and pathological states, defensive shrinking of the field of consciousness (as in phobias), alienation, loss of purpose, and intense suffering without the skills to endure and manage it. A major part of human suffering comes from rigid identification with defensive and disturbed patterns of behaviour and emotion, identification with very fragile personality structures and self-concepts, and generally speaking maladaptive attachments to self-concepts that are just defensive social facades, pessimistic views of oneself based on traumatic experiences, physical and emotional deprivations and the like. Emotions, as Cortright (2007) put it, are 'experience amplifiers'. They increase the conscious experience and tend to promote very strong memories. So the therapeutic approach within transpersonal psychotherapy places some heavy emphasis on the process of detaching from our usual, rather poor, sense of self and finding more about what and who we are, thanks to modified states of consciousness that, as already noted before, dramatically change our perception of ourselves and the world around us. To transpersonal psychotherapy, *the royal road to healing implies deep changes in identity and identity structure thanks to transformative experiences through healthy, expansive, modified states of consciousness.*[416]

Psychosynthesis places great importance on the use of active techniques in psychotherapy, in which the therapist encourages and guides the client, helping the client learn how to practice these techniques by himself, even outside the consulting room. Assagioli described the active techniques as belonging in three groups: psychophysical, psychological, and psychospiritual.[417]

The active techniques include symbolic visualization; guided imagery; using positive evocative words which combine visual, auditory, and motor images; and meditations developed for this purpose by Assagioli based on his studies of the Hindu philosophical and spiritual tradition of Vedanta and the Upanishads.

> Transpersonal psychotherapies are gaining acceptance and even prominence in the field of experiential therapy. They are often eclectic, combining aspects of existential, Gestalt, humanistic, and energy psychology with a focus on the ultimate potential development of humankind through expansion of consciousness.

Although almost no therapeutic techniques are unique to transpersonal therapy, there are a number commonly associated with it primarily because of their theoretical and practical compatibility. Five such techniques are briefly examined: (a) analysis of the personal drama, (b) "crazy wisdom" such as Sufi tales, Native American coyote stories, and Zen lore, (c) the use of symbol and metaphor, (d) synchronicity awareness, and (e) meditation. They share in common the potential to catalyze an experience in which the listener transcends the narrow identification with an egoic point of view, allowing the observing subject to become the object of observation.

Analysis of the personal drama. Fadiman defined personal dramas as "predictable, repetitive, and complex patterns of behavior performed either with or without the presence or participation of others," and he believes that they are "an unnecessary luxury and interfere with full functioning".[418] The personal drama is really just another way of describing *the personality*, that is the unique combination of conditioning, personal history, ego, beliefs, thoughts, and identifications that give a person a sense of personal identity, a sense of 'I-ness'. As such, the thrust of therapy is to help the client to disidentify from the restrictions of the personal drama and to attach their identity to the total self instead. This begins with the therapist letting the client know that the personal drama is being observed but that the 'actor' is not being confused with the person. This technique has a lot in common with Frankl's[419] "paradoxical intention", used by Haley[420] and re-named therapeutic paradox or "prescribing the symptom."

Paradoxical intention is a technique in which a therapist encourages a client to deliberately initiate or exaggerate a neurotic symptom. Usually, the act of trying intentionally to create the behavior renders him/her unable to do so. The client experiences distancing from the power of the symptom, and ultimately detaches from the symptom altogether.

Other examples of systems developed to help people identify and disidentify from internal ego states that engage in unhealthy dramas include Berne's Transactional Analysis[421] with parent, child, and adult ego states, and Zimberoff's[422] Victim Triangle with victim, persecutor and rescuer.

Crazy wisdom. Our shadows can sometimes be tricksters.

> The Trickster within can be an immature defensive aspect who tricks in order to deceive, redirecting attention from what is too challenging (too painful or too unattainable) toward an enchanting distraction. In this case, the Trickster has free reign to create mayhem. However, the Trickster can also be a Magician.

It takes a trickster to outmaneuver a trickster, and this is the role of the Magician within, to expose the shadow for the destructive infantile narcissist that he/she is. The Magician knows how to trick his own self-conceit and self-deceit: he tricks the Trickster in himself by depriving it of its one-sidedness. This is precisely the purview of what is called "crazy wisdom" – the overlapping roles of these two sides of the inner trickster. "Crazy wisdom literally means 'wisdom gone wild'. Yet one must first develop some wisdom before it can go wild, manifesting as natural, primordial simplicity and spontaneity."[423] When these two archetypes are conjoined, the transcendent function[424] (Jung's term for the inner compass that directs one toward healing and wholeness through complementarity between the conscious and the unconscious) manifests a new perspective with a novel way of presenting it incorporating elements of surprise, humor, and irony. This alliance takes place when the trickster stops resisting, gives up attachment to limiting beliefs, and vows to "fight no more forever". Again, the trickster shadow needs an inner self helper resource to navigate past its tendency toward infantile narcissism, to provide containment, direction, and transcendence.

Buddhist crazy wisdom refers to someone who seems to be

intoxicated with an unbounded, luminous, loving energy. It is only crazy from the viewpoint of ego, custom, or habit. "The sharpness that cuts through neurotic mind seems to be like a two-edged razor that cuts in both directions simultaneously, so the only thing that exists is the sharpness itself. It's not like a needle, not like an axe. It cuts both the projection and the projector at the same time. That is why there is a craziness aspect: the user gets cut by that razor as well as what he is using it on. That makes it humorous, too."[425] One Zen story tells of a master being asked what death and the afterlife hold for humans. After much furrowing of his brows, he finally produced the wise answer, "You need to ask that of a dead Zen master."

> If people are holding on too tightly to chastity, then they need a little prodding, they need some tickling, some humor. Remember, if a teaching is not threatening to the ego, the armored archetype within us, then it's not doing its job. So if people are fixated on chastity, a display of licentiousness will be useful. If someone thinks licentiousness is the path, then emphasize chastity. Sobriety, drunkenness. Logical thought, crazy thought. . . .
>   I was recently at a teaching in San Rafael with Lama Tharchin Rinpoche, and after everyone was settled he said, "You know that we all have Buddhanature. And that means that at some point we'll all become fully awakened." There was a big pause, and then he said, "Are you ready? Maybe in the middle of the talk tonight, you will become fully enlightened. Are you ready? It could be very inconvenient. What about all of the plans that you've made about where you'll go after the teaching? You're depending on not waking up, aren't you? Maybe you shouldn't have made so many plans."[426]

Native American wisdom is filled with stories about the coyote, an exasperating teacher. In one story he almost drowns trying to eat some berries reflected in a stream. We laugh at his foolishness until the humbling realization dawns of our own tendency to do the same foolish thing, e.g., pursuing an unattainable mirage of the perfect body or satisfying revenge. His wiliness sneaks up on us to confront our unexamined assumptions and beliefs. Trickster Coyote usually, in spite of his bumbling ways, is in the end able to create something new and improved out of the old.

Sufi mystics have many teaching stories featuring Mullah Nasrudin, who is a lot like his cousin Coyote. One day the Mullah's wife sent him to buy some bread. When the Mullah arrived at the bread shop he saw a long line waiting to buy bread. He thought he would do something to get in front of the line. He shouted, "People, don't you know the Sultan's daughter is getting married tonight and he is giving away free bread?" The multitude ran toward the palace as the Sultan was generous to a fault and loved his daughter more than anyone. The Mullah was now in front of the line and was about to buy his bread when he thought to himself, "Mullah, you are truly a fool. All the citizen's are getting free bread tonight and I am about to pay for it." So he ran to the palace and when he got there was thoroughly beaten by the disappointed people. In this story, the good Mullah reminds us of how often we believe our own fabrications, inflations, and fantasies, usually to the detriment of ourselves as well as others.

> These examples of crazy wisdom sneak up on the defenses of the ego and, with surprise and humor, allow for a sudden elevated perspective, a transcendence. There are magical moments in our work and in our life when such a whimsical yet poignant observation can trigger sudden insight.

Use of symbol and metaphor. Kate Maguire uses metaphor in her work with survivors of torture and extreme experiences. She says that metaphors "help the individual to live with his or her experiences, to own them; they help to communicate pain which is one of the most difficult things to do; they help the listener to listen without being traumatised; they prevent the listener from stealing the experiences for themselves, being the voyeur; they convey so much in such few words; they are bounded by form but boundless in interpretation; they can bring beauty out of horrific pain. . . . they will be the bridge between your souls. They are disarmingly spiritual."[427]

Primary process language (e.g., symbolic, poetic, metaphoric, mystical, archaic, childlike) allows direct access to the unconscious, bypassing the limitations of the conscious, analytic, rational intellect and its defenses.

Synchronicity awareness. Jung's famous treatise, "Synchronicity: An Acausal Connecting Principle," written in collaboration with the noted physicist, Wolfgang Pauli, hinges on his concept of synchronicity, which he defines as "the simultaneous occurrence of two meaningfully but not causally connected events" or, alternatively, as "a coincidence in time of two or more causally unrelated events which have the same or similar meaning", "equal in rank to causality as a principle of explanation."[428] Most of us can recall a personal experience of an uncanny coincidence accompanied by a spontaneous emotional response of awe, wonder, or warmth and the certitude that something meaningful or significant had just occurred. According to Jung, when the emotionally charged archetypal level is active, synchronistic events with symbolic meaning are more likely to occur. Synchronistic events can be analyzed in the same way as dreams, i.e., through the twin Jungian techniques of amplification and active imagination.[429]

Meditation, contemplative psychotherapy. There are many possible connections between Eastern contemplative practices and Western psychotherapy. Bazzano[430] suggests from his own practice that there are four significant elements to the experience of meditation:

- Meditation is no longer associated with goals or expectations but is the appreciation of what is;
- Meditation is not a search for 'answers' but allows space for deeper questioning and enquiry;
- Meditation allows an unraveling of content (thoughts, feelings, emotions) via an unraveling of the observer himself: a fluidity of experiencing which opens the observer/ experiencer to a clearer insight into the self as process rather than a solid, self-existing entity;
- Meditation allows a deeper acceptance and trust in the wider process of life itself.

These attributes correlate quite precisely with the qualities associated with existential psychotherapy, or more generally with most transpersonal therapies.

Between the 1960s and the 1990s, use of meditation as a therapeutic tool developed in distinct ways within the humanistic, psychodynamic, and cognitive–behavioral schools of therapy. Behavioral approaches focused on meditation as a psychophysiological relaxation tool and as a means for behavioral self-management (Benson, 1975; Shapiro & Walsh, 1984), giving only limited consideration to the spiritual. In contrast, the humanistic and transpersonal perspective viewed meditation as a means of producing heightened states of experience in the pursuit of self-actualization, self-transformation, and cultivation of compassion for others (Kornfield & Walsh, 1993).[431]

Incorporating some form of meditative experience into a therapeutic milieu can affect individual clients in numerous ways beyond potential spiritual advancement. Meditation has beneficial physical effects, such as to heighten parasympathetic relaxation, slow heart rate and decrease blood pressure. This may be useful in treating anxiety and stress-related illness. Meditation usually heightens emotional well-being. These effects tend to also assist individuals in managing their behavioral choices, and can be especially relevant in the treatment of compulsions and addictions. Bringing newfound peace into relationships is another common result of meditation practice. In fact, that heightened ability to experience empathy, compassion, and loving kindness toward others applies to oneself as well. A word of caution is appropriate: meditation as an intervention and growth process is cumulative and can be slow in producing tangible results.

A sudden zap works in your microwave oven. You put your food in, you zap it, and it gets cooked instantly. However, in the realm of mindfulness and meditation, you can't expect a transcendental microwave oven. No achievement happens all of a sudden. There is a process of growth, a gradual process of developing ourselves. No one is going to save us on the spot. Our progress is up to us.[432]

Archetypal Center Core Selves
Most people have had the experience of accessing some form of reliably wise guidance within, an aspect of oneself that is free from cognitive distortions and is in fact conflict-free. Accessing such an internal resource is a staple of humanistic, existential and transpersonal therapy. Remember that, in *Psychosynthesis*, Assagioli hypothesized the existence of "a

permanent center, of a true self situated beyond or above the [conscious self or ego]." [433] He viewed this, which is termed the Higher Self or the Transpersonal Self, as the very core of the human psyche.

How might we conceptualize this inner resource, and what means can be used to find and solicit input from it? By definition it exists beyond ego, since it springs from the unconscious well of inner selves. While possible selves are personalized representations of one's important life goals and imaginable possible futures, they must be conjured by an aspect of self whose purview extends beyond that of the ego. It is this inner resource that is capable of outmaneuvering the ego's defenses and habits and self-limiting beliefs. Let's use the term archetypal center core.

Allison[434] introduced the concept of the internal self helper (ISH) in working with multiple personality disorder/ Dissociative Identity Disorder (DID) and Comstock[435] expanded it with an accompanying theory of inner guidance and the center. An inclusive conceptualization of a center core was proposed by Gainer and Torem[436] and Torem and Gainer[437]. They identified it as containing the safe space[438], ISH, and a variety of inner strengths. They thought these personality energies promote rationality and adult logic within the internal family of selves[439].

> Center core phenomena vary greatly in both manifestations and actions. They appear to fall into distinct divisions in terms of subjective experience, observable manifestations, functions, and effects. Apparently, they become subjects of attention only when the individual is in trance—be it formal hypnosis or spontaneous trance. Comstock's (1991) foundational review of ISH and inner guidance was a milestone in identifying the history and characteristics of personality energies she classified as central. Both Comstock (1991) and Fraser and Curtis (1984) believed that there was a kind of center core energy that was different from the ISH. Fraser and Curtis (1984) called it the center subpersonality; Comstock referred to it as "the center" (Comstock, 1991, p. 169); and Fraser (1991) eventually named it the center ego state.[440]

Archetypal center core energies have been described by many clinicians. In the 20th and 21st centuries they include the center subpersonality (Fraser & Curtis, 1984); Watkins and Watkins (1997) center core; Rossman's (1987) inner advisor; Schwartz's (1995) self; Ginandes' (2006) empowered healing guide; Feinstein and Krippner's (2006) inner shaman; Brown and Fromm's (1986) ideal parent; Flint's (2006) subconscious; McNeal and Frederick's (1993) inner strength and Frederick and McNeal's (1999) inner wisdom; and Krakauer's (2001, 2006) inner wisdom. Frederick and McNeal (1999) and Frederick (2005, 2010) have previously referred to archetypal center core phenomena as archetypal selfobjects and transcendent archetypal selfobjects. These terms have been replaced in this article because of their unnecessary awkwardness. The term "transcendent" does not imply that these are spiritual energies (although some believe they are), but rather relates to Jung's (1939, 1960) "transcendent function," the ability to maintain complementarity and balance between the conscious and the unconscious.[441]

Archetypal center core phenomena present as a unique intrapsychic experience. Frederick[442] suggests these qualities, in general:

1. They usually require a hypnotic trance state for activation;
2. They are perceived multimodally as visualizations, thoughts, emotions, kinesthetic sensations, or any combination of these;
3. These phenomena are experienced as profound and archetypal;
4. They are transcendent in the specific sense that they promote conscious-unconscious complementarity (Gilligan, 1987; Jung, 1960);
5. The experience is often beyond verbal description;
6. A single, brief subjective experience may produce notable symptom alleviation; and
7. Archetypal selfobjects have a range of effects only one of which is inner guidance (Comstock, 1991).

Carl Jung made contact with inner guides who came to him in visions from deep imagination throughout his life. As a successful physician and analyst in his mid-thirties, Jung had several spontaneous visions when he was alone in his study contemplating the profound nature of disturbing dreams he had. These encounters with archetypal figures brought intense insights that he recorded and that eventually became the narrative in The Red Book.[443] He also records many of these encounters in his autobiography, *Memories, Dreams, Reflections*[444], including those he experienced as a young man and also when he was 69 and recovering from a heart attack. Jung developed a visual technique that he found helped him to go deeper into these visions, which he later called *active imagination*. This technique was a realistic visualization of descending a great distance down into the earth, as much as 1000 feet, he said. He encountered an old man and a woman who turn out to be the biblical figures Elijah and Salome.

Over time, Jung holds conversation with Elijah who eventually changes into another figure, Philemon. Philemon teaches Jung about the nature of human consciousness, including the workings of Jung's own psyche. Jung begins to realize that these inner figures are autonomous, that they exist apart from him and yet can only manifest in the world through him. Jung knows that what is revealed to him does not originate from him; it is the inner figure that seems to hold the knowledge and to be willing to share it with Jung.

> Philemon and other figures from my fantasies brought home to me the crucial insight that there are things in the psyche which I do not produce, but which produce themselves and have their own life. Philemon represented a force which was not myself. In my fantasies I held conversations with him, and he said things which I had not consciously thought. For I observed clearly that it was he who spoke, not I. . . . Through him the distinction was clarified between myself and the object of my thought. He confronted me in an objective manner, and I understood that there is something in me which can say things that I do not know and do not intend, things which may even be directed against me.
>
> Psychologically, Philemon represented superior insight. He was a mysterious figure to me. At times he seemed to me quite real, as if he were a living personality. I went walking up and down the garden with him, and to me was what the Indians call a guru.[445]

> Here we see clearly the transcendent function at work in Jung's life, bringing complementarity and balance between his conscious and unconscious, introducing him to archetypal wisdom figures available to him through deep introspection. Current examination of this phenomena, which we are calling archetypal center core energies, highlight several particular forms.

One might be called *inner strength*[446], an experience connected with the deep, innate human psychobiological energies of survival. Its outstanding characteristic is fearlessness, and so it brings confidence to the ego struggling with overpowering emotional circumstances or facing daunting choices. Another is *inner wisdom*[447] which brings out unconscious reservoirs of wisdom that appear to be inherent and fit within age-old, multicultural traditions of inner guidance. The messages of inner wisdom point to judicious, reality-based approaches to problems, and frequently inner wisdom asks pregnant questions whose purpose is to activate the individual's problem-solving abilities.

Another archetypal center core energy is *inner love*[448], although it does not really fit into the inner guidance tradition because it has neither advice to give nor any direction to share; it is simply open to giving and receiving love. The Inner Shaman[449]; Empowered Healing Guide[450]; representations of ideal parents[451] and the "fully-realized" persona of someone who has died[452] could also be considered as archetypal center core phenomena, contributing to secure attachment, internal self-soothing, the ability to tolerate separation, increased healthy separateness, and increased creativity.

Inner strength, inner love, inner wisdom—indeed all of the archetypal center core phenomena—are a protective-evocative form of ego strengthening which activate resource states from the unconscious.[453] Indeed, these archetypal center core phenomena behave like Jung's archetypes, as we have seen, in that they are transpersonal and part of the intricate psychic mental structure.[454] They are also part of the conflict-free sphere of the ego that had been identified and extensively described by Hartmann.[455]

I propose that we adopt the provisional term conflict-free ego sphere for that ensemble of functions which at any given time exert their effects outside the region of mental conflicts. We do not yet have a systematic psychoanalytic knowledge of this sphere. Adaptation obviously involves both processes connected with conflict situations, and processes which pertain to the conflict-free sphere. Of the fields studied or influenced by psychoanalysis, education and sociology, for instance, stand to gain by our broadening our horizon in the direction of the conflict-free sphere and adaptation.[456]

Archetypal center core phenomena provide containment for the individual's uncontrolled anxieties and reactivity. They have nurturing qualities, serving as trusted and resourceful elders. They provide respect and unconditional acceptance, which can help to neutralize shame. They promote integration of the individual's disparate parts (e.g., persona, shadows, complexes) and healthy conscious–unconscious complementarity.[457] They bring elements of novelty, surprise, a sense of awe and of the numinous.[458] In short, center core phenomena offer secure attachment to an infallible inner resource.

Are archetypal center core phenomena ego states? This does not appear to be the case. They do not appear to have been created to meet some satiation as ego states are. They conform to the culture only to a limited extent; they are seldom based on our parents, teachers, or other significant figures in our early lives; they are not born of trauma or of the need to attach. They appear to be innate, conflict-free energies whose presence as inner resource states has made human survival and growth possible. When the therapist makes the use of archetypal center core phenomena a necessary element of ego state therapy, of trauma therapy, and/or of therapy in general, the patient will have an opportunity to achieve a greater sense of self-efficacy, greater mastery, a higher level of self-care, greater stabilization, reduced dependency, and progress with developmental repair.[459]

When center core energies are accessed and used in therapy, which may require the induction of a non-ordinary state of consciousness such as hypnosis:

- *They are organizing and stabilizing.* This has been noted by Comstock[460], Torem and Gainer[461], Gainer and Torem[462], and many others.
- *They are liminal and archetypal.* Center core activity may initiate long-term change by leading the client to the threshold of new and transformative realizations, new behaviors, interactions that lead to new thoughts and experiences.

Among all the possible inner voices competing for attention, how do we recognize those that are legitimately archetypal center core phenomena, distinguishing them from other inner voices? Myrtle Heery's research on subjective reports of inner voices is instructive. Heery[463] distinguishes three categories of inner voices on different developmental levels (pre-personal, personal, transpersonal):

1. inner voices experienced from childhood onwards which can be understood by the therapist as fragmented parts of the self, parts of the ego or subpersonalities referred to in clinical hypnotherapy as ego states. (Ego States, as the name implies, refer to aspects of the ego, and do not therefore fit the category of transpersonal experience, which is considered to be experience beyond ego awareness);

2. inner voices characterized by dialogue in decision making, i.e. inner growth advisors that seem to be archetypes experienced as other than self, and which can be interpreted as an early aspect of later full transpersonal experience;

3. inner voices that are not like advising archetypes, but like fluid energy that opens channels towards and beyond a Higher Self. Such higher transpersonal experiences are more likely to be reported by those with deep and prolonged experience of hypnosis, self-hypnosis or meditation, according to Heery.

An example of an altered state therapy that liberates inner resources is Krakauer's[464] Two Part-Film Technique. In a hypnotic trance state, this technique allows the client to experience two very different ways of viewing and dealing with problem situations or relationships. One is the all-too-familiar defensive responses; the other is suggested by the client's own internal resource of wise counsel, the *inner wisdom*. Krakauer explains the effectiveness of her Two-Part Film Technique as springing from the actions of positive, wise, and caring unconscious internal resources that belong to an aspect of the personality she calls *inner wisdom* as well as the *collective heart*. With this technique the therapist trains the client to use self-hypnosis, minimizing input from the therapist and emphasizing the client's access to self-generated imagery and ideas. The inner resource state — *inner wisdom* — is capable of clarifying defensive cognitive distortions and helping to change undesirable behaviors. Krakauer differentiates her technique from those in which the therapist actively directs resource states. Instead, an internal dialogue is evoked in which the parts, or ego states, communicate their suffering, confusion, and developmental limitations to *inner wisdom*. The archetypal entity *inner wisdom* is then able to gain greater understanding and empathy for the painful problems of the ego states. This permits *inner wisdom* to offer meaningful alternative choices that are free from cognitive distortions. When the client leaves hypnosis and re-enters the waking state, he/she is able to reflect on the information obtained from *inner wisdom* and to choose a different perspective and path of action. Each time the patient accesses *inner wisdom* and is able to recognize wiser, less trauma-based, less dissociative choices, he/she takes another step toward developmental repair and wholeness. An important key in this process is inner dialogue between ego states and center core phenomena, an almost identical procedure as Jung's active imagination.[465]

Spiritual Wounding and Restoration

Transpersonal psychotherapy attends to spiritual wounding and repair in a direct way that most other approaches, including humanistic or person-centered therapy, often don't. Our many years of work with trauma survivors and PTSD have shown repeatedly that a splintered or devastated ego leaves the individual disconnected from his or her soul and therefore stranded in life without a "lifeline" to the numinous Divine. A chronic state of shock—the result of trauma embedded in the nervous system—can be the difference between being a 'slave' of God, an 'employee' of God, or a 'lover' of God, in the terminology of Orthodoxy. Shock can take the form of too much sympathetic nervous system activation (fight or flight response), or too much parasympathetic nervous system activation (freeze response), Spiritual shock manifests as *spiritual numbness* (on the parasympathetic extreme)—an inability to fully experience awe, reverence, ecstasy or surrender, or as *spiritual distraction* (on the sympathetic extreme)—a redirection of one's spiritual energy out into the mundane world.[466] In each case, the individual's chronic shock state serves to maintain a barrier to real, felt spiritual experiences, and some form of transpersonal intervention is called for.

Spiritual Distraction (sympathetic shock) may take the form of:

- "Spiritual busyness" or filling up one's time set aside for spiritual practice with activity, pursuit, efforts to achieve *some particular experience*, e.g., to become the "best ever" meditator, yoga teacher, Catholic, Christian, Buddhist, etc. This distraction is one of attending to what seems to be most *urgent* spiritually but not necessarily to what is in reality most *important*.
- "Spiritual crusades" or fighting for a dogmatic principle or against an external perceived evil. It is often easier to identify, judge and condemn an external threat than it is to honestly face an internal one.
- "Spiritual materialism," in which "we can deceive ourselves into thinking we are developing spiritually when instead we are strengthening our egocentricity through spiritual techniques."[467] This is a case of the ego driving the spiritual bus.

Spiritual Numbness (parasympathetic shock) may take the form of:

- "Spiritual suicide," in which one chooses to fall asleep spiritually, to hide from the challenging existential questions of a relationship with the Divine through mindlessness and monotony.
- "Spiritual depression," in which one denies anger and resentment toward God and redirects it inwardly, feeling

disappointed in oneself and despondent in life. One may be confusing spirituality with dogma and religion, and one's anger is in actuality directed at religious authority.

- "Spiritual bypass," in which one confuses dissociation, visions from the astral plane and the efforts of spiritual practices with a true awakening. These experiences are used instead to avoid intimacy in relationships and engaged participation in society.

Heart-Centered Hypnotherapy[468] and Altered State Psychodrama[469] are transpersonal therapeutic modalities well suited for repairing spiritual wounding and restoring a healthy spiritual connection. The age regression capability provides access to the original sources of traumatization, and the deep trance state allows direct contact with archetypal center core resources. While traditional therapy has mainly focused on the left brain, trying to cognitively understand complex emotions, behavioral patterns and relationship difficulties, it has often discounted the importance of how deeply spiritual many people are and at the same time ignored how essential it is to work with the body and its energy systems. Heart-Centered Hypnotherapy provides a protocol that incorporates a wide-ranging set of specific components:

1) discovery and resolution of deeply embedded feelings and behaviors through a deep theta brain wave trance state;

2) insight on long-standing life patterns and early imprinted beliefs through age regression;

3) a transpersonal approach providing access to profound pre- and perinatal experiences, future progressions, and direct experience with the archetypal forces known to depth psychology;

4) access to heightened somatic awareness and clearing of the body's shock (the residue of trauma trapped in the body's nervous system);

5) healing through the ancient chakra system to cleanse and release previous unhealthy and stagnant energies, and through which a deep release and cleansing happens on all levels;

6) applications of developmental psychology to promote inner child work and to encourage higher stages of adult development;

7) direct encounter and dialogue with archetypal center core energies that serve as inner resources; and

8) inclusion of the client's own preferred spiritual connection.

While exploring the deep subconscious mind, therapists as well as clients often feel their heart opening up with feelings of love and joy. When combining hypnotherapy with humanistic and transpersonal psychology, most clients describe a warm loving experience centered in the middle of their chest. They are describing the fourth chakra or Heart Center, the body's central energy center in the context of the ancient East Indian chakra system.

Chapter Eight

Transpersonal Coaching

Transpersonal therapy is the realm of repairing damage to an individual's psyche, including soul and spiritual damage. In that process, one may well reach a tipping point at which the emphasis shifts from repairing damage to building new capacities. Coaching incorporates the added dimension of adult development for *optimal* functioning. Here, too, there is the challenge of transcendence.

Stepping into your greatness means *transcending unnecessary limitation*. Some people no doubt hear grandiosity and egotism in the concept of "stepping into your greatness." Abraham Maslow warned about the self-defeating trap of the fear of one's own greatness. "We fear our highest possibilities (as well as our lowest ones). We are generally afraid to become that which we can glimpse in our most perfect moments, under the most perfect conditions."[470] He also suggests that this fear serves a positive purpose: it is a defense against grandiosity, arrogance, sinful pride, hubris. To invent or create, to step into one's own greatness, one must have the "arrogance of creativeness." But if one has *only* the arrogance without an offsetting humility, then the "self-crippling" becomes destructive. Maslow uses Aldous Huxley as an example of someone who accepted his talents and used them to the full, while looking out at the world with wide eyes, with unabashed innocence, awe and fascination, "which is a kind of admission of smallness, a form of humility."[471] This sense of humility is another foundational ingredient of higher stages of human development; it activates self-transcendence, or transcending the ego.

We all carry within us deeply imprinted assumptions about what we are capable of, and incapable of. Those assumptions are built around generalizations (early conclusions) of other people's beliefs. As children we accepted as gospel truth what the adults in our lives told us, or communicated to us in nonverbal ways.

And those beliefs continue to be a primary influence on our perception of life and of ourselves, limiting the choices we make.

Transcending these limitations calls on our capacity to stand outside of our conditioned perspective, to see the world and ourselves more objectively. With such a viewpoint, one is more open, more accepting, less egotistic. One finds a deeper sense of meaningfulness, purpose, and connection. We see transcendence at work in selfless service or self-sacrificing altruism, in the humble acceptance of the opportunity to use one's natural gifts for the greater good of all.

Viktor Frankl[472] asserted three primary sources or types of pathology – somatogenic, psychogenic, and noogenic. The first two are physical and emotional, but the third is existential. This neurotic pathology arises from a perceived emptiness of purpose in life. According to Frankl, the predominant human motivation is the will to meaning; when profound meaning is not perceived, the individual becomes in Frankl's term 'existentially frustrated' or what Pascual-Leone calls 'existentially hopeless'.[473] Frankl used this story to convey the vital importance of purpose, or meaning, in a human being's life:

> Generally, one assumes that a boomerang always returns to the hunter; but actually, I have been told in Australia, a boomerang only comes back to the hunter when it has missed its target. Well, man also only returns to himself, to being concerned with his self, after he has missed his mission, has failed to find a meaning in his life.[474]

Research by Crumbaugh and Maholick[475] validates the perspective that psychopathology tends to increase with perceived lack of purpose in life. Conversely, when a person experiences meaning in his/her life, mental health tends to follow. Clearly, meaning in life and mental health are important components contributing to or detracting from one's motivation. We will revisit the importance of meaning in life as part of the discussion on posttraumatic distress and posttraumatic growth.

The transcendence involved in development to optimal functioning yields transparency; looser and more flexible ego boundaries; and 'postambivalence', i.e., total wholehearted and unconflicted love, acceptance, and self-expression.

What Maslow called postambivalence, Jung called an unconditional "Yes" to that which is. In his autobiography *Memories, Dreams, Reflections*, Jung said, "Something else too, came to me from my illness. I might formulate it as an affirmation of things as they are: an unconditional 'yes' to that which is, without subjective protests – acceptance of the conditions of existence as I see them and understand them, acceptance of my own nature, as I happen to be."[476]

Strengths and Transcendence

In facilitating adult development, we emphasize the vital importance of focusing on a client's strengths, passions, and values. It is those strengths that provide the raw materials, and passions that provide the engine of motivation to achieve. Every coaching interaction should include reference to the client's strengths. That can be assessed informally through discussion, or in a structured way through an assessment tool such as the Values in Action Inventory of Strengths (assessment available for free at www.viastrengths.org from The Mayerson Foundation, creators of the VIA Institute). The instrument is a powerful pathway to greater self-awareness of strengths. It is one of the transpersonal coach's most important tasks to help clients discover their greatest strengths, and then to remind them of those strengths frequently.

The Values in Action Inventory identifies an individual's signature strengths, and how to use them in our working and social lives to help us achieve "a good life", while using them to help others will put us on course for achieving a "meaningful life." Listed here are the six virtues, or core values, and the signature strengths that support each.[477] Note the prominence of transcendence as one of the signature strengths.

1. Wisdom - the ability to take stock of life in large terms, in ways that make sense to oneself and others
- **Curiosity in the world** - an ongoing, intrinsic interest in both their inner experience and the world around them. Curious people tend to be attracted to new people, new things, and new experiences, and they are rarely bored
- **Love of learning** - motivated to acquire new skills or knowledge or to build on existing skills or knowledge.

They feel good when they are learning new things, even though they may occasionally become frustrated when the material is challenging

- **Judgment, critical thinking and open-mindedness** - the willingness to search actively for evidence against one's favored beliefs, plans, or goals, and to weigh such evidence fairly when it is available
- **Creativity, ingenuity, originality**, practical intelligence, street smarts
- **Perspective** - Providing wise counsel to others

2. Courage
- **Valor and bravery** - Acting on convictions without shrinking from threat or difficulty
- **Perseverance**, industry and diligence - voluntary continuation of a goal-directed action in spite of obstacles, difficulties, or discouragement
- **Integrity, honesty**, genuineness - A regular pattern of behavior that is consistent with espoused values (i.e., "practicing what you preach")
- **Zest, passion and enthusiasm** - Approaching life with excitement and energy; not doing things halfway or halfheartedly; living life as an adventure; feeling alive and activated

3. Humanity and Love
- **Kindness and Generosity** - generosity, nurturance, care, compassion, and altruistic love
- **Loving** and allowing oneself to be loved
- **Social intelligence**, personal intelligence, emotional intelligence

4. Justice - Civic strengths that underlie healthy community life.
- **Fairness and equity** - Giving everyone a fair chance, treating people the same according to a sense of justice
- **Leadership** - Organizing group activities and seeing that they happen
- **Teamwork**, citizenship, social responsibility, loyalty - Working well as a member of a group or team; being loyal to the group; doing one's share

5. Temperance
- **Self control** - Being disciplined, controlling appetites and emotions

- **Prudence**, discretion, caution - Prudence is a cognitive orientation to the personal future, a form of practical reasoning and self-management that helps to achieve the individual's long-term goals effectively. Prudent individuals show a farsighted and deliberate concern for the consequences of their actions and decisions, successfully resisting impulses and other choices that satisfy shorter term goals at the expense of longer term ones, having a flexible and moderate approach to life, and striving for balance among their goals and ends
- **Humility and modesty** - Letting accomplishments speak for themselves, not seeking limelight
- **Forgiveness and mercy** - a series of changes that occur within an individual who has been offended or hurt in some way by another person. When individuals forgive, their thoughts and actions toward the transgressor become more positive (e.g., more peaceful or compassionate) and less negative (e.g., less wrathful or avoidant)

6. Transcendence
- **Appreciation of beauty and excellence** - ability to find, recognize, and take pleasure in the existence of goodness in the physical and social worlds
- **Gratitude** - Being thankful for the good things that happen
- **Hope, optimism and future-mindedness** - Expecting the best and believing one can work to achieve it
- **Spirituality**, sense of purpose, faith, religiousness - a concept of an ultimate, transcendent, sacred, and divine force that guides an individual's daily life experience
- **Playfulness and humor** - Seeing the light side, bringing smiles and laughter

'Coaching Hypnosis'

In transpersonal psychology, hypnosis is appropriate and useful beyond the clinical purposes of repairing traumatic damage through hypnotherapy. It is a powerful tool within the context of adult development, growth, and coaching. 'Coaching hypnosis' may be referred to as the deliberate use of hypnotic strategies and principles as an adjunct to accepted coaching process. The inclusion of hypnosis, NLP techniques, and hypnotic strategies and principles in coaching is not only appropriate but highly effective.

Suggestion and suggestive techniques. Suggestion and suggestive techniques, while traditionally associated with hypnosis and Neurolinguistic Programming (NLP), can be usefully applied by the coach in almost any format of interaction with a client. In other words, hypnosis is not a requirement for suggestive influence. Professionals with training in hypnosis and NLP will be familiar with the importance of properly structuring suggestions. We will review the technology of constructing effective suggestions, following the elaboration provided by Steckler[478] and Yapko[479].

1. **Keep the suggestions simple and easy to follow**. Complicated and sequential suggestions engage the client's conscious mind, rendering unconscious process less available for access.
2. **Use your client's language**. The coach's words and language may not have the same meaning for the client. Further, the coach can miss important cues in the role of the client's unconscious as expressed by the words the client selects. This is especially true for idiosyncratic usage. "Pissed off" is not the same as "angry". Yapko cites an example of a client who used the word "telegraph" in what seemed an unusual way. In trancework with her, it evolved that her father had received a "telegraph" to go to war, never to return, a memory lost to consciousness by the client, but one which affected her trust in male relationships into the present.
3. **Have the client define everything**. What constitutes a "phobia" or "depression" for the coach may not be the same experience for the client. If the client defines what he or she means, both connotation and denotation are alike for coach and client.
4. **Use the present tense and a positive structure**. It is important to phrase suggestions in terms of what a person can do, rather than in terms of what they can't do. "I am now an organized person . . ." rather than "I want to get more

organized." Also, link the present to the future: "As you are doing this, you can also begin to do that."

5. **Encourage and compliment the client**. A respectful regard for the client is crucial. Encouragement, rather than attack or critical reproach, allows the client to move to a position of acknowledging personal strengths and resources, allowing for self-generated change.

6. **Determine ownership of the problem**. It is difficult to facilitate change in people who see themselves as "victims," who are "other-blamers." Helping people to discover that they can control their reactions to life events is in fact one component of the hypnotic experience, helping to establish an acceptance set for subsequent owning of responsibility.

7. **Determine the best modality for the trance experience**. People experience the world through their senses, and Bandler and Grinder[480] have hypothesized that people utilize a preferred sensory mode in their thinking, and further that they express this preference in their language. Some people think in pictures, while others favor the auditory modality, remembering conversations with clarity or recalling their inner dialogue during particular experiences. Still others express themselves in kinesthetic terms, remembering primarily the feeling components of experience. While each person processes experience in terms of all modes, identifying a client's preferred mode can allow the coach to couch communications in the words of the favored system, increasing the likelihood of facilitating client change because of the improved communicative rapport.

8. **Keep the client only as informed as is necessary to succeed**. An advantage of hypnotic communication is its ability to make contact with the client's affective rather than cognitive domain. While this may present an ethical dilemma at one level, Yapko advocates handling this on a sensitive case-by-case basis. He notes that telling a client about using a confusional technique to disrupt a maladaptive thinking pattern will effectively destroy the gain of the technique. Dealing with affect inevitably has a greater impact than dealing strictly with intellect: "I know (cognitive) I shouldn't feel this way, but I do (affective)."

9. **Give your clients the time they need**. Everyone responds according to their own pace, and it is crucial that the coach remain patient and flexible with the coaching agenda.

10. **Get permission before touching your client**. Always ask before intruding on personal space. Respect the client's physical integrity. Touching without permission may also reorient the client outwardly, diminishing the inward focus of trance.

11. **Establish anticipation signals**. To avoid startling clients, always say, "In a moment I am going to . . ." Anticipation signals foster trust in the hypnotic communication.

12. **Use a voice and demeanor consistent with your intent**. It is a therapeutic contradiction to urge relaxation in a stressed, tense voice. Further, soothing tones discourage intellectual analysis, thus further facilitating trance.

13. **Chain suggestions structurally**. Hypnosis can be utilized to build a link between what the client is doing and what he will do. This can be done with "and" or "but" ("You are sitting here and beginning to feel relaxed"); or with implied causatives such as "as," "while," and "during" ("As you notice yourself breathing more comfortably, you can begin to remember your birthday"). However, the strongest link is the causative predicate, suggesting a current behavior will cause a future one ("Thinking of your birthday will make you remember other holidays").

14. **Be general specifically**. Avoid the use of detail in suggestions. The more specifics one provides, the more likelihood of the client's contradicting the suggestion.

15. **If desirable, substitute other terms for hypnosis**. Some clients are afraid of "hypnosis" but welcome the idea of progressive relaxation, focused imagery, and other hypnotic techniques by other names. Possible additional alternative labels are deep relaxation, controlled relaxation, visual imagery, guided imagery, guided fantasy, guided meditation, or mental imagery. However, as Yapko points out, if a focused state of attention is narrowed to suggestions offered, and influence then occurs, hypnosis is present.

Use of suggestion is not manipulation. Manipulation involves the intention to get someone to do what you want.

Coaches use suggestions for the sole purpose to meet the client's agenda, not their own. It is goal-directed communication when a coach says, "This will help you improve your performance – I can already see the difference!" while offering the client feedback about improvements to his public speaking.

An individual is more receptive to suggestion in a hypnotic trance state than when she is in her everyday cognitive mindset. One way of capitalizing on this receptivity is to use *presuppositions*. You get the client thinking that something desired has already happened, is now happening, or is inevitably going to happen. A coach might communicate the presumption that something is about to happen, establishing a positive expectancy for the client by saying, "Allow a time to come to you when you felt confident, and when you are there raise a finger to let me know" (presupposing that an appropriate time will come). Another example of using this technique is to present a choice, either of which accomplishes the task, such as "Would you like to discuss this today or during our next meeting?" or "'I wonder where you'll start to implement your clear priorities first. Will it be at work with your clients or at home with your family?"

We communicate the presumption that something is happening when we say, "That's right, now continue relaxing" or "Allow this sense of purpose to spread throughout your body." And the coach suggests to the client that something has already happened when she says, "Notice the calm excitement you are feeling as you breathe deeply and recall that experience."[481]

These suggestions presented as presumptions are important in the wording of guided imagery or hypnotic facilitation. A coach trained in the use of hypnosis is very familiar with phrases such as, "Now you are beginning to feel confident and well-organized as you sit at your desk and review the day's top priorities," or "Beaming confidence, you recognize the respect that each colleague sitting at the conference table has for you." Notice how important it is to use descriptive language to bring the client's awareness directly into the situation being imagined, and to link the task with strong emotions.

Repetition is a powerful reinforcement for any suggestion. The coach's suggestions will be more successfully received and acted on when the main message is repeated several times throughout the coaching session, thereby repeatedly directing attention to the intended goal or idea.

State suggestions as a positive, gearing them toward a desirable goal rather than away from an unwanted one. Rather than "Don't let others' judgments about you stop you from following your plan", the client will respond better to "You love the sense of freedom that comes with absolute confidence in the rightness of your plan."

Self-hypnosis. Research findings show that many individuals with little or no previous experience with hypnosis expect that hypnosis induced by a professional would be experienced as involuntary, but that self-hypnosis would be experienced as voluntary.[482] Therefore a coach who intends to utilize hypnosis in the engagement may want to introduce the client to self-hypnosis to empower a sense of self-efficacy and to diminish possible resistance.

Self-hypnosis is an accessible and effective means of following through on many of the practices a coach may facilitate for the client, either during the coaching session or in between sessions. For example,
- Practicing/rehearsing skills
- Facilitating learning
- Regaining control
- Maintaining motivation
- Accessing resources
- Goal attainment

Rehearsal. Hypnosis is an excellent vehicle for exploring an individual's internal imagery and conclusions that may be unconsciously influencing a client's everyday choices in life. If the coaching focus at any one point in time is on interpersonal relations, dealing with conflict, approaching competition, or one's personal level of organization, it may be very useful for the client to understand what unconscious influences are at work. Of course it is important to access positive, supportive associations as well as any negative, inhibiting ones needing to be eliminated.

An example of incorporating hypnosis into coaching is using it to neutralize negative elements and promote adaptive responses in rehearsing competitive situations.[483] Understanding the source of a current performance deficit is half the process of resolving it, and in the hypnotic trance state, in age regression, the coach can effectively assist the client to access early conflicted experiences and to release the original debilitating beliefs and conclusions (e.g., "Other people are unreliable", or "Conflict is scary and I always lose", or "Competition is threatening because it means the winner is boastful and the loser is humiliated").

Then the second half of the healing process is to find early experiences of success in the area of current focus, and to amplify and anchor viscerally that experience. Perhaps the client remembers a time in grade school when she won a spelling bee and was jubilant while remaining gracious with the other children competing in the spelling bee. We then want to anchor that resource state with a word or phrase, a color, an image, or a somatic experience. It becomes a powerful inner resource which can be called on in a rehearsal of the problematic situation in the client's present day life. In hypnosis, we would implement a mental rehearsal technique in which the client recalls herself in a current day challenging situation that felt like failure, and give the suggestion to let the memory fade. Now, in a moment, she would go back into that same situation, and first find compassion for herself in light of the early conditioning she has now uncovered. Next, still in that same situation, she is encouraged to use her anchors to recall her resource, her inner strength, and her new perspective, to feel the strong presence of her compassionate, secure self.

Because our visceral experience is so much a part of the pattern of behavior we want to change, we can use hypnotic and self-hypnotic techniques to de-condition the automatic reactions and replace them with more adaptive responses. Perhaps the client's heart tends to race and her hands begin to perspire when confronted with a conflictual situation at work. We can again use the anchors already established to calm that automatic sympathetic nervous system response in a rehearsal of an actual work-related conflict. The client can experience in mental rehearsal a calmness, an alert but open perspective, a composed heart and dry confident hands.

If it is useful with a given coachee, the TV technique[484] can be used to review troublesome situations "with the emotional volume turned down," enabling a client to more objectively identify elements of success as well as obstacles to problem-solve.

Finally, Hornyak[485] suggests utilizing hypnosis to develop protective buffers for highly challenging environments. It is a fact that there will be people and situations that we would prefer to avoid but cannot. It may help the client in such a situation first to use the anchors she rehearsed to establish confidence, calm, and to not take it personally. Then it may be helpful for her to create a metaphor such as learning to "take your sail out of their wind" or participating in the situation with the dispassionate perspective of the TV technique. The client may want to visualize the daunting boss or co-worker as an immature child, or as a particular animal to accurately remember who one is dealing with and to neutralize their impact. The client could create an imaginary structure such as a protective bubble, or suits of armor to protect herself and reduce the absorption of toxicity from others.

> Applications that rely on age-progression include: rehearsing recently taught coping strategies; rehearsing benefits and gains in order to increase motivation; and identifying problems that may arise and managing them in advance.

Age-progression and age-regression. We have discussed a number of ways that age-progression and age-regression can be adapted to fit a coaching approach. For example, age regression was utilized to go back to times in the client's life when they expressed their signature strength with confidence, or dealt successfully with transitions. Likewise, age-progression is an integral part of an *anticipated memory* conjured in a guided imagery process, or of the various processes we have elaborated in work with the potential future self.

As well, time projection imagery can be included to demonstrate to coachees that they can tolerate current difficult or challenging situations, moving the perspective ahead to a time when he/she can imagine the current challenge has been mastered or resolved.[486]

In an age-progression experience, the client can imagine and explore an image of his/her future. What do they want to do or feel? What is it like? What is needed to get there? Are there any anticipated difficulties? From the vantage point of this imagined future, the client may find it easier to recognize clear goals and what success looks like and feels like. What resources and personal skills are needed? What coping mechanisms will need to be developed in order to make this vision a reality?

When looking back from this potential future, what would make you think, "I handled this well." Within the non-defensive state of hypnosis, a client may be more open and receptive to feedback from that future self than she is from her current day self.

Age regression applications include accessing resources that 'once were' and building on them; accessing desired resources or skills that already exist in another area and 'transferring' them to the immediate need; and reviewing previous performance in order to build on positives and develop what's missing. For example, a client may have been out of the work force for a period of time and lack confidence in her ability to do well in a job interview. The coach could take her back to a time that she did very well in a similar situation, and she could anchor the feeling of confidence.

Chapter Nine

Transpersonal Psychology in Higher Education

> Whereas traditional psychotherapy can be taught to any reasonable student of human psychology, transpersonal psychotherapy cannot. The arena of the transpersonal cannot be approached *just* intellectually – like love, it has to he believed in and/or experienced to some extent.[487]

Dr. Robert Frager, one of the founders and a professor at the Institute of Transpersonal Psychology, now Sofia University, has suggested that there are three elements to a good, balanced, transpersonal education: (1) rigorous academic training, (2) professional competence in counseling and therapy, and (3) a transformative experience.[488]

> How we educate has everything to do with how effectively individuals and cultures develop themselves in the face of life's dynamics, e.g. expanding their perception of themselves to include the deeply nuanced self that they are, and an ability to move their attention from themselves to others and their environment and ultimately to their world.[489]

> Any education, therefore, that would address the whole person—the embodied mind in its psychological depths— would have to make a place for *symbolic ways of knowing alongside empirical and rational ways of knowing.*[490]

Transpersonal psychology is a relatively rare specialization within the field of psychology. There are only a few graduate programs in the United States offering advanced degrees in transpersonal psychology. Several of the well-known programs include **Antioch University** (founded in 1852); the **California Institute of Integral Studies** (founded in the 1950s by Alan Watts and Dr. Haridas Chaudhuri as the American Academy of Asian Studies, and renamed the California Institute of Integral

Studies in 1980); the **John F. Kennedy University Graduate School for Holistic Studies** (founded in 1965); **Meridian University** (founded in 1993, Jean Houston, Chancellor); **Naropa University** (founded by Chögyam Trungpa Rinpoche in 1974); **Saybrook Graduate School** (founded in 1971 by Abraham Maslow, Rollo May, Carl Rogers and other leaders of the humanistic psychology movement); **Sofia University** (formerly the Institute of Transpersonal Psychology, founded in 1975). We will use two Schools as representative examples in the following examination of a transpersonal curricula and educational approach. A recent entry in the field is **The Wellness Graduate School of Psychology**.

Sofia University (Institute of Transpersonal Psychology)

Dr. William Braud is Professor and Dissertation Director, Institute of Transpersonal Psychology, and has offered many germane ideas for how to successfully structure a graduate school of transpersonal psychology. The *content* of course curricula offered by the school are transpersonal in nature, and the *educational approach* is transpersonal, i.e., has an experiential and whole-person learning emphasis. That also includes the importance of an open, nonauthoritarian, nondogmatic community of students, faculty and staff, providing in the curriculum and in the institution's cultural orientation, opportunities for training and balancing of body, emotion, mind, spirit, community-relations, creative expression, ecological awareness (ecopsychology), and diversity (appreciation of diverse ways of being in the world).[491] In this way, all of the many 'multiple intelligences'[492] are addressed and honored. As well, multiple varieties of consciousness[493] are acknowledged and methods of inducing and navigating through them developed: ordinary and non-ordinary, waking and dream state, conscious and unconscious.

> At the core of the model [of transpersonal education] is an emphasis on the balanced development of the whole individual, including physical, emotional, mental, and spiritual growth and integration. The model is designed to provide students with tools for working with others at all levels and, more important, to facilitate each student's growth and development. Knowledge of psychological theories and

techniques are important, but even more important is the state of consciousness, the being of a teacher or a therapist. This model can be viewed as part of the life-long growth of the individual, and its completion understood more as a foundation for further development than as the conclusion of learning.[494]

A basic tenet of depth psychology, existential, Gestalt and transpersonal psychology, is that the most fundamental preparation of a successful practitioner or facilitator is personal growth and development. All the theoretical knowledge, memorized protocols, and rote mimicry of a gifted clinician will never make up for lack of personal mastery and emotional and spiritual maturity. In experiential therapeutic encounters, knowledge is a function of being. Aldous Huxley made the point:

> Knowledge is a function of being. When there is a change in the being of the knower, there is a corresponding change in the nature and amount of knowing . . . Nor are changes in the knower's physiological or intellectual being the only ones to affect his knowledge. What we know depends also on what, as moral beings, we choose to make ourselves.[495]

It behooves the graduate program preparing clinicians to: attend to their personal mastery and emotional and spiritual maturity, to optimize their preparation to do qualitative research in psychology, and to function well as transpersonal psychotherapists. Just as the training of transpersonal clinicians includes personal development, so too does the training of transpersonal researchers.

"Together with the deep personal meaningfulness of the research participant to the researcher, encouraged in transpersonal psychology, phenomenological research challenges the very sense of identity of the students, and turns into a process of personal transformation. Adding spiritual practices to the training of transpersonal researchers thus becomes an aid and a container for this transformation."[496]

More specifically, what are the areas of capabilities that should be included in this training, and what methodologies would be most effective in producing the desired results? We can certainly benefit from the work at the doctoral degree program of the Institute of Transpersonal Psychology, operating since 1975, which has developed a regimen of training of the mind, heart, and intuition.[497]

> These practices work with the 'felt' sense of self, and open the access to interior spatial phenomenological correspondents of all psychological processes such as perception, cognition or motivation, that is the direct perception of the interior structure or contents of the self. Tantrik practices combine awareness with directing attention to particular zones of interior space, known as chakras, centers, or meridians. According to several co-researchers, these practices provide a faster maturation of awareness and a better aptitude to knowledge than traditional types of Buddhist mindfulness. The payoff may consist of a rapid opening of unconscious, known as spiritual emergency. Avoiding this rapid opening was a matter of special concern in development of the training. . . .
>
> The training consisted of three stages. These were offered at the introduction to qualitative research, during participation in a research group focused on a particular research topic, and within the advanced methods seminar. The overview of the whole process is followed by a detailed description of methods.
>
> As always in meditative training (Goleman, 1977), mindfulness practice formed the foundation. The particular types of mindfulness differentiated the modalities of awareness, such as sensory, emotional, intellectual, and imaginal and also discriminated between the subjective "I"-consciousness and the activities of "seeing" or "feeling." . . .
>
> The developed awareness of the interior mental processes helps to prepare for the second stage of training, the self-reflective questionnaire which identifies the best-suited research paradigm. The third stage of training, offered as the part of the advanced methods seminar, consisted of the technique of focused introspection on the sense of self in the chest. This technique opened the interior map of the psyche and refined the awareness of its subtle elements. Overall, this succession reflected the naturally occurring cycle of spiritual practice, from elementary forms of awareness to self-reflection, and then to more advanced forms of self-awareness.[498]

Awareness of one's assumptions has been established in the Stage 1 practices. Stage 2 of the training consists of work with a self-reflective multiple-choice questionnaire to identify the paradigmatic "predisposition" of one's mind. The questionnaire is based on the Handbook of Qualitative Research[499], and allows students to identify and bracket any unconscious identification with the natural scientific approach, and also to curb the tendency to logical *a priori* theory building. In other words, it alerts the individual to any agenda which might lead to "cherry picking" data or to assuming an interpretation of the data prior to the analysis phase of the investigation. The full questionnaire consists of nine questions, which cover the phases of research such as formulating the pilot study, clarifying research questions, style of engagement with the material, outcomes, etc.—the full procedure for qualitative research.

Stage 3 consists of body-based focusing, which opens the Gnostic "mind of the heart." The concept of the "mind of the heart" originates from the discoveries of the ancients that the phenomenological emergence of meaning happens in the inner space of the chest, in the heart chakra. Here is the experiential domain of the "knowledge by presence", that is direct apprehension of the contents and structures of consciousness, bypassing the physical senses and the intellect. The focusing techniques of meditation on the "mind of the heart" or "spiritual heart" enhance the awareness of the interiority of the psyche, and lift the habitual identifications with unexamined concepts, thus facilitating "bracketing" (differentiating between the various manifestations of consciousness) in phenomenological enquiry. The training in Stage 3 uses two consecutive practices. The first practice, "Opening the Eyes of the Heart," trains the relocation of the center of awareness into the chest by sequentially moving the inward-seeing eyes from their sockets in the skull down into the center of the chest, thus gradually developing an awareness of the interiority of consciousness. The second practice, "Heart–Mind, Researcher's Mind," encourages the deep mapping of the contents of consciousness through guided introspection on the sense of self.

Louchakova reports that there is a common sequence of awareness that opens through this introspection process.[500] It usually starts with the sense of self, and then the following succession emerges: sensory experiences; layer of rising emotions, subtler sensations of energy, and breath; layer of "talking" mind; layer of images; stillness, nothing, unknowing, like in a deep sleep; layer of sheer intellect, meanings, and vast space and subtle mental states, archetypes, and essential relations. Finally, it was possible that an eighth layer was reached: absorption of awareness in pure subjective consciousness.

The Wellness Graduate School of Psychology

The Wellness Graduate School of Psychology has utilized Kundalini chakra meditation in combination with Jungian techniques such as active imagination to develop introspective skills and challenge individuals to transcend self-imposed limitations.

The meditation regime begins each day together at the residential retreat seminars with a 30-minute meditation focused on the primary seven chakras in the body. The meditation is usually guided, and encourages intimate exploration of the body's energy systems, including the branches of the autonomic nervous system and awareness of one's personal assumptions; exploring unconscious identifications and agendas through internal dialogue; and connection with intrapsychic center core resources.

Ritual, by inducing altered states of consciousness and establishing non-ordinary expectations, can provide forms of knowing not otherwise possible[501] and can facilitate transformative change, especially in liminal contexts.[502] The Wellness Graduate School utilizes several ceremonial experiences, or rituals, to create liminal space and encourage non-ordinary states of consciousness. One is hypnosis and self-hypnosis, which is an elegant way of approaching the transpersonal. Another is a unique form of dream work called Dream Journeying.[503] Another is the Native American *inipi* (sweat lodge) ceremony, and occasionally the Native American *hamblecha* (vision quest) ceremony, both of which are totally optional. Ritual is used to open the circle and again to close the circle when archetypal energies are invoked for deep introspective or psychotherapeutic processes; this provides a symbolic way of acknowledging the presence of these energies, the fact that they are present at the invitation of the participants, and their containment during the discreet time of their presence. Soul retrieval is another ritualized process, utilized within the context of both therapeutic and contemplative practices, to enhance the individual's sense of wholeness and connection with the greater self.

Hypnosis and self-hypnosis. The School utilizes these techniques for clinical training in therapeutic intervention and treatment, and also in a coaching context for rehearsal as well as discovering and exploring inner resources such as archetypal center core phenomena and future selves.

Dream Journeying. Dream work is an important aspect of the clinical training, especially at the doctoral level. Dream work is clinically approached in the altered state psychodrama modality, with characters (roles) determined by elements in the dream rather than people in the client's life. So the identified client (protagonist) enacts the dream, encountering the people or buildings, animals or plants, heroes or villains that populated the dream. In the process of that re-enactment, the client has an opportunity to encounter and dialogue with those denizens of the client's unconscious. Recognizing these dream elements as metaphorically representing aspects of him/herself, the client's self-image (identification) expands to incorporate them: for example, I am the dreamer, and the angry policeman, and the frightened teenager, and the forest in which the scene takes place.

The additional dream work process available to students in the doctoral program is Dream Journeying, which has already been discussed. It, too, is a way for participating individuals to transcend the ego and explore the transpersonal self.

Active imagination. Early in the doctoral program, students are trained in the art of active imagination as created by Carl Jung. This is an exquisitely powerful transpersonal experience of meeting and dialoguing with intrapsychic energies, be they emotions, beliefs, memories, judgments, introjects, shadows or compelling archetypal center core phenomena.

Inipi (sweat lodge) ceremony. The Native American inipi (sweat lodge) ceremony is a valuable cross-cultural experience that builds group cohesion in a transpersonal context, and is one of the ego-transcending experiences offered at The Wellness Graduate School of Psychology.

We have been introduced to the sweat lodge by our Native American friends. We often complete our seminars of deep healing work with a sweat lodge, which represents the womb of mother earth. The lodge is built in the shape of an igloo, constructed with a frame made of willow saplings. Blankets are then arranged over the frame to keep it warm, dark, and moist inside. A fire is built outside the lodge and volcanic rocks are placed inside the fire to heat for several hours until they glow red-hot. People begin to gather outside the lodge and then go in one by one after being smudged (purified) with burning sage.

We enter from the door in the east and walk around clockwise inside in a circle to the edge of the door. Each person sits close to the next until the whole lodge is filled with people. The person who "pours the water" is the Native leader who may sit in the west facing the door and the fire outside, or in the east. There is also an altar outside the door with sacred artifacts, feathers, pipes, and herbs such as sweet grass, cedar, and sage to put on the rocks.

The sweat lodge is a sacred place to sing and pray and celebrate life. There are four rounds, each one beginning and ending with Native prayer songs to open the heart and call in helpful spirits. Between rounds the door is opened for air and to bring in more hot rocks. This continues until all have prayed and are spiritually cleansed. When the door is opened for the last time, each person files out and forms "a receiving line" around the fire. We go around and greet and hug each person to welcome them from their incubation in the lodge back into the world again. This is usually a very profound experience for everyone.

Hamblecha (vision quest) ceremony. The Native American *hamblecha* (vision quest) ceremony is a very sacred test of 'selfness' and commitment to one's spiritual path, regardless of an individual's specific faith. It is the commitment of time set aside, outside of time, to lament for a vision. We spend a great amount of time in preparing ourselves for this ceremony. We ask the Creator (God) or one of Creator's many spirit helpers to answer the prayers we offer up, to bring a vision of greater purpose in life, and to help us become a better person in our walk on this earth.

During the time of preparation, at least six months in length, each person puts together a string of prayer ties which consists of small pieces of cloth in the colors of red, yellow, black and white that represent the four directions and the four races of mankind. In these squares of cloth we put a pinch of tobacco (which is considered sacred by Native American people) and then tie them together (all the while praying) onto a prayer string. This is then used to surround the small space which the person will occupy for the four days and four nights of the actual ceremony "on the mountain", away from the hustle and bustle of everyday life.

The individual brings a sleeping bag to keep warm, his/her prayer ties, and perhaps fears of going without food and water for four days and nights, and fears of the "critters" that could possibly attack. Some of the deepest fears may be about being alone and isolated for four days, being bored and disappointed, or of having an experience that is *too* powerful. The sacred space that a person is placed in, protected by the prayer ties that are draped around it, at times feels safe and at other times can feel confining. The individual spends four days and nights out in nature, with no distractions like reading material or anything to 'do', with only oneself, the content of one's mental activity, and the energies of the environment – physical and spiritual. Nights are usually physically and emotionally challenging, and a quester may well greet the morning sun with joy, welcoming its warmth and the familiarity of daylight.

> One learns to pray, to discover the power of faith, and to consciously contact Creator. As layers of fear peel away, the existential distinction between personal and transpersonal is gradually revealed. I am not my fear: who am I? I am more than the contents of my mental activity: who witnesses the stream of thoughts? I am not alone: who and what accompanies me on my journey? My destiny is more significant than any plans I might conjure for my life: what is the source of a newer, more expansive vision of my purpose?

On the last morning the individual is brought in from "the mountain" to the base camp and into the sweat lodge for the final closing ceremony. When individuals leave their space, everything is removed, leaving no visible signs of their presence on Mother Earth. Then food is offered to break the fast, offering another opportunity to learn about "savoring the moment" and "*being* instead of *doing*."

During the four days and nights, supporters in camp are intensely praying, sweating in the lodge, singing beautiful Indian songs and drumming. Alone out in that sacred space, the quester is indeed not alone.

For most individuals, this ceremony is a profound once-in-a-lifetime opportunity to immerse in a rich spiritual experience.

Soul retrieval. Soul retrieval is another important tool in our approach to healing and ego-transcendence. At the time of a traumatic experience, one or more "pieces" of a person's soul can essentially break apart from the rest of the soul and leave the person. This disconnection from parts of the soul can lead to feelings of emptiness or of "something missing," or a sense from others that this person "is a lost soul." Modern psychology often refers to dissociated parts of the self and explains that integration is an important part of therapy. And more than that, we've learned from both ancient and modern shamans that soul retrieval has always been recognized as one of the main functions of the shaman or healer. This spiritual work is accomplished in the "trance state," and therefore naturally fits in with hypnotherapy protocols that incorporate the soul. When we bring someone into the trance state and have her visit an event in which pieces of the soul disconnected, we can have her literally look for and retrieve those pieces. After sessions like these, people will tell us that they feel "whole" or "complete" for the first time since the event, which often means "since before they can remember."

Assessments to Evaluate Progress

Assessments to evaluate progress toward stated objectives should describe where one has been, where one is now, and where one is going, and should yield indications of what seems to be working well or poorly, and which areas are in need of greater attention. The particular assessments that may be used grow out of the nature and goals of the journey one is undertaking, whether psychospiritual or academic. And, of course, assessments need to be valuable not only to the student being evaluated but also to the program and methods employed by the educators, to be used for program evaluation and revision.

Any methods used to assess and evaluate transpersonal educational effectiveness, i. e., psychospiritual health, well-being, and growth, must also conform to the principles of the experiential and whole-person nature of the education itself. For example, the assessment intention developed at the Institute for Transpersonal Psychology "assessed qualities and characteristics that were parts of, or related to: self- actualization, self-transcendence, a transpersonal (i.e., not exclusively egoic) self concept or identity, openness and interconnectedness, surrender and acceptance, change, mood, body awareness and somatic knowing, environmental awareness, spirituality, values, mindfulness, discernment, compassion, appreciation of differences, personal growth, integration, individuation, and possible transformative changes."[504]

Assessing individuals' psychospiritual growth needs to take into account the nonlinear path of such growth. For example, Ruumet's helical model of psychospiritual development suggests that one continually cycles back through, or revisits, earlier or 'lower' personal areas and issues in the course of developing increasingly greater access to later or 'higher' transpersonal qualities.[505] Acknowledging the paucity of transpersonal psychometric tests, Friedman and MacDonald define transpersonal assessment as follows:

> Transpersonal assessment may be defined as an activity requiring professional judgment whereby the practitioner and client work collaboratively at arriving at an expanded conception of the client, including viewing nonordinary states and both their antecedents and consequences as potentially, but not necessarily, beneficial, for the purpose of enhancing the client's growth and development of self-awareness and health. In the process of developing such an understanding of the client, the practitioner relies upon transpersonal theory in a systematic way (e.g., through the use of standardized measures of transpersonal constructs) and examines his/her potential biases as an essential aspect of the assessment.[506]

They go on to emphasize that "our definition of transpersonal assessment also allows for the inclusion of alternative assessment methodologies such as divination techniques (e.g., Tarot cards, *I Ching),* shamanic or shamanistic practices, mediumistic practices (cf. Krippner & Welch, 1992) and, in general, the systematic use of nonordinary states of consciousness by the clinician to generate information about a client"[507], and to suggest that any such assessment methodology should be documented as valid and clinically useful.

Friedman and MacDonald offer their own instrument that meets the criteria they established: The Self-Expansiveness Level Form (SELF). It is an objective measure of the transpersonal concept of self-expansiveness, referring to the extension of the sense of identity or self, from the focus of the individual in the here-and-now as a biologically constituted organism toward the capacity of that organism to transcend all limitations in sense of self.[508] The SELF is based on a space-time grid, a type of map, against which the individual self can be measured. The SELF consists of three scales. The Personal Scale is a measure of identification with the here-and-now state of the person from a conventional, non-transpersonal frame of reference. A Middle Scale, a set of rather neutral extensions beyond the personal level but not quite reaching what was seen as a transpersonal level. The Transpersonal Scale provides information most clearly relevant to the transpersonally oriented clinician. There is an overall number obtained to measure the individual's degree of transpersonal identification. The SELF has well established reliability and validity.

The authors explain that the absolute value obtained on each scale becomes more meaningful when interpreted in relationship to the values obtained on the other scales.[509] For example, moderate identification with the personal level is very different in meaning when compared to a low identification versus a high identification on the transpersonal level. The first instance, moderate personal with low transpersonal identification, suggests an individual who is fairly conventional in their pattern of self identification with an average level of personal acceptance and little transpersonal acceptance. The second instance reflects a pattern where transpersonal identification exceeds personal such that the meaning of the moderate personal identification becomes suspect. Is this individual, for example, actually showing some degree of alienation from the self at the personal level in comparison to their high score on the transpersonal level? Thus, although both of these individuals have the same degree of identification on the personal level, their responses to the transpersonal level leads to a different perspective on the meaning of their personal level scores.

Academic objectives, i. e., traditional areas of academic performance or achievement and content knowledge, are evaluated more conventionally within specific courses. Student academic skills include familiarity and facility with the content, approaches, and methods of psychology and transpersonal psychology, critical thinking, and didactic writing. Students identify, practice, and develop these skills in the assigned readings, discussions, assignments, and writing requirements of all formal courses, and clinical performance in professional skills course.

Research Methods in Transpersonal Psychology

Among the questions of interest to psychologists are those having to do with optimal mental health, self-actualization, love, happiness, meaning, authenticity, altruism, awe, a sense of the mystical and the sacred, and the so-called "farther reaches" of healthy human experience (Maslow, 1971). As well, these interests may extend to an array of related difficulties and challenges, such as apathy, alienation, existential emptiness, despair, and transpersonal 'pathologies.' These, and many related concepts, share a quality of being difficult to quantify and capture for research purposes.[510]

Typically, the research strategies advocated by many transpersonal psychologists, e.g., Braud and Anderson[511], emphasize the more radical empiricist, pluralistic epistemology (which includes qualitative methods, experiential methods, and alternative modes of knowing) rather than the quantitative, behavioral, and cognitive methods common to most traditional academic researchers. Basically there are two main groups of qualitative research.

The first is basic research akin to "pure" science. Grounded theory, for example, systematically and depthfully explores life-world experience, noting data that has given rise to themes, and cross-referencing these insights. Traditionally, grounded theory research also has incorporated two external kinds of data such as test scores or observations. Empirical (psychological) phenomenology is another basic research approach. The investigator reads descriptions of living through a situation, and systematically explores what is being said about how the person is relating to self, world, and others. All data must be accounted for, and common themes are brought together in a holistic summary typically accompanied by examples from each research subject. . . .

Practical qualitative research is the second general group. Here, understandings of life-world events are a starting point for exploring their relation to various outcomes. For example, a particular experience within psychotherapy can be qualitatively researched and then identified in transcriptions or by client report, and still later be related to indicators of process and/or outcome.[512]

In grounded theory the researcher's own prior experiences with the topic being investigated, including judgments, assumptions and bias, is known as the researcher's *theoretical sensitivity*.[513]

Transpersonal research endeavors are characterized by expansiveness and inclusiveness, as well as sensitivity and nuance. One aims to confront the whole of what one is researching with the whole of one's being, in order to acquire descriptions and understandings of one's topic that are as rich, deep, 'thick,' and complete as possible.

Expansiveness and inclusiveness are realized in the researcher's use of multiple modes of knowing in collecting, working with, and communicating data and findings and in the researcher's radical empirical stance toward the subject matter. Radical empiricism is, of course, an epistemological stance advocated by William James (1912/1976), in which one includes only what is based in experience, but includes everything that is based in experience.

The multiple modes of knowing include not only familiar 'left-hemispheric,' theoretical, rational, linear, analytical, verbal research skills, but also less frequently emphasized, but equally important, complementary, 'right-hemispheric,' experiential, body-based, sensory-based, intuitive, imagistic, and holistic techniques and skills. The transpersonal researcher adapts transpersonal, psychospiritual skills and practices such as mindfulness, discernment, compassion, and appreciation and honoring of differences (in all domains) for use in research projects. The researcher can supplement these, in all phases of research, with skills such as intention-setting; attention-focusing; bodymind quieting; extended and nuanced uses of vision, audition, proprioception, and kinesthesia; imagery, visualization, and imagination; direct knowing, intuition, and empathic identification; play; and accessing typically unconscious materials and processes (through dream incubation, active imagination, and other techniques). Forms of creative expression and embodied writing (Anderson, 2001) may be used in communicating research findings. . . .

The transpersonal researcher is concerned not only with the acquiring of new information (what Clements, 2004, has called 'changes of mind') for the researcher and for expanding the knowledge base of the discipline, but also with the potential transformation (which Clements has called 'changes of heart') of everyone involved in the research enterprise. Those who might be transformed by a research project include the investigator, the research participants, those who receive the research findings (the research project's 'audience'), and, ultimately, society at large.[514]

Complementarity

Rychlak has suggested that psychology, and indeed all scientific research, should use a principle of complementarity, a familiar concept in physics, where it refers, for example, to the finding that light can be both particle and wave.[515] Rychlak proposes that the psychological version of complementarity offers four different theoretical perspectives for studying psychological, behavioral, and social phenomena. One perspective is taken from physical science and deals with psychological phenomena as physical phenomena, a second is grounded in biological systems, a third in social systems, and a fourth in values, meaning, and purpose. Thus humanistic and transpersonal research have a legitimate place in Rychlak's framework, as do physical, biological, and social processes.

Whatever the *methods* of research, research *conclusions* "should be empirically based; research should strive to be free of personal biases, prejudices, and dogma; other individuals should be able to agree that conclusions are justified by the data; and criteria should be provided for evaluating competing knowledge claims."[516]

"The way has never been more open for researchers to work back and forth between qualitative evidence and more fully mathematical, quantitative measures. To do so with integrity, care must be taken to retain the contemplative and compassionate in the best qualitative work while at the same time holding quantitative methodologies to the rigorous requirements of fundamental measurement."[517]

Qualitative measures in research might include an analysis of themes in written narrative accounts of personal experience by participants in an experience or behavior under study. Then among these consistent reports, specific categories of experience may begin to emerge.

The transpersonal psychology researcher needs instruments that measure important goals of humanistic and transpersonal psychotherapy, such as personal growth, interpersonal interaction, client agency, the development of comfort with emotion, the resolution of negative emotion, emotional expression, ego-transcendence. A commonly used outcome measure in the assessment of humanistic treatment is the Personal Orientation Inventory (POI), developed by Everett Shostrom, a humanistic psychologist. It is a personality measure meant to assess level of self-actualization that was derived empirically from comparisons of clinically-nominated actualized and nonactualized groups.[518]

Bruner was one of the first cognitive psychologists to articulate the distinction between the narrative and the paradigmatic (or abstract) dimensions of knowing.[519] The narrative mode tells a specific story, is based on the spatial and temporal location of an experience, placing it in the qualifying set and setting, and is therefore context-rich. The paradigmatic-abstract mode aims at being context-free in order to gain the power to generalize beyond any particular set and setting. Narratives are based on the logic of imagination that suspends common-sense categories and that provides access to *state-specific understanding*. That is, narratives and stories conjure a response from the listener or reader, and that response allows for a level of understanding that may not be possible without being in the state resulting from the response. Stories may elicit sadness, recognition of injustice, hope, or the lightness of humor. And in the state created, the listener or reader is receptive to a deeper understanding than may be possible from being told facts and concepts. This is the case with "crazy wisdom", symbol and metaphor, dreams and synchronicity awareness as discussed previously.

Abstract paradigmatic thinking relies on the logic of rationality and consistency and makes use of formal abstractions, concepts, constructs, general information, and prototypic knowledge independent of particular context.[520]

Another difference between narrative and abstract knowing is the relationship between the knower and the known, and whether what we experience as 'I' is autonomous or placed in a part-to-whole relationship. It is largely a distinction between passive and active ways of expressing the connection between the knower and the known. For example, a passive way of relating "I am thinking" would be "the thought came to me." "I composed a song" is experienced as "a song came to me." Experiences in altered states of consciousness often appear better described by the passive verbal description.[521] Likewise, many of the experiences involved in transpersonal psychology or psychotherapy are similarly better described passively. And research into those experiences would best utilize a passive descriptive mode in order to capture the true essence of the felt experience, which is likely as a part-to-whole relationship. Indeed, the very meaning of transpersonal is to convey the human experience as transcending the personal, individual, autonomous 'I'. And from this perspective many approaches that would be irrational to analytic abstract paradigmatic thinking become acceptable: paradox, irony, possible simultaneous multiple realities[522] and mutually exclusive events, dream logic and the seemingly impossible.

Cross-culturally, transpersonal psychologists have learned, and put into practice, that both of these approaches to knowing, and therefore to research, are valid, and that neither is superior to the other except in certain applications. The narrative approach is most useful in exploring (researching) spontaneous or directed-knowing experiences such as dreaming, shamanic journeying, encounters with psychoidal energies, ecstatic body-oriented practices, trance-induced age regressions or progressions, meditation and peak experiences. The paradigmatic-abstract mode of knowing, and of research, is best when the subject under study can be physically observed, counted and measured. The field of transpersonal psychology has encountered difficulty in properly documenting outcomes of therapeutic or educational interventions using paradigmatic-abstract modal research methods. Fortunately other more appropriate research methods are being developed. Now we will investigate several of these alternatives.

A recent book by Rosemarie Anderson and William Braud titled *Transforming Self and Others through Research: Transpersonal Research Methods and Skills for the Human Sciences and Humanities*, offers a great deal of practical information about moving beyond the medical model quantitative research methods that are no longer adequate to measure the subtleties of humanistic and transpersonal psychotherapy.[523] It introduces qualitative methods, focusing more directly on the phenomena itself, in a more naturalistic approach, which can give a clearer, perhaps more vivid picture of the subject of the study. And yet a further step is possible: to build into the design, as the study's focus, significant participation and opportunity for change in everyone, researcher and participants.

To be successful, a transpersonal researcher will need to train the ego to collaborate with liminal (threshold) experience and spiritual sources, developing intention, attention, quieting and slowing, auditory and visual skills, kinesthetic and proprioceptive skills, direct knowing, intuition, empathic identification, accessing unconscious processes and materials, and play and the creative arts.

Another recent book offers a fascinating exploration of five different approaches to qualitative research: *Five Ways of Doing Qualitative Analysis: Phenomenological Psychology, Grounded Theory, Discourse Analysis, Narrative Research, and Intuitive Inquiry*.[524] Five eminent researchers provide an in-depth understanding of five approaches to qualitative research by each analyzing the same written and interview data from their respective point of view. The five approaches are those of phenomenological psychology (Frederick J. Wertz), grounded theory (Kathy Charmaz), discourse analysis (Linda M. McMullen), narrative research (Ruthellen Josselson), and intuitive inquiry (Rosemarie Anderson).

Organic Inquiry

William Braud summarizes another quite unconventional transpersonal research approach, informed and inspired by feminist, Jungian, spiritual, and mystical traditions.[525] Organic inquiry is an emerging approach to qualitative research on psychospiritual growth, in which the researcher crosses the egoic threshold into a *liminal* realm to gather useful experience unavailable to the individual ego in ordinary reality. The liminal is a state beyond ego where the ego is barely perceptible, a less structured and less familiar state, where experience may be witnessed, but not created or controlled by ego. Once useful data has been gathered, then the researcher returns to cognitively integrate that data into the ongoing inquiry process. The psyche of the researcher becomes the subjective 'instrument' of the research, working in partnership with liminal and spiritual influences as well as with the experiences of participants. Braud summarizes the approach[526]:

> In my view, Organic Inquiry is one of a very small number of truly transpersonal research approaches, in terms of its aims and the resources accessed during its conduct. Here are some of its most important features:
> - its offering of a format for including trans-egoic, liminal, or transliminal (see, e.g., Sanders, Thalbourne, & Delin, 2000; Thalbourne, Bartemucci, Delin, Fox, & Nofi, 1997) influences within a context of disciplined inquiry;
> - the overarching importance of the psychological and spiritual preparation and adequateness (adaequatio; see Schumacher, 1978, pp. 39–60) of the researcher, and the importance of the active use of transpersonally-relevant resources (e.g., contemplation, dreams, intuition, synchronicities, dialogue with an inner figure or muse) in such preparation;
> - the notion that research may result in transformation (of the investigator, research participants, and reader/audience) as well as information;
> - the inclusion of alternative modes of knowing such as feeling, sensing, and intuiting in all phases of the research project;
> - its emphasis on the use, value, and power of stories;

- its valuing of describing the context of discovery as well as the context of justification (see Reichenbach, 1938; White, 1998) in research reports;
- its indication of the need for letting go of egoic control and preset methodological structures in the service of new knowledge;
- its emphasis on the power of intention;
- its formal invitation to the readers/audience of its research report to involve themselves fully in what is being presented to them—to involve their hearts as well as their heads;
- its suggested indicators of transformation (increased access to and appreciation of Self, Spirit, and Service); and
- its various methodological innovations, including the use and comparisons of early and late researcher stories, creation of a group story as a nomothetic summary of study findings, bodily indicators of validity (e.g., chills, tears, feelings of certainty; Rosemarie Anderson, 1998, 2000, had previously suggested similar processes of sympathetic resonance as validity indicators), the concept of transformational validity, and the use of early reader reactions as a test for the latter (similar to Rosemarie Anderson's, 1998, 2000, earlier suggestion of the use of resonance panels for validation purposes)."

Clements outlines the procedure of organic inquiry using a metaphor of the growth of a tree, likening this form of research to growth within the larger context of nature, a process that both includes and transcends human understanding. "By choosing the approach, the researcher commits to an archetype of transformation that must be actively facilitated, but may not always be controlled. Trans-egoic sources, like dreams, synchronicity, or creative expression that originate beyond ego, may be invited, but they may not be directed."[527]

> The five characteristics of organic inquiry – sacred, personal, chthonic, related, and transformative – are to be seen as cumulative rather than successive.
>
> *Sacred: preparing the soil.* Before a seed is planted, the earth is prepared. Similarly, participation in the organic approach calls for spading up one's old habits and expectations to

cultivate a sacred perspective. *Personal: planting the seed.* Planting the seed represents the initial experience of the topic by the researcher. The best topic will have passionate meaning because it has been the occasion for the researcher's own psychospiritual growth. *Chthonic: the roots emerge.* Just as the developing roots of a tree are invisible and beyond control, an organic inquiry has an underground life of its own because of its subjective and spiritual sources. Like a living tree, the process is allowed to evolve and change. *Related: growing the tree.* Participants' stories are like branches that join to and inform the trunk story of the research itself. *Transformative: harvesting the fruit.* The fruit of organic inquiry are the transformative changes it offers, changes of mind and heart, particularly for its readers.[528]

Clearly, organic inquiry requires a researcher who has prepared for the task. He/she must have already worked on their own processes of psychospiritual development. Discernment is essential; he/she must be able to determine the differences in the data between subjective and objective, spiritual and material, self and other. Researchers must know their own personalities and psyches so as not to confuse an understanding of the data. If these remain unreflected, the results of the study, the purity of the data, will be hijacked by psychological defenses and personal agendas. Researchers must have healthy egos in order to step beyond them and equally strong intellects to assess the validity of the organic process and clearly articulate the resulting knowledge.

Phenomenological researchers are likely to agree that the enquiry requires patience, receptivity, sustained focused attention, emotional harmony, inspiration regarding the subject matter, and some degree of characterological maturity. Similarly, epistemology in many spiritual systems concludes that great intellectual power has to be necessarily combined with a heart full of love. Resulting knowledge is "not simply cerebral, but belongs to the realms of heart-intellect" (Nasr, 1992, p. xiii). This specific preparedness of the "heart–intellect" is especially important for research in transpersonal psychology with its consideration for the breadth of human experience.[529]

Ritual and ceremony are ancient ways of knowing, and therefore of research. In the same way that narratives provide access to *state-specific understanding*, ceremonies are culturally determined, functioning to connect the action of the participants with the 'greater' narrative, the symbols that illuminate the identity of the group that they belong to. Ritual presents a moment in time and space where the person is called to join and partake of the intentionality of the group by entering into a prescribed state.[530] The ritual circumscribes liminal space, outside of time, where mysteries are not described or explained, but rather ingested and digested. Ceremony establishes a mindfulness, reinforces a part-to-whole relationship with all the forces at work in the environment, and demonstrates the vital role of the individual in maintaining order in the world. Ceremony and ritual are legitimate avenues to discovering deeply embedded truths, and therefore can play an important role in documenting and preserving those truths. Is that not the purpose of research?

Chapter Ten

The Shadow in Transpersonal Psychology

We have discussed earlier the potential Achilles heel of transpersonal psychology's tendency to become so fascinated with the *states* of consciousness to the point of overlooking the traps of ensnarement laid by the *contents* of that consciousness.

> The shadow side of transpersonal psychologists' preoccupation with states of consciousness in their own right is their limited understanding of some of the important contents and structural elements of the psyche, particularly the archetypes. Transpersonal psychology to date has seemed too absorbed in the states themselves to explore their inner nature adequately. It's a bit like mapping a territory without bothering to find out who is living there.[531]

Any peak or transpersonal experience is often felt to be an encounter with a 'bigger than life' extraordinary supernatural force. Jung used the terminology for that power of 'mana', a Polynesian word, and identified a mana personality as a dominant of the collective unconscious, the well known archetype of the mighty man or woman in the form of hero, chief, magician, medicine-man, saint, the ruler of men and spirits, the friend of God.[532] Working with such powerful archetypal energies is the stock in trade of shamans, meditators, dream workers, and all explorers of the far reaches of one's psyche.

These mana-personality archetypes in the collective unconscious represent age-old human experience (or more probably longing for experience). Who doesn't want a benevolent, kind, generous, protective "Father Knows Best"? Who doesn't want an all-loving, all-forgiving, all-nurturing Great Mother? And what father or mother doesn't want to see themselves or be seen as just that? It is seductive for an individual to identify with these ideal icons literally, and when they do big trouble is sure to follow. Jung cautioned that ego inflation is one of the main dangers when coming into contact with 'transpersonal' content, the 'numinous', or the 'collective unconscious'. In other words, persons with a strong spiritual experience might identify to such an extent with it, i.e., appropriate the mana, that they lose sight of their limitations, their personal problems and ongoing need for personal development.

These universally relatable primordial images serve as a gauge against which to measure real life experience, totems to expand our concept of what is possible. It is when we attempt to concretize that image, to embody it in a human being that problems develop, because the promise of "extraordinary potency" is just too seductive for most people to resist. Jung said, "It is indeed hard to see how one can escape the sovereign power of the primordial images. Actually I do not believe it can be escaped. One can only alter one's attitude and thus save oneself from naively falling into an archetype and being forced to act a part at the expense of one's humanity. Possession by an archetype turns a man into a flat collective figure, a mask behind which he can no longer develop as a human being, but becomes increasingly stunted."[533]

Another alternative trap is for the ego to project such a lofty status onto someone else and blindly follow the anointed one, opening oneself to hero worship and/or the martyr's 'good fight' against demons. It is not difficult to find examples of either of these misplaced ways of managing an encounter with the numinous transpersonal. We only need look at the pomp and panoply of royalty, of the church, of the military, or the medicine man in his mask, to see that construction of the appearance of power is probably as old as humankind. And we need only look to the disgraced guru, the fallen church leader, the politician exposed for corruption, or their disappointed followers to see the disastrous results of ego inflation.

A third defensive approach is to replace the powerful archetypal force with stereotypes - Jung speaks of the gods as having "become diseases," through literal interpretations.[534] Here the magical is reduced to the mundane, the numinous to data. The ego has subtly wrested control from the powerful archetypal mana forces, making them the subject of study and the objects of analysis. "If the ego presumes to wield power over the unconscious, the unconscious reacts with a subtle attack, deploying the dominant of the mana-personality, whose enormous prestige casts a spell over the ego. Against this the only defense is full confession of one's weakness in face of the powers of the unconscious. By opposing no force to the unconscious we do not provoke it to attack."[535]

And so the spell cast over the ego can take the form of either identifying with or projecting the mana, the power; or interpreting the life out of the profound archetypes; or alternatively what has been called 'spiritual bypassing', in which the individual focuses on spiritual experience as a short-cut to resolving or just plain avoiding psychological developmental tasks in the face of transpersonal encounters.[536]

Yet there is another exquisite facet to this dance of identity that is life-affirming, that contributes to ego strengthening *and* to ego transcendence. The alignment of the ego with a "bigger than life" energy/entity is tantamount to an *initiation*, absent a healthy, socially appropriate, formalized initiation *rite*. All primitive societies and tribes have their rites of initiation, often very highly developed, which play an extraordinarily important part in their social and religious life. Through these ceremonies boys are made men, and girls women. Initiation ceremonies are a magical means of leading man from the animal state to the human state. They are clearly transformation mysteries of the greatest spiritual significance.[537]

For the ego to recognize its encounters with the transpersonal as initiation opportunities, to approach the numinous with awe and humility, is to embark on a journey of transformation that requires some form of practice. "Such development normally entails that such a spiritual experience has to be realised in many steps, which may be cumbersome, difficult or boring. Otherwise there is the danger that a false, fragile and demanding ego will use the experience to compensate for its own shortcomings. This may well protect the ship from sinking, but will also prevent it from sailing."[538]

Challenging an 800-Pound Gorilla

Transpersonal psychology began as a reaction to the status quo within the academic, scientific discipline of psychology. It was intended to offer an alternative, and to attempt to reform the discipline with a new expanded vision of the possibilities of what can be studied and understood. Harald Wallach offers a critique of the lack of success in that endeavor over more than four decades.

> Hence, at least part of the transpersonal enterprise is in fact an implicit or explicit *challenge to the entire history and set of methodologies by which science and scientific psychology* is done. The point is: you do not challenge a 800-pound gorilla with a thin stick. He either laughs at you or simply breaks your stick. If you want to challenge the whole history, tradition, and academic self-understanding of modern day psychology, you had better beef up your arsenal and know what you are doing. Rarely do transpersonal psychologists seem to understand what they are doing. In order to challenge the mainstream view what needs to happen is a thorough understanding of the presuppositions that the mainstream operates on, a profound critiquing of these presuppositions, and the provision of very, very good data indeed that could actually give adherents to the mainstream view enough reason to think twice about what *they* are doing.
>
> None of this has happened. The critique of the mainstream from transpersonal quarters has been mild and not very profound.[539]

Of course, Wallach's premise seems to be based on an either-or dualistic viewpoint, that for transpersonal psychology to justify its existence it must replace what has come before, or at least significantly alter its trajectory in a new direction. There can be little argument that it has failed to do so. Asserting that is an existential condemnation of the paradigm, however, may be overstating the case.

The shadow which is being exposed here is that of an overly ambitious and idealistic self-assessment. What started out as a Fourth Force in psychology may represent a niche specialization instead. Honest and objective self-evaluation is the antidote for grandiose self-delusion.

II. Transpersonal Psychology: Maps of the Terrain

Chapter Eleven

Optimal Functioning

A relatively common perspective in our society today is that as human beings we can develop further, become more fully human, advance toward optimal functioning. The questions arise:

- What is it that is developing to higher levels – intelligence? consciousness? ego? body awareness? aesthetic refinement? Self?
- How do individuals progress to advanced stages of development?
- Do the majority of adults fail to achieve the most advanced stages of personality development, and if so, why?
- What factors facilitate such exceptional development in adulthood?
- What type of person is most likely to progress to advanced stages of development?
- What is the nature of the identities such individuals create for themselves?

As we have repeatedly observed, a common perspective in transpersonal psychology and spiritually oriented human potential paradigms highlights three primary realms of human development. They are variously termed *pre-personal* subconscious, *personal* self-consciousness, and *transpersonal* superconsciousness[540]; 'normal', self-actualization, and transcending self-actualization[541]; the 'slaves' of God, the 'employees' of God, and the 'lovers' of God in the Eastern Orthodox Christian tradition[542]; natural, cultural, and existential in the Sufi tradition[543]; ego growth, soul embodiment, and spirit realization[544]; or as it was succinctly stated by Teilhard de Chardin: "First, *be*. Secondly, *love*. Finally, *worship*."[545]

These realms are based on the three worlds within which we live: the Lower Unconscious, Middle Unconscious, and the Higher Unconscious.[546] The underworld and the upper world both represent spiritual dimensions of human life, what Viktor Frankl[547] called the "spiritual unconscious" (a full discussion of this topic can be found in Hartman & Zimberoff, 2008b). Aspects of ourselves develop in each of these worlds, and a discussion of the higher levels of human development must include all three. Gerard Bruitzman has summarized these three levels of development using Plato's Allegory of the Cave.[548]

> . . . it is important to realize that no one can see beyond their current level of understanding in a particular sense or faculty and in their particular aggregate of ten relatively functioning powers. We refer to Plato's Allegory of the Cave, an example of the Great Chain of Being and Knowing, to explain what we mean. Plato points out that there are some people captivated by the passing shadows on the cave wall, some people who break their chains to discover the reasons for the passing shadows, and some people who break out of the cave altogether to discover the true source of light (Cousineau, 2003). Let's call these three broad groups of people: prisoners, who work to maintain their normal existence and cannot accept the surreal claims of freedom fighters and light bearers; freedom fighters, who want to help prisoners to break free of their chains but in turn cannot accept the incredible claims of light bearers; and light bearers, who do what they can to relieve the suffering of prisoners addicted to their shadows and freedom fighters addicted to their causes.

> . . . all of us have our particular karmic mix of prisoners, freedom fighters and light bearers within ourselves across our various levels of skill in each sense or faculty.

So we will examine these important fundamental questions first regarding the ego layer of the human psyche, and its potential expansion into the others. Again we will encounter a threefold conceptualization of that development: pre-personal, personal, transpersonal; prisoners, freedom fighters, light bearers; slaves of God, employees of God, lovers of God.

As one develops to higher levels of ego maturity, the ego moves away from focusing on its traits and toward a consolidation of identity. Qualities associated with higher stages of ego development include a consistent sense of presence, an authenticity, and a lightness or ease of being. Descriptions of people functioning at an optimal level include increasing flexibility, conceptual complexity, and tolerance for ambiguity; recognition and acceptance of internal contradictions; a broader and more complex understanding of the self, others, and the self in relation to others; internalized self-control and emotional self-regulation; transcendence of ego boundaries; transparency; "postambivalence" i.e., total wholehearted and unconflicted love, acceptance, and self-expression.

Vertical and Horizontal Development

We can conceptualize the ego aspect of growth and development on both vertical and horizontal perspectives. An example of vertical development involves integration of the parasympathetic and sympathetic nervous systems, the heart and the brain, and the chakras from the root chakra of survival to the crown chakra of transcendence. Vertical development also indicates one's relationships with soul and spirit, with the deep unconscious and with sublime levels of divine energy. Integration also occurs horizontally, for example, left brain and right brain. We know how different those two hemispheres are: the right brain is intuitive, synthesizing, creative, holistic, and more agile in novel situations while the left brain is rational, analytical, sequential, objective, and more active in routine processing. Horizontal development also indicates the quality of relationships with others, with the environment, and with oneself.

Remember Ken Wilber's distinction of the two different vectors of growth, *transformation* (the vertical ascent through different stages of consciousness) versus *translation* (making sense of the world from whatever stage you happen to be at, in the healthiest way possible). Jane Loevinger identifies the distinction between vertical and horizontal assessment in the field of intelligence, and applies that clarity to assessing ego development.[549]

For many contemporary personality theorists, Piaget has become more important than Binet. Rather than quantifying intelligence in terms of proportion of adult status achieved, as Binet and his followers did, Piaget adopted a premise like the one that opened this discussion, namely, the qualitative nature of psychological data. He saw even intellectual achievement in fundamentally qualitative terms. Piaget was interested in children's mistakes, not in their correct answers. When he saw the same mistakes repeated, even by children in different countries, he postulated that the child's reasoning is governed by a mental structure, not just sheer amount of ability or training.

Conceptual complexity in the field of ego development is distinguished from sheer intelligence or intellectual level by an emphasis, instead, on the emotional and motivational implications of ego functioning.

Stages and States

Ken Wilber has masterfully mapped the terrain of human development in all its complexity, utilizing accumulated knowledge from fields such as anthropology, mythology and psychology, gathered from both the West and the East. Expanding on Piaget's concept of mental structure, Wilber clarifies the distinction between Maslow's stages of development and the experiences (peak or mundane) that make up one's moment-to-moment experiencing:

> "Structures" or "stages" of consciousness represent an attempt to measure our growth and maturity, and Maslow was determined to recognize the great potential that human beings could aspire to – the farther reaches of human nature. Stages have been studied in the West by developmental psychologists like Jean Piaget, Lawrence Kohlberg, Carol Gilligan, and Jean Gebser, all of whom have created sophisticated models of development that can be generically summarized as moving from "ego-centric" stages, to "ethno-centric" stages, to "world-centric" stages, and beyond. These stages are experienced in succession—that is, you have to move through "stage 3" of psychological development before you can hit "stage 4".
>
> "States" of consciousness, meanwhile, have been extensively studied in the East, and represent our various degrees of freedom in this and every moment. These states are ever-present, meaning they can be experienced at any time in our lives, and are often accessed through spiritual practices like meditation or prayer; through physical practices like

athletics or yoga; through deep intimacy, sexuality, and relationships; through altered- or drug-induced states; or even completely spontaneously while walking down the street or taking a shower.[550]

An important difference between states and stages is that stages of development are inclusive (each new stage building upon and incorporating the last), while states of consciousness are not—they are exclusive in the literal sense of the word, meaning you cannot be happy and sad, drunk and sober, or liberated and contracted at the same time. We cannot skip stages of development (you must grow through stage 3 before you can master stage 4); states of consciousness are much more fluid, and any state can be experienced at just about any time, however briefly or randomly. States of consciousness will always be interpreted based on the stage of development a person happens to be at when he or she has the experience; a transcendent state might be interpreted as pathological by someone operating at the pre-personal stage of development.

Thus Maslow differentiated between *peak experiences*, a state that may be fleeting and even random, and *plateau experience*, a more consistent perspective based on peak experiences that persist over time which therefore defines a stage of development.

There is a process of development for every individual toward the "optimal expression of being human," and, as with other developmental lines, it proceeds in sequential stages, each one building on and incorporating the earlier stages in such a way that no stage can be skipped and the sequential order of the emerging stages is a relatively fixed aspect of the human experience. In between these stages are transitional experiences, special windows of opportunity for transcendent growth: *transitional spaces*.

Remarkably, one example of a transitional space can be a traumatic experience. A predictable element in traumatic experiences that turns out to be transformative is that a corrective experience intervenes in the course of events to bend the trajectory toward healing and growth. Sometimes those corrective experiences occur through the intervention of the environment: someone is there to create safety, or circumstances allow for a benign outcome. And sometimes the corrective experiences are sought after, developed, nurtured, and grasped. We may be able to identify a facilitative agent, either serendipitous or sought, that helps to account for the dramatic advancement often observed at such moments.

If we can identify likely circumstances under which the trajectory is bent toward growth and healing, then we can vigilantly be prepared to maximize the opportunity when it occurs. The transitional spaces between developmental stages seem to be such especially opportunistic moments. Those ages in childhood development tend to be around birth, 3, 7, 12, and 16. Those ages coincide with milestone events in brain development, in cognitive development, and in ego development. They are also, not coincidentally, the most common destinations for age regressions in hypnotherapy.

If as facilitators in age regression therapy (or in adult therapy) we know what the opportunity is for growth from the existing ego development stage to the next, we may be able to help the client to tailor the corrective experience to meet the criteria of the most auspicious facilitative agent. In other words, while we are working to correct the erroneous emotional self-beliefs ("I am bad", "I am stupid"), we may also be able to advance the factors contributing to advancement to the next ego development stage ("I see that I am eager to form social bonds, not to avoid getting caught but to create security", signifying development from the Self-Protective stage to Conformist). Let's look at the Ego Development theories behind this statement to enumerate the sequence of stages of development.

And so we now turn to the question of how one's point of view changes as one progresses through stages of ego development. We will address the questions that were posed at the beginning of this chapter.

Postconventional Personality – Ego Development
Jane Loevinger devoted her career to studying and developing a theory of Ego Development and creating a measurement of it. Loevinger said, "The striving to master, to integrate, to make sense of experience is not one ego function among many but the essence of the ego."[551] Loevinger's notion

of the ego as a self's "guiding fiction" is adapted from Alfred Adler's work.[552]

"The ego is conceived as a master trait of personality, with a core organizing function. At the same time, that organizing function is also grounded enough to be applicable to life as it is lived in everyday social relations. It is appealing to conceive of a core organizing function, something that acts as a rudder for inner and outer forces."[553]

Ego development can be described as being an increasing differentiation in the balancing of concerns about self and other. At early stages of ego development, one is concerned with being hurt and being controlled by other people, whereas at later stages one is concerned with hurting other people, and still later, with compromising one's own achievements by being overly concerned with other people.[554] It is important to note that individuals of different developmental levels organize their experience in profoundly different ways, and not necessarily determined by age. A younger person can be wiser or more mature than an older person. Martin Luther King, Jr. reached an advanced level of maturity by the youthful age of 39, his age at the time of his tragic murder.

Ego development has been described as the development of character.[555]

"Many would identify as [Loevinger's] most valuable contribution the conception of ego development and the delineation of the stages, which helped us to go beyond the fragmentation of trait psychology and to look at personalities as meaningful wholes."[556]

". . . one may debate whether what Loevinger described should be called *structures*, *stages* (hard or soft), or simply *levels*. But there is no doubt that, like Piaget and Kohlberg, Loevinger focuses on coherence and meaning in describing personality development and insists that the specific manifestations of a stage—traits or behaviors that they may be— acquire developmental sense from their relations to the whole, while the whole transcends in meaning each of its elementary components."[557]

> There are three central tenets of Loevinger's theory: the unitary nature of the ego, the ego representing an integration of diverse personality characteristics (cognitive functioning, personal and interpersonal awareness, and character development), and the sequentiality of ego stages (albeit is possible to reverse the sequence).

According to Manners and Durkin:

Loevinger (1976, 1997) described four domains as representative and inextricably interwoven aspects of the ego: character development, cognitive style, interpersonal style, and conscious preoccupations. *Character development* incorporates impulse control and moral development in terms of the basis for moral behavior and the types of moral concerns. *Cognitive style* represents level of conceptual complexity and cognitive development. *Interpersonal style* represents the attitude toward interpersonal relationships and the other person, the understanding of relationships, and the preferred type of relationship. *Conscious preoccupations* refer to the predominant foci of the person's conscious thoughts and behavior, such as conformity to social rules, responsibility, and independence.

The concept of a 'developing' ego refers to the progressive redefinition or reorganization of the self in relation to the social and physical environment and is conceptualized in terms of developmental change in the four domains described previously (Loevinger, 1976, 1997). For example, the character development moves from being impulsive and fearful of punishment by others if caught doing wrong (lower ego stages) to self-regulation and internalized standards (higher ego stages). The cognitive style develops from conceptual simplicity at the lower stages to conceptual complexity and tolerance for ambiguity at the higher stages. The interpersonal style develops from an exploitive approach at the lower stages to a respectful interdependent approach at the higher stages. The conscious concerns develop from bodily feelings and self-protection at the lower stages to affective differentiation, individuality, and communication at the higher stages.[558]

In general, ego development is characterized by increasing flexibility; recognition and acceptance of internal contradictions; a broader and more complex understanding of the self, others, and the self in relation to others; internalized self-control and emotional self-regulation. However, the nature of the relation between ego development and intelligence remains unclear. Research has not resolved whether the relation between intelligence and ego development remains the same through all the ego stages or whether higher levels of intelligence are necessary for, or facilitate, higher ego stages. Likewise, the relation between ego development and psychopathology is unclear; while a person at any level can be emotionally unstable, we do know that the form and expression of their dis-ease can be affected by their level of ego development.

Following are some general research findings regarding higher stages of ego development. Having an open-minded, unconventional approach to beliefs and values is associated with higher levels of ego development.[559] Tolerance, defined as being nonjudgmental toward the beliefs and values held by others, is also associated with higher ego development.[560] Appreciation of artistic and cultural products and activities is associated with higher ego development.[561]

Westenberg and Block showed that psychological mindedness (introspectiveness, self-knowledge, and a general awareness and examination of motives in self and others) increased with ego level, as does resiliency (defined broadly as the capacity for flexible and resourceful adaptation to internal and external stressors).[562] Those higher in ego level also tend to have a more internal locus of control.[563] Individuals at higher ego levels have a greater capacity to form and maintain intimate relationships with others.[564]

Adults at higher ego levels, especially women, often tend to behave in ways that do not conform to traditional gender roles.[565] It seems that a hallmark of high ego development is an integration of both masculine and feminine strengths: "Self-development at higher levels apparently goes hand in hand with an awareness of emotional interdependence and granting of appropriate autonomy to others as well as to self. If this seems a complex blend of caring and autonomy, . . . it is precisely this complexity that the individual at higher ego levels is successfully mastering."[566] More evidence for this integration of masculine and feminine characteristics comes from McAdams, Ruetzel, and

Foley, who showed that ego level was related to having both instrumental and interpersonal goals.[567]

Loevinger conceptualized the ego as a unifying frame of reference that underlies all of our thoughts and actions; ego development is the process of gaining psychological maturity.[568] Viewed as the master trait, ego development encompasses changes in impulse control and character, interpersonal relations, conscious preoccupations, motivation and cognitive style combined into a complex matrix of personal and social integration. Her model includes nine qualitatively distinct milestones of development, each representing increasingly mature organizations of the self and relationship with the environment (Table 2).

The stages are sorted into three tiers, *Preconventional*, up to stage 3, *Conventional*, stages 4 to 6, and *Postconventional*, stage 7 and above. *Preconventional* development is marked by low impulse control and fear of punishment, whereas *conventional* development is characterized by social conformity and respect for rules. Hallmarks of stage 6, *Conscientious*, the final stage of the conventional development, are to interiorize ethical standards and value long-term goals.

At least 80% of the population functions consistently at the preconventional and conventional levels. Stage 5, Self-Aware, is the modal level for adults in our society, with the mean — at least for well-educated adults — falling between Self-Aware and Conscientious.[569] Evidence indicates that most adults do not progress to postconventional levels of ego development. Two large surveys of adults of various ages have both reported 8% of participants at or above the Individualistic level in ego development; these same surveys reported only 2–3% of adults scoring at or above the Autonomous level.[570] Susanne Cook-Greuter has suggested a fourth tier of development, a postpostconventional stage, which she designates as ego-transcendent, with less than 1% of the population functioning at that level.[571]

A Four-Tier Model of Human Development

4 Tiers of Development Cook-Greuter; Wilber	% of population	Ego-Development Stages Loevinger; Cook-Greuter
Postpostconventional Ego-Transcendent	Less than 1%	*Transcendent Self*
Postconventional	9%	10. Unitive
		9. Construct-aware
		8. Autonomous/Integrated *Mature connected self*
		7. Individualistic
Conventional	80%	6. Conscientious *Separate individual self*
		5. Self-aware
		4. Conformist *Communal self*
Preconventional	10%	3. Self-protective
		2. Impulsive 1. Presocial *Undifferentiated self*

Table 2 (from Cook-Greuter, 2000)

Development to Postconventional stages, stage 7 and above, requires a significant paradigm shift. Stage 7, *Individualistic*, requires significantly greater sophistication and psychological mindedness, an understanding that individual differences make it hard to proscribe rules and judgments globally. At stage 8, *Autonomous*, individuals become orientated toward self-expression and authenticity. Stages 7 and 8 correspond approximately to Maslow's notion of self-actualization.[572] According to Cook-Greuter, stage 9, *Construct-aware*, is marked by an interest in the process of *how* one makes meaning, as well as the way in which we arrive at our sense of self and outer reality.[573] At stage 10, *Unitive*, individuals maintain a present-centered flow of awareness and tolerate ambiguity with ease.[574]

> Maslow's final stage of development beyond self-actualization, *transcending self-actualization*, could correspond to stage 9, *Construct-aware*, or above, or perhaps Cook-Greuter is accurate in asserting that it represents a fourth tier beyond even the *Unitive* stage.

The paradigm shift that is required to develop to postconventional stages and above is difficult because it is "illogical" by Western linear, rational criteria, and therefore it is culturally sanctioned. Conventional Western psychology views the construction of a permanent, separate self identity as the measure of healthy human development. Cook-Greuter comments: "According to this view, adulthood is achieved when people can successfully use abstract reasoning to deal with their everyday experience, and when they see themselves as independent, goal-oriented, responsible agents of their own lives while granting others the same right to separate personhood. Mental development up to this point establishes increasingly more clearly defined boundaries between subject and object world, between knower and known, between observer and observed in an effort to construct an ever more accurate, objective map of reality based on scientific, rational criteria."[575]

The third tier, postconventional, requires going beyond the modern, linear-scientific mindset and beyond the conventions of Western society by beginning to question the unconsciously held norms and assumptions about reality acquired during socialization and schooling. Cook-Greuter continues:

> Based on evidence from my research, postconventional development reverses the overall process of separation and differentiation of the earlier ego stages. The rigid boundaries between knower and known are gradually deconstructed and merged. The dismantling occurs in two steps. The first step is generally referred to as the *systems view* (Bertalanffy, 1968; Bateson, 1972; Koplowitz, 1984; Senge, 1990); the second step is called the *postautonomous* (Cook-Greuter, 1990) or *unitary view* of reality (Koplowitz, 1984, 1990). . . .
>
> The main advantage of the systems over the conventional, linear view is that people now realize that their perspectives are local, partial, context-dependent and culturally conditioned. Systems thinkers are aware of themselves as participant observers, or as inevitably part of the problem

space. In other words, they realize that each person sees a slightly different aspect of the underlying territory. . . . However, systems thinkers do not yet understand how profoundly all humans are conditioned into the language habit (Cook-Greuter, 1995). They are not aware how they automatically privilege some aspects of experience by being part of a language community and ignore, or are oblivious, to others regardless of the social-political context.

Only a small percentage of people develop a reality perspective that goes beyond the fully equilibrated systems view or Autonomous/Integrated stage. Few theories of development postulate forms of reasoning that are even more differentiated and abstract than the systems view.[576]

In the postautonomous or unitary step of development beyond the conventional, individuals come to transcend the overall stance of the systems thinker. Turning further inward, they start to see how self-limiting are their own thought and language habits, and their ego's defensive maneuvers. They become aware of the profound splits and paradoxes inherent in rational thought, even from a systems view, of the linguistic process of splitting everything into polar opposites with assumed value judgments. Black and white, good and bad thinking is replaced with a much more nuanced perspective.

"Although systems thinkers may have intimations of the ramifications that arise when one begins to conceive of the self and reality as constructed, they fend, at the same time, automatically against any knowledge of their own impermanence and insubstantiality. As the process of self-awareness deepens and reasoning becomes further differentiated at the Construct-aware stage, access to intuition, bodily states, feelings, dreams, archetypal and other transpersonal material increases."[577]

Research has indicated that some of the factors associated with developmental advances include meditation, psychotherapy, formal education, complexity of work, and dispositional factors, such as giftedness, ego resilience, and openness to experience.[578]

It should be noted that Noam[579] and Labouvie-Vief[580] have questioned the unitary nature of Loevinger's conception of the ego, arguing that it attempts to combine into a single construct two independent though interacting dimensions: self-complexity, which is a predominantly cognitive process, and self-integration, which is a predominantly affective and interpersonal process.

We will examine more thoroughly the conception of the ego soon.

Individuals at the higher ego levels tend to be open to unfamiliar ways of thinking, have the capacity to process information in new and complex ways, and generate original ideas.[581] In fact, people develop those qualities *only* when the environment fails to meet their expectations, forcing flexibility and resourcefulness.[582] We now examine the mechanism of posttraumatic growth.

Posttraumatic growth

One of the known "windows of opportunity" for growth is traumatic experience. "Posttraumatic growth is the experience of positive change that occurs as a result of the struggle with highly challenging life crises. It is manifested in a variety of ways, including greater life satisfaction[583] as well as an increased appreciation for life in general, more meaningful interpersonal relationships, an increased sense of personal strength, changed priorities, and a richer existential and spiritual life."[584]

When an individual encounters adversity, be it accidental or malicious, sudden or lingering, there are at least four potential consequences.[585] One possibility is a downward slide in which the initial detrimental effect is compounded and the person eventually *succumbs*, defeated. A second possibility is that the individual *survives* but is diminished or impaired permanently. A third potential outcome is that the individual returns to the pre-adversity level of functioning, that is to say he or she *recovers*. The fourth possibility is that the person may surpass the previous level of functioning, and he or she *thrives*. The thriving outcome has been studied extensively, and is generally called *posttraumatic growth*. The following graphic representation (Figure 1) is taken from Carver[586], who adapted it in turn from O'Leary & Ickovics[587].

There has been significant research into the phenomenon of a growth "benefit" resulting from traumatic experience. After difficult life experiences, some people express ways that they have benefited from their misfortune, finding "a silver lining in the cloud." The most common perceptions of benefit reported by survivors of trauma are strengthened family relationships, positive personality changes, and changes in life priorities.[588]

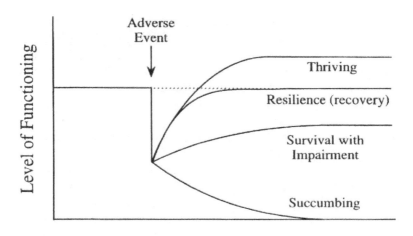

Time

Figure 1. Four Outcomes of Adversity

Calhoun and Tedeschi[589] report that perceived growth from traumatic events tend to fall into three general domains: (1) changes in perception of self, to more self-reliance and capability of coping with difficult challenges; (2) changed relationships with others, to an increase in interpersonal emotional closeness, an increase in one's freedom to express emotion, and an increase in sympathy and understanding for others' suffering; and (3) changes in philosophy of life, to a deeper appreciation for life, new life directions and priorities, increased experience of existential wisdom, and greater interest in and openness to spiritual and religious matters. They indicate that the precipitating event, which can lead either to traumatic distress or traumatic growth, must be of sufficiently "seismic" proportions to shake the foundations of the individual's assumptions about life, and perhaps to shatter them. The potential for growth lies precisely in the need to reevaluate and rebuild one's basic assumptions about and view of the world.

Experiences sufficiently "seismic" to shake or shatter the foundations of the individual's assumptions about life call into question his/her understanding of meaning, or meaninglessness, in life. This signals a direct appeal to one's soul to awaken and engage.

We examine this conceptualization in the chapter on eudaimonic growth and self-authorship.

Lines of Development, Multiple Intelligences

Howard Gardner realized that all people have some areas in their life in which they are stronger than other areas, and that assessing development would need to account for that diversity.[590] Gardner initially formulated a list of seven intelligences. The first two have been typically valued in schools; the next three are usually associated with the arts; and the final two are what Gardner called 'personal intelligences'.[591]

- **Linguistic intelligence** involves sensitivity to spoken and written language, the ability to learn languages, and the capacity to use language to accomplish certain goals. This intelligence includes the ability to effectively use language to express oneself rhetorically or poetically; and language as a means to remember information. Writers, poets, lawyers and speakers are among those that Gardner sees as having high linguistic intelligence.

- **Logical-mathematical intelligence** consists of the capacity to analyze problems logically, carry out mathematical operations, and investigate issues scientifically. In Gardner's words, it entails the ability to detect patterns, reason deductively and think logically. This intelligence is most often associated with scientific and mathematical thinking.

- **Musical intelligence** involves skill in the performance, composition, and appreciation of musical patterns. It encompasses the capacity to recognize and compose musical pitches, tones, and rhythms. According to Gardner, musical intelligence runs in an almost structural parallel to linguistic intelligence.

- **Bodily-kinesthetic intelligence** entails the potential of using one's whole body or parts of the body to solve problems. It is the ability to use mental abilities to coordinate bodily movements. Gardner sees mental and physical activity as related.

- **Spatial intelligence** involves the potential to recognize and use the patterns of wide space and more confined areas.

- **Interpersonal intelligence** is concerned with the capacity to understand the intentions, motivations and desires of other people. It allows people to work effectively with others. Educators, salespeople, religious and political leaders and counselors all need a well-developed interpersonal intelligence.

- **Intrapersonal intelligence** entails the capacity to understand oneself, to appreciate one's feelings, fears and motivations. In Gardner's view it involves having an effective working model of oneself, and to be able to use such information to regulate one's life.

Subsequent research and reflection by Gardner and his colleagues has identified three particular possibilities for candidates for inclusion as additional intelligences: a **naturalist intelligence**, a **spiritual intelligence** and an **existential intelligence**. He has concluded that the first of these "merits addition to the list of the original seven intelligences".[592]

- **Naturalist intelligence** enables human beings to recognize, categorize and draw upon certain features of the environment. It combines a description of the core ability with a characterization of the role that many cultures value.

Subject Becoming Object

Maturity through the various stages of development can be described as a process of "subject becoming object." In other words, with more maturity, one can see in himself what was previously invisible because the observing ego was identified with it, leaving no witness to observe from outside. When one's shadows are dominant, the individual identifies *as that point of view*: I am defensive about certain things, I believe that *I am* alone or a victim or unworthy. Identified with a state, trait or belief, there is no internal objective observer. With greater ego maturity, I begin to recognize these as stances and beliefs which may be accurate or not, but in either case do not define who I am. For example, I am actually not alone (perhaps I begin to recognize spirit helpers, guardian angels, or the companionship of the natural world). Being less attached to an identity determined by circumstance and behavior, I have less to defend. Previously, we could not hold certain aspects of ourselves as objects in awareness, and thus our identity remained embedded in these fragments of self. That small piece of us remained strongly identified with a previous stage of consciousness, one that the rest of the self may be ready to grow beyond.

These fragments of self, or split-off subpersonalities, are arrested at whatever stage of development was in place at the time of the split. In most cases that was very early in life, at a very young and immature age. It is also possible for some subpersonalities to be highly advanced. The average person has a dozen or more subpersonalities, variously known as parent, child, adult ego state[593]; topdog, underdog[594]; false, actual, real self[595]; id, ego, superego[596]; future selves, best possible self[597]; and many other variations.

> The worldview and the self-construal looks immensely different depending on which self is acting as observing ego: is it the False Self (the broken or illusory self image), the Actual Self (the "authentic" or healthily-integrated self at any particular stage of development), or the Real Self (the timeless Self behind and beyond all manifestation).

Salman puts the collaborative subject/object relationship into a Jungian perspective, representing the culmination of the individuation process.

> With a willing participation in the fullness of one's life, several factors come to light, viewed through the prism of analytical psychology, as contributing to the realization of wisdom: (1) a lived experience of both the archaic and the creative wisdom of the unconscious psyche, (2) the individuation of a Self-oriented ego, unique but in the service of the whole personality, and connected to universal aspects of reality, (3) the transformation of fate into destiny, and (4) the capacity to marry the primordial images of the unconscious psyche to the rational consciousness of ego awareness. All of these factors come together to yield an experience of meaning which reaches into both subjective and objective dimensions of experience and reality.[598]

It turns out that all people experience this state everyday: in their dreams. "The secret of dreams is that subject and object are the same."[599] Not by accident did Jung refer to the Self, the unity or totality that provides a blueprint for one's optimal development, as a "dream of totality".[600] Jung said,

The dream is a little hidden door in the innermost secret recesses of the soul, opening into that cosmic night which was psyche long before there was any ego-consciousness, and which will remain psyche no matter how far our ego-consciousness may extend. . . . All consciousness separates; but in dreams we put on the likeness of that more universal, truer, more eternal man dwelling in the darkness of primordial night. There he is still the whole, and the whole is in him, indistinguishable from nature and bare of all egohood.[601]

> This becomes a process of unpacking a nested Russian doll, continually finding a new and smaller doll inside the last one. Just when I thought I had become the subject witnessing an aspect of myself as object, I find another deeper and more subtle consciousness that is witnessing *that* identified self.

Wilber comments: "But a strange thing has now happened, for I realize that the real self within is actually the real world without, and vice versa. The subject and object, the inside and the outside, are and always have been nondual. There is no primary boundary. The world is my body, and what I am looking out of is what I am looking at. . . . the inside world and the outside world are just two different names for the single, ever-present state of no-boundary awareness."[602]

Subsumed under the one concept of ego are both the perceptions and the organization of those perceptions. Yet Loevinger insisted that "There is just one dimension," which she called ego. We will look more carefully now at the frame of reference, or map, as a relationship between these two subsumed aspects.

We all experience ourselves as both an object and as a subject, as a 'me' and an 'I'. McAdams explains it well:

The ego, or I, is the process of "selfing," of apprehending subjective experience and making something out of it. The most cherished thing selfing makes is the Me, the self-as-object, the concept of the self that is recognized and reflected upon by the I. Thus, as [William] James suggested, the *duplex* self is both I (process) and Me (product). The ego is the I part. The ego reflects upon the Me. The ego knows the Me. The ego synthesizes the Me out of experience. The ego makes the Me. . . . Furthermore, positioning the ego in this way sheds considerable light on both the structure of personality and its development over time.[603]

The I-self has been called the existential self, experiencing self, or implicit self. The Me-self has been called the categorical self, the empirical self, the object of consciousness, the explicit self, self-perceptions or most commonly the self-concept.[604] Beyond that "split" ordinary adult ego structure lies a potential and optional advanced ego, which we might call the transcendental ego or ultraself.[605]

It is extremely useful to acknowledge that the ego actually makes many Me's[606], contained within what we are calling the 'ego realm' or what Jung called the 'ego complex.' Each Me may fall within the general category of the ego's *personas* and *shadows*. James Hillman describes the process as building the me's out of accumulated spare parts from here and there, with the 'I' determining whether to reject a given constructed me or not just as the body's immune system decides whether to reject an organ transplant or a skin graft.[607] In *Everyday Zen*[608], Charlotte Joko Beck relates an old koan about a monk who went to his master and said, "I'm a very angry person, and I want you to help me." The master said, "Show me your anger." The monk said, "Well, right now I'm not angry. I can't show it to you." And the master said, "Then obviously it's not you, since sometimes it's not even there." Who we are has many faces, but these faces are not who we are.

> I may not know *who* I am (i.e., the many faces of me), but I always know *that* I am (i.e., the I, the self-as-subject).

The 'me' is built out of parts from here and there; e.g., introjects from parents or early authorities, social and cultural norms. The 'I' is an enduring presence with "subject permanence" that ultimately accepts or rejects the imported parts.[609] The 'I', like the body's immune system, has the capacity to discern what is native essence and what is foreign, to claim the former and to reject the latter. As ego development progresses, defining the object 'me' becomes less important and transcending the object 'me' (immersion in the subject 'I') becomes the focus. Recall Maslow's reference to what he called self-forgetfulness in moments of peak experience, i.e., becoming less dissociated than usual into a self-observing ego and an experiencing ego.[610]

Higher stages of ego development bring a predictable change in the relationship between the subject and object and how their developmental trajectories interrelate. From the Impulsive to the Conscientious stages, ego development focuses on fashioning a Me intricately adorned with desirable traits to establish exactly where the Me stands in relation to others and to support the I's striving for personal goals and individual accomplishments. Beginning with the Conscientious stage of ego development, individuals are clearly separating their Me-conceptions from the dictates of social convention. The I-perspective is truly becoming author of the Me, based on internalized principles and standards. At the Individualistic level, the ego adopts a thorough "developmental" perspective on life, recognizing the me-construction as a past-present-future developmental sequence.

The Autonomous stage brings an increasing tolerance for ambiguity and conflict, and a strong focus on self-fulfillment over personal achievement. The Integrated stage brings what Loevinger calls "the consolidation of identity"; as the ego moves away from traits it moves in the direction of identity.[611] "Thus, the ultimate psychosocial demand becomes the consolidation of identity for the storytelling I."[612]

> Consolidation of identity, the current authors suggest, is a unifying of the I-perspective and the Me-conceptions; storytelling and living the story are collapsed into one smooth operation. Bringing the I and Me together is to construct one's life and to live it seamlessly, providing life with unity and purpose amid ambiguity and conflict.

MacIntyre characterized self-fulfillment as living the most enriching or noble or satisfying story one can reasonably construct.[613] This is one way to conceptualize the experience of flow, mindfulness, or the witness perspective. The ego functions to invent, experience, and narrate the story. Now the ego has expanded its perspective to incorporate not only the Middle Realm, kingdom of trait refinement and personal goals and individual accomplishments, but also the Lower Realm of soul embodiment and story creation, as well as the Higher Realm of spirit realization, story narration and the enlightening "moral of the story."

Alexander et al. propose that a systematic practice for experiencing transcendence may be fundamental for "unfreezing" development so that postconventional levels can be attained.[614] This sets in motion a major developmental transformation toward what they term a "postrepresentational" tier of development. One feature of this transition is a growing realization of one's identity in terms of nonconceptual awareness of the subject of experience, rather than in terms of concepts about oneself as object. Cook-Greuter has presented evidence of a rare advanced stage like this, in which one is not identifying oneself with any of the changing contents of awareness. She refers to this as a "fluid, postobjective" self view.[615]

Advancement to higher levels of ego development requires the ego to surrender its sense of autonomy. Taft suggested the term *ego permissiveness* to convey the ego's willingness to tolerantly relinquish some of its (self-perceived) power in order to allow the actualization of the potentialities of the pre-conscious and unconscious aspects of the personality, just as a permissive parent or leader takes the repressive pressure off subordinate elements in the system so that they can grow.[616] Ego permissiveness connotes a reduction of ego control in the interests of self-expression and growth. Some dimensions of ego permissiveness are (1) peak experiences (a state of loosened identifications and fluid ego boundaries); (2) dissociated experiences (the experience of an 'altered state of consciousness' in which consciousness is dissociated from, yet still aware of, emotions, external perceptions, or somatic experience); (3) acceptance of fantasy (relatively easy suspension of disbelief); and (4) belief in the supernatural (belief in the reality of supernatural phenomena, outside the normal world of perception and logic; tolerance for logical inconsistencies and paradox).

> Ego development to higher levels requires surrendering the illusion of its own autonomy, the outcome of being permissive and quiet.

Advancement to higher levels of ego development is synonymous with growing in authenticity. In its strong sense, Jim Bugental notes, "authenticity amounts to [nothing less than] the resolution of the subject-object split, the self-world dichotomy."[617]

Self, Possible Future Selves, Best Possible Self

Any study of the self presents fundamental dilemmas because the subject studying is also the object studied and, moreover, the observing ego is only a part of the total subject of investigation: Michael Fordham observed that " ' . . . a concept of the totality is particularly difficult to construct', [Jung] noted; 'Indeed it is impossible'."[618]

Possible selves represent the broad range of imaginable possible futures; they are personalized representations of one's important life goals.[619] Possible selves hold the place of what might still be. One's *best possible self* is one's most cherished future self, one's best possible imagined outcome.[620]

Possible selves encompass not only the goals we are seeking but all of the imaginable futures we might occupy. *Lost possible future selves* represent the self in the future which might have once been held with promise, but which are no longer a part of a person's life.

The elaboration of the *best possible self* narrative relates to enhanced ego development because developing highly complex life plans is an accomplishment unique to the developed ego.

The elaboration of the *lost possible self* narrative also relates to enhanced ego development. Part of maturing may be the ability to place one's choices in the context of all the roads not taken. Our ability to honestly reconsider what we once valued may be a hallmark of maturity; the capacity to face one's lost possible self in a detailed way is a sign of maturity.[621] Such a capacity reveals a person's willingness to admit to imperfection, to erroneous assumptions, to failed expectations, in short, to humanity. The process of deliberately introspecting on one's previously valued life dreams and actively working to invent or reinvent alternative future selves is reflected in enhanced ego development. The potentially painful task of considering 'what might have been' is an important aspect of maturity.

Individuals who fail to disengage from unattainable goals tend to show depressive symptoms and limited opportunities for new goals.[622] A hallmark of successful self-regulation may be the ability to flexibly pursue goals, and to disengage from life goals that no longer include the possibility of fulfillment.[623]

Ken Wilber discusses three kinds of self: the False Self (the broken or illusory self image), the Actual Self (the "authentic" or healthily-integrated self at any particular stage of development), and the Real Self (the timeless Self behind and beyond all manifestation).[624]

> What are the factors in the personality makeup of highly developed individuals that bring them closer to transcending the authentic Actual Self and embodying the Real Self, i.e., acknowledging their various possible selves, and realizing their best possible self?

We review research conducted by Angela Pfaffenberger.[625] Persons at postconventional stages of development define development and talk about their growth in significantly different ways than persons in the conventional tier of development. A number of different aspects distinguish reliably between postconventional and conventional participants' narration of growth stories. Pfaffenberger reports three major themes emerged in a recent research project: complexity of narrative, interiority, and intention with commitment.

> *Complexity.* The most noticeable aspect in the narratives and interview materials was that as the ego stage increases, the complexity of the story increases. The complexity of the story appears to be linked to the complexity of cognitive-emotional integration. . . . Higher development appears to be linked to a willingness to fully participate in a wide variety of activities, the ability to see those activities and events as beneficial opportunities for growth, and an ability to make finely shaded differentiations in one's experience. Postconventional participants exhibited a willingness to accept the complexity and the often-accompanying ambiguity in their lives.

> *Interiority.* In addition to complexity of the growth story, the main element that reliably distinguished between conventional and postconventional participants was interiority. The narratives of postconventional participants showed a high degree of introspection and inner awareness. An inner orientation was often expressed in vivid descriptions of lived experience. . . . In the stories of postconventional participants existential themes often surfaced, such as understanding that

life is finite and that you need to make a choice about what to do in order to create meaning. The majority of postconventional participants conveyed directly or indirectly that they felt that meaning in life arose from the fact that they explored who they were and what their contribution consisted of. The stories of conventional participants showed an entire absence of themes in regard to finding one's inner self and attempting to express that consistently. . . . postconventional participants showed more diversity, and often slight incidences could lead to introspection and self-knowledge. Many postconventional participants described specific growth episodes that had no element of external difficulty but instead they talked about choosing to stay with an inner sense of unclarity or discomfort.

Intentionality. A consistent theme throughout the postconventional narratives was the expressed valuing of growth, the desire to grow, and the commitment to act on this desire through efforts that often involved persistence, discomfort, and exertion. Simultaneously, there appeared to be a departure from more external, culturally formed values, such as financial success and professional achievement. The intentionality has several aspects that usually occurred in combination, and it appears to be one of the key aspects of understanding higher development.

Postconventional participants value growth and seek it intentionally. To this end, they use a variety of means, such as (1) join a community of likeminded individuals, which is termed here a *discourse community*, (2) they adopt a consistent theory of growth, and (3) they maintain specific practices that enhance their inner awareness and carry them out consistently for many decades.

> We have seen that ego development brings with it increased compassion, tolerance, empathy, maturity, and the capacity for interpersonal connectedness, but does it necessarily lead to an immediate sense of subjective well-being, fulfillment, meaningfulness, or mental health?

Ego development is independent of well-being or psychological adjustment.[626] "The complex ego, overwhelmed by conflict and ambivalence or left disillusioned by life's difficult lessons, misses central aspects of maturity such as self-acceptance and contentment. True maturity incorporates both the complex sensibility implied by ego development as well as the context of positive feelings and resilience implied by well-being. If we consider these two facets of maturity as important indicators of adult development, we might ask how a person accomplishes each.[627] And precisely here is the opening for the transpersonal aspect of growth and development to contribute to a beyond-ego self, balanced between ego maturity and well-being. We shall turn to this question now with an exploration of eudaimonic growth.

Chapter Twelve

Eudaimonic Growth and Self-authorship

The essence of eudaimonia is the idea of striving toward excellence based on one's unique potential. *Daimon* (held by the ancient Greeks to be a kind of spirit given to all persons at birth) refers to potentialities of each person, realization of which leads to the greatest fulfillment. Each person is obliged to know and live in resonance to his daimon, thereby progressively actualizing excellence consistent with innate potentialities.

Well-being is experiencing a high level of positive affect, a low level of negative affect, and a high degree of satisfaction with one's life. The first two conditions could easily fit the definition of happiness, and therefore a *hedonistic* approach to life. However, life satisfaction adds a separate element. Life satisfaction may be defined as living well or actualizing one's human potentials, referred to as *eudaimonia*.[628] In other words, "well-being is not so much an outcome or end state as it is a process of fulfilling or realizing one's *daimon* or true nature— that is, of fulfilling one's virtuous potentials and living as one was inherently intended to live."[629]

The eudaimonic viewpoint can be traced to Aristotle's view of the highest human good involving virtue and the realization of one's potential, dating back to 350 BCE. That tradition has been embraced and elaborated on by the work of psychodynamically and humanistically oriented psychologists such as Jung[630], Allport[631], Assagioli[632], Maslow[633], and Rogers[634]. One compilation of the characteristics of psychological well-being includes these six: self-acceptance, personal growth, relatedness, autonomy, relationships, environmental mastery, and purpose in life.[635] To summarize these qualities, self-acceptance means long-term acceptance and positive self-regard, including the darker side of failures and weaknesses; personal growth aims at self-realization, actualizing potentialities, and continually confronting new challenges; relatedness involves participating in shared activities, feeling understood and appreciated, and communicating about personally relevant matters; autonomy means acting with the experience of choice, and is made up of the components of self-determination, independence, and the regulation of behavior from within; positive relationships include intimacy, love, empathy and affection; environmental mastery includes acting on and changing the surrounding world, participating in significant endeavors that go beyond oneself; and purpose in life involves the search for meaning and direction in life, generative contribution to community, and living authentically.

Bauer, McAdams, and Pals suggest that eudaimonia, the good life, is comprised of pleasure, a sense of meaningfulness, and a rich psychosocial integration in a person's understanding of himself or herself.[636] The authors report that people with intrinsic goals for personal growth, meaningful relationships, and community contribution tend also to display psychological well-being. Further, the researchers indicate that when people's goals include integrative growth, i.e., growth involving deeper understanding and integration of new and old perspectives, they tend to display a high level of ego-development and psychological well-being, especially on the dimensions of purpose in life and personal growth.

A quiet[637], permissive[638] ego is prepared to transcend the hedonistic approach to life in order to reach the eudaimonic experience. Now we explore the process of self-authorship, made possible by these qualities of ego that encourage and allow transcendence.

Self-evolution and Journey Toward Self-authorship

Robert Kegan is a developmental psychologist at the Harvard Graduate School of Education. His theory of self-evolution traces the emergence of increasingly complex forms of meaning making during adolescence and adulthood.[639] The development of one of these forms is self-authorship. This theory has two distinctive features. First, Kegan approaches the description of human development holistically. Thus the forms of meaning making explicated in his theory include multiple dimensions: cognitive knowledge (How do I know?), intrapersonal identity (Who am I?), and interpersonal relationships (How do I relate to others?). The second distinctive feature of Kegan's theory is that the core of his theory is the subject-object relationship and how this changes as meaning-making structures evolve.

> "Object" refers to those elements of our knowing or organizing that we can reflect on, handle, look at, be responsible for, relate to each other, take control of, internalize, assimilate, or otherwise operate upon. . . . "Subject" refers to those elements of our knowing or organizing that we are identified with, tied to, fused with, or embedded in. We have object; we are subject.[640]

Of course, some incidents in life are experienced as more meaningful than others. Thorne et al. found an association between tension and meaning making.[641] Bluck and Gluck found that most wisdom narratives provided by participants in their research highlighted negative or challenging situations that led to an uplifting resolution or lesson (what we might call the "when life gives you lemons, make lemonade" phenomenon).[642] They also found that individuals' wisdom narratives tend to be generalized across longer temporal periods, linking a set of related events together rather than focusing on a single isolated incident.

Bauer and McAdams[643] demonstrate that the ways in which individuals make sense of transition narratives in their lives are linked to their stage of ego development[644] and social-emotional development[645]. They analyzed narratives about important transitions in their research subjects' careers and religions for integrative themes (reflecting statements about a new understanding of self or others), intrinsic themes (an emphasis on personal happiness and fulfillment), agency, and communion.

They found that transition stories that stressed integrative lessons about personal mastery or enhanced status (agency) were more highly correlated to ego development, while transition stories that focused on personal growth in relationships were more linked to greater subjective well-being (i.e., social-emotional development). Similar to Thorne et al.'s results, Bauer and McAdams found that relationship memories that expressed enhanced belonging and happiness were not as likely as memories of striving or conflict to generate insight and self-understanding. However, the one type of memory that correlated with both ego development and social-emotional development was relationship memories that involved struggle and resolution. The authors suggest that perhaps we come closest to the 'good life' through meaningful relationship experiences that ultimately teach us the greatest priorities in life (e.g., the near fatal illness of a child or the positive resolution of a marital crisis).

The evolution to more complex meaning-making structures arises from elements that were formerly subject becoming object, or moving what was unseen and unexamined to a place where it can be seen and examined. Kegan describes this as the growth of the mind: "liberating ourselves from that in which we were embedded, making what was subject into object, so that we can 'have it' rather than 'be had' by it".[646]

> As previously unexamined assumptions are evaluated more objectively, new choices become possible. The new perspective has rebalanced what is subject and what is object, such that what was subject in the earlier form becomes object in the next. This charts the development of the form of meaning making Kegan calls self-authorship.

With this capacity, one can be "the author (rather than merely the theater) of one's inner psychological life."[647]

Baxter Magolda framed the development of self-authorship as extending along a continuum.[648] At one end of the continuum are those who use a meaning-making structure with an external orientation. For these individuals, the source of beliefs, values, identity, and nature of social relations exists outside the individual in the external world. These individuals rely on external authorities (actual authority figures or societal expectations) to determine what to believe, how to see themselves, and how to construct social relations. At the Self-Authoring end of the continuum are those who use a meaning-making structure with an internal orientation. For these individuals, the source of beliefs, values, identity, and nature of social relations exists inside the person in his or her internal psychological world rather than being dictated by those around him or her. The person reflects on, evaluates, and is an active agent in making choices about information from external sources to construct an internally defined belief system, identity, and way of relating to others.

When the internal voice sufficiently develops, it edges out the external voice. In between these ends is a form of meaning making that Baxter Magolda calls the "Crossroads," which reflects a mixture of external and internal orientations. People enter the Crossroads as they begin to question external authorities, work through the Crossroads as they process the tension between their emerging internal voices and external influence, and find their way out of the Crossroads when their internal voices have developed sufficient strength to coordinate external influence. That internal voice is now channeling the archetypal center core resource.

Self and Ego Boundaries

"... the experience of the self is always a defeat for the ego."[649]

Here Carl Jung generalizes his own internal struggle, bolstered by the experience of most of his European and American patients. However, the irascible ego clinging to its perceived autonomy may not be universally accurate for all people; the embedding of the ego into the Self may not always be experienced as a loss. A discussion of ego and self must be sensitive to differences that exist between various cultural worldviews, and between the sexes. We have previously observed, for example, that individuals influenced by an Afrocentric perspective or the Native American worldview recognize self as *extended self*, which includes all of the ancestors, the yet unborn, all of nature, and the entire community. And the extended self is also a *community within*, a centrifugal force emanating other complex selves that can interpermeate each other.

The relational aspects of women's development is somewhat similar, according to Wright, relying on permeable boundaries "to allow the simultaneous experience of self and other. The self-boundaries are permeable in the sense that they are open to the flow between self and other."[650] Due to this experiential difference, Wright postulated the following:

> Because women's prepersonal development differs from men's, it is not much of a stretch to postulate that women's transpersonal development may also differ. ... I propose that the connected self, with its permeable boundaries, cuts across

developmental lines in the prepersonal, personal, and transpersonal stages. Permeability affects all levels of experience. ... In terms of how it affects transpersonal development, it may subtly change the developmental path.

I speculate that because of permeable self-boundaries, women's experience of an isolated, unitary self already may be diminished. Awareness may naturally focus on the holographic, interwoven nature of reality. In this awareness, the hierarchical structures that the mind uses to reduce experience into comprehensible packets of reality can be more easily dissolved, and formlessness and ambiguity are better tolerated.

Boundary permeability may ease the path to union with a spiritual self. The merging and embedding of the self into God or Self may not always be experienced as a loss of self. Instead it may reflect a coming to "self/Self."[651]

And so this discussion of self/Self begins with a theoretical view that attempts to define the following aspects of each person's psyche[652]:

a. *Self* (the archetypal basis of personal existence). Called one's "inner nature" or "essential nature"[653], the Self is "the ordering and unifying center of the total psyche"[654].

b. *self-concept* (an idea of personal identity). The 'I' aspect of the self that organizes and assimilates one's perceptions and experiences into a coherent self-picture with which one then strives to be consistent.

c. *self-esteem* (feelings of personal worth). A barometer of how people *feel* about themselves (the affective component of the self), self-esteem is a reflection of how one evaluates the self.

d. *ego* (a barometer of psychological and emotional strength). The ego is actually part of the self. A major function of the ego is to obey the reality principle and to operate by means of the secondary process, which involves reality testing by realistic thinking, distinguishing between things in the mind and things in the external world.

e. *ego boundaries* (gauges of psychological and emotional resiliency). When people talk about someone having a weak or strong ego, they are implicitly saying something about the sort of boundaries that help to keep that individual's sense of self intact.

Where does the self begin? An 'emergent' and 'core self'[655] or 'proto-self'[656] or 'primary self'[657] are postulated to be the starting point in the human journey.[658]

> The primary self is 'empty' of phenomena, so that it is 'nothing but' potential. The primary self is a primitive form of the self, developing from soon after conception. Development begins from within; the self activates itself. A physiological analogy is the onset of the embryo's heartbeat. As the embryo's first observable activity, at about three weeks, the heartbeat initially originates within the heart itself . . . it is not a response to an external stimulus.[659]

> . . . in order to understand development we have to understand that complex systems are self-organizing: they 'prefer' states of equilibrium. However they can be pushed towards new states of equilibrium by particular forces, acting from within the organism or from the external environment. Thus development is understood as a progression through a series of stable states.[660]

It's an important detail, of course: which forces activate development, those acting from within the organism, as Fordham[661] and Bremner suggest, or those acting from the external environment. In Fordham's model, self-representations are understood as expressions of the wholeness of the primary self occurring in the developing ego, that is, conscious awareness. Fordham's and Bremner's position contrasts with developmental theorists, such as Daniel Stern and Peter Fonagy, who hold that the baby's self-representations are derived fundamentally from internalizing the experiences with the mother.[662]

In *Psychological Types*, Jung defines the self as the psychic totality: "the self is the subject of my total psyche which also includes the unconscious."[663] The self is the central organizing system, a superordinate whole in the psychic hierarchy with the ego and other psychic parts subservient to it. The central archetype of order distinguishes a particular archetype that has special integrative functions in relation to the ego and the archetypes, e.g., the archetypal central core phenomenon[664] and the conflict-free ego sphere.[665]

The Self is archetypal and the ego-complex is created, developing over a lifetime. The self and the ego complex operate in a cooperative symbiotic relationship. Figure 2 shows three models outlined by Edward Edinger.[666] On the left is the first of three main stages of the relationship between the Self and the ego–just after birth. Edinger points out that "The Self is the ordering and unifying center of the total psyche (conscious and unconscious) just as the ego is the center of the conscious personality."[667] The ego begins within the psyche as one with, and barely distinguishable from, the Self. Here the ego is present only as a potentiality. Edinger calls this the "state of primary ego-Self identity."[668]

In the center of Figure 2 is a model of the second main stage of this relationship. Here the ego is emerging as a separate system. A residual ego-Self identity still remains (in the overlapped area between the two). In this stage, the ego has developed self-consciousness, and has formed a sense of identity. The ego is leaving the Self but is still connected through an ego-Self axis. This stage occurs, for most people, during middle age.[669]

On the right of Figure 2, we see a model of the third and final stage. Here the ego has completely formed as a separate system and the ego-Self axis is at a maximum. Edinger acknowledges that this relationship "is an ideal theoretical limit which probably does not exist in actuality."[670] The sense of separation of the ego from the Self is completely conscious here, and the ego usually views the Self as something entirely different from itself, something bigger that the ego is part of and connected to. The goal of individuation, during the second half of life, is for the ego to assimilate to the Self and come to terms with it in a cooperative way.

The basic connection between ego and self is of crucial importance for both ego and self; ego cannot exist without the support of the self, and the self needs the ego to *realize* or *actualize* itself. This connection is depicted in the diagrams by the line connecting the center of the ego with the center of the self and labeled ego-self axis. This axis is the gateway or path of communication between the conscious personality and the collective psyche, a connection that must be relatively intact if the ego is to survive stress and grow. Damage to the ego-self axis impairs or destroys the connection between conscious and unconscious, leading to alienation of the ego from its origin and foundation.[671]

Paradoxically, healthy dialogue and cooperation along this axis leads to both greater separation and greater intimacy in the ego-self relationship.[672] We will explore this seeming paradox through a careful evaluation of ego boundaries.

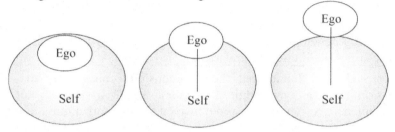

Figure 2: The Ego–Self Axis

The ego early in life has no boundaries; it experiences everything as self. The process of evolving an ego separate from self in order to establish the ego-self axis requires the ego to create boundaries.

Ego boundaries describe the demarcation between a person and his or her external environment, or between various internal aspects of psychic experience, i.e., the boundary between any two entities or processes in the mind (e.g., thoughts, feelings, perceptions). The ego boundary concept has also been used as a means of conceptualizing altered ego states[673], creativity[674], and dreams[675].

For some people external ego boundaries may be so constricted and rigid as to allow in almost no life experiences or contacts that are new, different, unusual, or potentially threatening. Examples of this kind of rigid ego boundary can be seen in individuals who are habitually close-minded, autocratic, self-centered, and fixed firmly in their ways. But in healthy people, ego boundaries are flexibly adaptive; that is, the boundaries can be permeable and open up to allow in new experiences, or they can close up and stand firm to keep threatening experiences out. Unlike individuals with constricted ego boundaries, those with flexible ego boundaries tend to be more open-minded, democratic, relational, and situationally adaptive. People with this kind of flexibility tend to resemble Rogers'[676] fully functioning person or Maslow's[677] self-actualizing individual.[678]

The same dynamics apply to internal ego boundaries, so that at one end of the spectrum people compartmentalize thoughts and feelings, keeping them separated and distinct from one another. Ernest Hartmann refers to these ego boundaries as 'thick'.[679] Boundaries that are 'thin' allow different mental processes to be connected, to overlap, and to blend. Hartmann recently developed the Boundary Questionnaire which measures the structure of one's boundaries.

> He has found that these dimensions consistently dis-criminate among adult behaviors along a number of dimensions, ranging from defensiveness, hypnotizability, and fantasy proneness, as well as to the ability to recall dreams and the tendency to experience frequent nightmares. In numerous studies, females consistently score significantly thinner ego boundaries than males.

A clear relationship exists between one's boundary dimensions and one's dream content and structure, because the dream is a thin internal boundary state in which memories, thoughts, affects, and images are frequently combined. Adults and adolescents with thin boundaries, in contrast to thick boundary individuals, report a higher rate of dream recall and a greater tendency to be affected by their dreams during waking hours.[680] Certain psychic boundaries separate dream mentation from waking thought, i.e., in order to recall a dream, one must transfer the dream material across the boundaries which separate the dream state from the waking state. Thin boundaries may provide relatively easy transfer, facilitating dream recall, while thicker boundaries may impede dream recall by walling off material from consciousness, thereby hindering the transfer of information.

There is a clear developmental pattern to the dynamics of ego boundaries. In adolescence, there is an almost universal thick boundary between the young person and the external world. In other words, adolescents erect thick boundaries between themselves and the world, regardless of the nature of their internal ego boundaries. Hamachek[681] suggests that during this time, the adolescent's sense of cohesion and stability is threatened by the frequent occurrence of bizarre emotions, turbulent moods, and by the overall effects of 'psychic restructuring'[682] due to enduring periods marked by self-consciousness and fragmentation[683]. In response, the adolescent ego may attempt to safeguard its cohesiveness and continuity through the construction of defensive boundaries which separate the self from the world.[684]

Hamachek offers examples of this thickening of external boundaries: behaviors which shield the adolescent from his or her environment, such as the adolescent listening to extremely loud music, undergoing periods of extreme introspection or sullenness, or engaging in bizarre or deviant behavior which separate him or her from society at large.[685] Yet, unlike the almost universally thick external boundaries, internal ego boundaries do in fact vary among adolescents so that, for example, the ability to recall dreams varies as it does with adults.

In time, the defensive outer boundaries for some become less rigid as the ego develops the capacity to better regulate instinctual drives, whereas with other adolescents they may remain relatively rigid.

Ego Development on the Road to Transcendent Actualization

The concept of transcendent actualization was introduced in transpersonal psychology by Maslow, who viewed it as an optimal way to give spiritual meaning to one's life and to live this meaning in everyday life.[686] *Transcendent actualization* refers to a self-realization founded on an awareness and experience of a Spiritual Center, also called the Inner Being or the Self, the source of our highest tendencies, such as altruistic awareness, will, and love.[687] This is represented by Edinger's third and final stage in the evolution of the ego-Self axis in which the ego views the Self as something bigger and wiser that the ego is part of and connected to.

Transcendent actualization is defined as a developmental process whereby individuals (the I) commit themselves to living in harmony with their Inner Being (the Self). To achieve this harmony, they must expand their unitive consciousness of beings and events and realize the unifying values of Being in their daily lives (Metamotivation; Hamel, 1997). This is what is meant by the actualization of the Self, the fundamental prelude to which is integrating and transcending the fears and desires of the ego (Desjardins, 1972; Firman, 1993).[688]

> That is why in order to actualize the Self, a fundamental change is required in the person's identification; he/she must transcend identification with the ego. In other words, transpersonal growth is required.

The ego – a synonym for the 'personal me' – cannot directly access the Self because it lives in the belief that its own private thoughts, sensations, and emotions, accurately reflect reality, oblivious to the self-induced illusion it creates and promotes.[689]

Transpersonal growth refers to the intrapsychic relationships characterized by "(a) nonordinary or objective consciousness or metacognition: an acute awareness of beings and events based on spiritual intuitions, ethical considerations, inspirations, and higher order feelings; and (b) metamotivation: motivation based on the unification of the dualities of the personality and the realization of profound or spiritual values."[690] Transpersonal identity consists in living in touch with the Self, that is, a source of love, wisdom, and creative inspiration within the individual, according to Assagioli.[691]

In transcendent actualization, the objective is no longer growth of the ego, but rather the realization of the Self, the most authentic core of the person. The Self represents the totality of the psyche, it encompasses conscious and unconscious, personal and collective. This brings us into an awareness and the potential for dialogue with the *imaginal* realm, what Jung refers to as the *psychoidal* level of the unconscious. This level of encounter is most difficult to engage because it so deeply challenges the ego's positions of control and authority.

The psychoid has to do with a realm of experience of deep regression and primary process, where the capacity to distinguish inner and outer, subject and object, fantasy and reality is blurred; the realm of paradox. Here we meet the instinctual, animal, primordial within – the archetypes that *animate* us. Try as we might, we cannot force the pre-verbal, pre-cognitive into the rational and conceptual. We must accept it as *precognition*, for in this timeless realm past and future are also irrelevant.

Marie-Louise Von Franz, a close associate of Jung's, uses an apt metaphor for the challenge of bringing contents of the psychoidal unconscious into conscious awareness. She is referring to an individual's inferior function, his/her least developed and most unconscious capacity. The metaphor applies to any contents of the deep unconscious.

A mistake some people make is that they think they can pull up the inferior function onto the level of the other conscious functions. . . . It is absolutely impossible to pull up – like a fisherman with his rod – the inferior function. . . . Trying to fish it up would be like trying to bring up the whole collective unconscious, which is something one just cannot do. The fish will be too big for the rod. So what does one do? Cut it off again? This is regression. But if you don't give in, there is only the other alternative – the fish will pull you into the water! At this moment comes the great conflict . . . It is having the humility to go down with one's other functions onto that lower level. This, then, produces a stage between the two layers at about the level where everything is neither thinking nor feeling nor sensation nor intuition. Something new comes up, namely a completely different and new attitude towards life in which one uses all and none of the functions all the time.[692]

> The World of Spirit is inhabited by all the beings and natural forces that cannot be seen in our human world. This is the Great Collective. They exist independently of any individual, and indeed of humanity itself. Yet they require interaction with humans in order to fulfill their purpose, which is to evolve and develop fully. In order to interact, these great forces must cross the barrier between realms; they incarnate in a physical form, becoming embodied as a dream element, a vision, a visible form in nature, a somatic sensation or disease symptom. They use the power of imagination to cross over.

In this encounter, the Self is vulnerable and needs to be protected by the ego. The transcended ego attends to the Self, willingly undergoing the personal risks of *dis*embodying and allowing itself to become *dis*enchanted by the physical world. The ego must be strong enough to withstand (1) internal uncertainty and sabotage by an autonomous complex or shadow which is destructive to both the ego and the vulnerable Self, and (2) external judgments or hostile influences from others in one's life, also destructive to the vulnerable Self.

The World of Humanity exists independently of the Great Collective. Yet we require interaction with these great forces in order to fulfill our purpose, which is to evolve and develop fully. In order to interact, we must cross the barrier between realms; we *dis*embody, using the power of imagination to cross over.

These two worlds meet in the liminal realm of transcendent actualization, combining aspects of both the psychoid and the psyche. If the ego is not engaged in collaboration, and identifies with or "claims as its own" the images and drives that emerge from the unconscious, it will be overpowered and incapable of working with them. However, as the ego attends to the inner figure *without* identifying with it, a collaboration of equals occurs. Jeffrey Raff describes that potential collaboration:

> The ego and the principle of consciousness it represents have gotten closer to the inner world of instinct and freedom. The ego has left behind a great many of its previous rules and laws, and moved closer to the spontaneous capacity to follow inner feelings and hunches. It has abandoned many of its previous positions to take into account the advice of inner figures of all kinds, and in its new freedom, has become more wild, and less domesticated. It has added some of the unpredictability of the unconscious, and moved closer to its own inner nature. At the same time, the unconscious has moved closer to the world of consciousness by casting off its chaos and confusion, and by allowing a certain level of harmony and order to affect it.[693]

In this mutual encounter, the ego is protected by the Self who has become a friend and confidant, an inner partner who exerts immense energy to encourage and support the ego's quest, allowing one to take sobering risks and to face defeat courageously or victory graciously. The Self may provide a timely insight or inspiration, or arrange a synchronicity that magically opens a needed doorway.

When the ego aligns with the Self, an integration of the spiritual life is activated, following two modes identified by Assagioli: a descending or an ascending movement.[694] The descending movement occurs by chance or grace, e.g., as in the case of creative genius, spiritual intuition, inspiration, sudden illumination, or the impulse to do a humanitarian or heroic act.

To initiate the ascending movement, however, requires initiative on the part of the ego. An active, deliberate process must be set in motion by the conscious actualized ego, seeking partnership with the Self to reach transcendent actualization. Through appropriate psychospiritual preparation, expanding self-knowledge, and developing internal strengths, the actualized ego demonstrates concentration, tranquility, equanimity (receptivity), energy and exploration (proactivity).

> Both modes, descending and ascending, are essential to transcendent actualization. Activating spiritual practice is aimed either at accessing transcendent realities ('ascent' paths) or at bringing spiritual energies down to earth to transfigure human nature ('descent' paths). Of course, this either/or understanding ignores the existence of a synthesis — immanent transcendence, embodied spirituality, or transcendent actualization.

Taitetsu Unno, one of the world's preeminent scholars of Shin Buddhism, discusses this seeming paradox

> The ideal of monastic Buddhism is transcendence of mundane existence, as if one were ascending to the mountaintop. In contrast, the praxis of Pure Land Buddhism takes place by descending into the valley, the shadow of the mountains. We find a similar contrast in Chinese civilization. Like monastic Buddhism, the Confucian ideal may be symbolized by the soaring mountain peaks, manifesting the highest achievements of the literati. And like the Pure Land, Taoism is found in the valley and lowlands, a haven for those who do not fit into conventional society for whatever reason. But it is in this valley that life and creativity flourish. In the words of the *Tao te ching*:
>
> > *The Valley Spirit never dies.*
> > *It is named the Mysterious Female.*
> > *And the Doorway of the mysterious Female*
> > *Is the base from which Heaven and Earth sprang.*
> > *It is there within us all the while;*
> > *Draw upon it as you will, it never runs dry.*
>
> In the valley fecundity is nourished and dynamic creativity is born. From its depth comes the life force that creates Heaven

> and Earth, immortalized as the Spirit of the Valley and
> identified with the feminine principle; its procreative vitality is
> inexhaustible. . . .
>
> The obstacles encountered are different from those
> encountered pursuing monastic disciplines on the Path of
> Sages because one must struggle with oneself in the midst of
> all kinds of entanglements in society.[695]

The same principle applies to the psychological realm; transcendent or transpersonal methodologies ('ascent' paths of Jungian work, subtle energy, soul work) or immanent body-centered and nature-centered modalities ('descent' paths of bioenergetics, Reichian work, breathwork, shamanic work). And the synthesis is immanent transcendence (mindfulness and bodyfulness) or transcendent actualization, which embodies the Hebrew concept *daveq u-meyuhady* meaning "united or connected and at the same time separate." Resolving the tension between any two apparent opposites means transcending the dichotomy while blending both on a higher level of synthesis. Two vital keys are clear regarding how one achieves such resolution: one is to recognize that opposites contain the seed of each other within, and the second is to withstand the tension of the opposites, without surrendering to one or the other, long enough to achieve synthesis.

Individuals approaching transcendent actualization "open themselves up to a higher level of experience, beyond the scope of what the ego can provide. Instead of being centered on themselves and the contents of their ego (their sensory, mental, and emotional experiences), they are turned toward the Self and its contents (spiritual intuitions, inspirations, altruistic impulses, ethical considerations)."[696] Hamel et al. elaborate on the qualities of one who is engaged in transcendent actualization:

The Four Components of Transcendent Actualization[697]

1. **In-Depth Perception.** Related to the Inner Being or Self, this first component of transcendent actualization denotes the ability to discern and explore the different aspects of one's life and life in general, going beyond appearances. Its fundamental property is discernment. The receptivity of the transcended ego to the Self is characterized by a vigilant attention, a deep knowledge of its personal

resources and boundaries, a meaningful knowledge of the reality facilitated by viewing the object from different angles, and a perception of realities that ordinary consciousness cannot perceive but that are common in contemplation.

2. **Holistic Perception.** Related to the Inner Being or Self, this second component of transcendent actualization denotes the ability to perceive one's life and life in general from a viewpoint independent of habitual attachments. Its fundamental property is detachment. The actualizing ego is open to the promptings of the Self, and to a global integrative vision of the essential core of reality independent of fears, desires, and beliefs.

3. **Presence of Being.** Related to the Inner Being or Self, this third component of transcendent actualization denotes the ability of one's personality to live in harmony with the Self. Its fundamental property is creative will. The ego moving toward the Self is characterized by an inner search of knowing how *to be* rather than only how *to do* and *to have*.

4. **Beyond Ego-Orientation.** Related to the Inner Being or Self, this fourth component of transcendent actualization denotes the ability to leave one's personal preoccupations behind to focus on others, a mission, an altruistic goal. Its fundamental property is the realization of profound spiritual values (such as love, goodness, courage, mutual support, honesty). The person proactively transcends one's egocentric boundaries, avoids continued self-preoccupation, and feels a sense of belonging to a greater whole than oneself. This generates feelings of humanity, the sacred, gratitude, humility, admiration, faith, and hope.

The 'Ultimate'

Jung commented on a state he referred to as 'the ultimate'. Jung's reference is in *Memories, Dreams, Reflections*, when he is describing his experiences following the break up with Freud. He wrote, "Only gradually did I discover what the mandala really is: 'Formations, Transformations, Eternal Mind's eternal recreation' . . . In them I saw the self—that is my whole being—actively at work. . . [in them]. I had attained what was for me the 'ultimate'."[698]

Fordham's comment on 'the ultimate':

. . . a reflection on 'the ultimate'. I take it to represent a state in which there is no past and no future, though it is present like a point which has position but no magnitude. It has no desires, no memory, no thoughts, no images but out of it by transformation all of these can deintegrate. There is no consciousness so no unconscious—it is a pregnant absence.[699]

> The 'ultimate' refers to mystic states, which both Jung and Fordham studied. Fordham refers to a phenomenon-less state, a "pregnant absence", which presents a contrast to Jung's idea of the 'ultimate'. For Jung, the 'ultimate' is the individuated self experienced as a unity that transcends the multiplicity of internal 'subjects' observing internal 'objects'. For Fordham, the 'ultimate' is the primary self, which precedes but contains the potential for and predisposition to develop a multiplicity of objects and relationships with them.

Collective Transcendence and Evolution

Just as individuals develop to higher levels of mastery, so too can groups, cultures, societies and civilizations. Indeed, one of the known catalysts for individual development is participation in a like-minded, mutually challenging group. Just as individual development to elite levels requires identifying self-limiting beliefs and unconscious behavior patterns, so too does group development. And just as individual development requires identifying and employing internal resources, so too does group development.

Cultural complexes can be defined as emotionally charged aggregates of ideas and images that tend to cluster around an archetypal core and are shared by individuals within an identified collective. Thomas Singer, a Jungian analyst, suggests that even cultural complexes can be healed.

> Describing deeply entrenched cultural complexes is a bit like trying to diagnose an illness of the collective psyche. And, it seems as though describing the illness leads to an automatic question—what is the cure? The standard Jungian answer to the cure for a complex is that one has to drink it to its dregs; one has to suffer it repeatedly until finally its toxic effects are digested and transformed in some alchemy of the psyche. . . .

Gandhi, Martin Luther King, Desmond Tutu come to mind as being the kind of leaders who have embodied a transcendent spirit for the collective psyche that leads to the vision of a real cure of cultural conflicts. . . . Some gifted individuals may have the ability to experience consciously the cultural complexes that divide groups into warring factions. They have the capacity to hold these cultural complexes in their psyche in such a way that an authentic experience of the transcendent comes alive in them, pointing to a resolution of otherwise intractable, emotional group conflicts. They actually carry the transcendent function for the group, with its potential for healing at the level of the collective psyche.[700]

Just as cultures and civilizations develop to higher levels of mastery, so too does the human species. Evolution of transcendent consciousness on earth was foreseen by Sri Aurobindo many years ago. Observing the relentless progressive increase in sentient awareness (consciousness) from unicellular organisms to human beings, Aurobindo argues that evolution is not done. It follows that human intelligence is not the highest possible manifestation of consciousness on earth. Aurobindo coined the term "supermind" to describe the next, higher level of consciousness that he believes will manifest on earth— first and partially, in human beings as far as human nature permits, but later and fully, through a biologically transformed life form that will exceed the human being in the capacity for consciousness as far as human beings currently exceed other animals.

Chapter Thirteen

The Oxherder Series

We have used modern Western language to describe adult development beyond conventional levels, transcending even the stage of actualization to what we are calling ego surrender. Many cultures across the expanse of history have represented such wisdom in their own colloquial language: Egyptians, Sufis, Kabbalists, Vedic scholars, Christian mystics, medieval alchemists, Native Americans, Tibetan and Chinese and Japanese monks, and so many others.

The Ten Ox-herding Pictures describe the path to self-development and enlightenment in the Zen tradition, a school of Buddhism that emphasizes the practice of meditation as the key to awakening one's true mind, Buddha-nature, and uncovering one's innate wisdom and compassion.

The pictures are the representation in folk images of practices for training the mind. They depict a young ox-herder, a novice practitioner, searching for and taming an ox, the original mind that the practitioner is trying to find.

The author of these "Ten Oxherding Pictures" is said to be a Zen master of the Sung Dynasty known as Kaku-an Shi-en belonging to the Rinzai school. The ten pictures are variations on the Kaku-an tradition, and the accompanying verses are by Pu-ming, translated into English.

The famous Zen master Dogen expressed the underlying simple truth succinctly:

The way of Buddha
is to know yourself,
To know yourself
is to forget yourself,
To forget yourself
is to be enlightened by all things.

1. Searching for the ox

In this first picture, the young ox-herder is in the wild running around aimlessly, lost in desire for gain and fear of loss, and in ideas of right and wrong. It is not the ox that is lost, it is the ox-herder. We, too, are anxiously looking for inner peace. The ox-herder is meditating for the first time in searching for his Buddhahood. We all have the innate Buddha-nature, indicating the potential to manifest our highest potential.

Alone in the wilderness, lost in the jungle, the boy is searching, searching!
The swelling waters, the far-away mountains, and the unending path;
Exhausted and in despair, he knows not where to go,
He only hears the evening cicadas singing in the maple-woods.

2. Seeing the tracks

The ox-herder finally sees some footprints. Here the practitioner is catching a glimpse of his original mind or innate Buddhahood. He has come to understand that the objective world is a reflection of the Self. Yet, he is unable to distinguish what is good from what is not, his mind is still confused as to truth and falsehood. He has not yet entered the gate.

By the stream and under the trees, scattered are the traces of the lost;
The sweet-scented grasses are growing thick--did he find the way?
However remote over the hills and far away the beast may wander,
His nose reaches the heavens and none can conceal it.

3. Seeing the ox

As the boy follows the tracks of the ox, he finally sees the ox half-hidden among the trees. The ox-herder is now manifestly present, his senses attuned to the search. This shows that if the practitioner studies and practices hard, he will find his true mind; he will find that it is no other than himself. One week we visit a temple, another week we talk with a teacher. We continue to read books to find a good way to practice.

On a yonder branch perches a nightingale cheerfully singing;
The sun is warm, and a soothing breeze blows, on the bank the willows are green;
The ox is there all by himself, nowhere is he to hide himself;
The splendid head decorated with stately horns what painter can reproduce him?

4. Catching the ox

The boy is trying hard to catch the wild ox with a rope. But the ox is unruly and does not want to be caught. The boy has to hang on tightly as the ox jumps fiercely and drags him around. Similarly, even though the practitioner has now had a glimpse of his true nature, he has not yet severed all delusions from his mind. It is a tough struggle to pacify all his wild thoughts.

With the energy of his whole being, the boy has at last taken hold of the ox:
But how wild his will, how ungovernable his power!
At times he struts up a plateau,
When lo! he is lost again in a misty unpenetrable mountain-pass.

5. Tending the ox

The boy is gently tending the ox and the ox is not wild any more. However, he is still holding on to the rope loosely because he knows that although the fight is over, he must remain vigilant. There is an endless train of thoughts cascading through the self-deceiving mind. Even if one makes great progress, one must continue to practice hard.

The boy is not to separate himself with his whip and tether,
Lest the animal should wander away into a world of defilements;
When the ox is properly tended to, he will grow pure and docile;
Without a chain, nothing binding, he will by himself follow the oxherd.

6. Riding the ox back home

The struggle is over; the boy is no more concerned with gain and loss. ox-herder is sitting leisurely on the ox playing the flute. Riding the trained ox, his eyes fixed on things not of the earth, the boy happily comes back home. If the practitioner controls his mind he will return to his true, original mind.

Riding on the animal, he leisurely wends his way home:
Enveloped in the evening mist, how tunefully the flute vanishes away!
Singing a ditty, beating time, his heart is filled with a joy indescribable!
That he is now one of those who know, need it be told?

7. The ox forgotten, the ox-herder rests alone

The ox has disappeared and the ox-herder is resting at home. After the boy returns home he sits alone forgetting about the ox. He is at peace with his mind, body and heart. When you know that what you need is not the snare or fishing net but the hare or fish, it is like gold separated from the dross. This means that even though the practitioner reaches a certain level of enlightenment, he should keep on practicing without rest.

Riding on the animal, he is at last back in his home,
Where lo! the ox is no more; the man alone sits serenely.
Though the red sun is high up in the sky, he is still quietly dreaming,
Under a straw-thatched roof are his whip and rope idly lying.

8. Both the ox and ox-herder are forgotten

Now the ox-herder and the ox are both gone. All confusion is set aside, and serenity alone prevails; even the idea of holiness is irrelevant. There is only an empty circle, representing the "emptiness" of interdependence and deep connection to the world. Emptiness is not a vacuum, a black hole, but rather the possibility of endless transformation. We are a flow of conditions; we do not have a solid, separate identity. Through complete emptiness the boy attains a state of enlightenment.

All is empty-the whip, the rope, the man, and the ox:
Who can ever survey the vastness of heaven?
Over the furnace burning ablaze, not a flake of snow can fall:
When this state of things obtains, manifest is the spirit of the ancient master.

9. Returning to the Origin

Now there is no ox and no boy, only the beautiful scene of the original, clear mind. Our life is ordinary and just as it is, but we look at it differently. We realize that everything expresses the truth of life and awareness, and is talking to us. The waters are blue, the mountains are green; sitting alone, he observes things undergoing changes.

To return to the Origin, to be back at the Source--already a false step this!
Far better it is to stay at home, blind and deaf, and without much ado;
Sitting in the hut, he takes no cognisance of things outside,
Behold the streams flowing-whither nobody knows; and the flowers vividly red-for whom are they?

10. Entering the marketplace with bliss-bestowing hands

The ox-herder, after years of practice, returns from the mountain to the village. We find spirituality everywhere; it is not confined to monasteries and secluded places. This last stage represents freedom, wisdom and compassion. The ox-herder goes to teach what he has realized to all sentient beings: that things and people are not as solid as or as separate as we think they are. So we have to learn to see things as they really are.

Bare-chested and bare-footed, he comes out into the market-place;
Daubed with mud and ashes, how broadly he smiles!
There is no need for the miraculous power of the gods,
For he touches, and lo! the dead trees are in full bloom.

Appendix

Glossary of Terms

Active imagination – The technique developed by Carl Jung to replace Freud's free association to access the unconscious. It is a method for exploring the meaning of dreams, but is also a way to explore the unconscious through non-dream imagination. Dreams and active imagination are dialogues that you enter into with the different parts of yourself that live in the unconscious.

Altered States of Consciousness – or non-ordinary states – A state of consciousness different from the ordinary states of waking, dreaming, and dreamless sleep. One's state of consciousness can be altered through substances (alcohol, drugs, anesthetics), accidents (head injuries), disease (dementia, psychosis), or intentional induction (meditation, hypnosis).

Analytical psychology – Analytical psychology is Swiss psychiatrist Carl Jung's term for his school of psychology, which presaged the development of transpersonal psychology. Analytical psychology emphasizes the primary importance of the individual psyche; a personal and a collective unconscious; inner aspects of the feminine (anima) and masculine (animus) in all people, men and women; categories or types of orientation (thinking, feeling, sensation, intuition) and attitude (introvert and extravert); and the personal quest for wholeness that is termed individuation.

Archetype – Jung's term for structuring patterns of experience within the collective unconscious, an inherited idea or mode of thought that is derived from the experience of the race and is present in the unconscious of the individual.

Authenticity – The quality of being genuine, not false or imitation; true to one's own personality, spirit, character, or essence.

Bardo – Tibetan word for the intermediate state between any two states, especially between one life and the next incarnation, but also between a stimulus and the response to it. Becoming aware of the interim creates an opportunity to make conscious choice rather than allowing conditioned or habitual reactions to take over.

Bioenergetic analysis or Bioenergetics – a system of physical and psychological therapy that increases well-being by releasing blocked physical and psychic energy, developed by Alexander Lowen and rooted in the work of Wilhelm Reich. Bioenergetic Analysis helps to release chronic muscular tensions, manage affects, expand the capacity for intimacy, heal sexual difficulties and learn new, more fulfilling ways of relating to others.

Character armor – Wilhelm Reich originated the concept of a person's somatic guarding against psychological threat to one's sense of self, exhibited in consistent reactive responses, tailored to promote a false sense of self, and born out of childhood rejection or trauma. It is manifested through muscular armoring, the chronic physiological manifestation of ego anxieties and emotional inflexibility.

Consciousness – On the simplest level, the state of being awake and aware of one's surroundings. A sense of one's personal or collective identity, including the attitudes, beliefs, and sensitivities held by or considered characteristic of an individual. Being conscious usually entails having a sense of selfhood, being the one who experiences: I may not know *who* I am, but I know *that* I am.

Cultural complex – Just as individuals have complexes, so too do groups, cultures, societies and civilizations. A cultural complex can be defined as an emotionally charged aggregate of ideas and images that tend to cluster around an archetypal core and are shared by individuals within an identified collective. They can be inspiringly positive or destructively negative; just look at the best and worst of group behavior throughout history and across cultures.

Depth psychology – Historically, the term depth psychology was coined by Eugen Bleuler to refer to psychoanalytic approaches to therapy and research that take the unconscious into account. More recently, depth psychology refers to approaches to therapy that are open to the exploration of the subtle, unconscious, and transpersonal aspects of human experience. A depth approach may involve the study and exploration of dreams, complexes, and archetypes. Depth psychology is non-pathologizing and strength affirming.

Ego – Ego is the part of the mind that mediates between the person and external reality (reality testing), and between one's own conscious and unconscious (a sense of personal identity). In the Freudian structural model of the human psyche, the ego is the organized, realistic part that mediates between the desires of the id (instinctual drives) and the moral dictates of the super-ego (socialized conscience).

Ego-self axis – In Jung's psychology, a maintained connection between the ego and the larger reality of the Self. The ego-self axis is the vital living connecting *link* between ego and self that ensures the integrity of the ego and the protection of the Self. The self is the ego's origin and source of energy and stability, the container for the ego's personal sense of selfhood.

Ego-self identity – The connection between ego and self is, in early phases of development, unconscious and enmeshed. A fetus or an infant has no ego boundary, and experiences everything as itself, i.e., the baby *identifies with* everything it encounters, including objects, emotions, and dream imagery. The ego (experiencer) and self (container for experiencing) are experienced by the ego as one.

Ego-self separation – The process of maturation is one of gradual separation of the ego's sense of identity with self, as it establishes boundaries to define what is 'me' and what is not 'me'. Ego-self separation ideally leads to a progressive reduction of ego-self identity, necessary for the child's socialization, without damage to the ego-self axis. When separation goes too far it becomes alienation, or when separation does not occur at all it becomes ego inflation, and either extreme causes damage to the ego-self axis. This leads to a developmental arrest or hindrance of growth, and requires repair through supportive corrective experiences. Eventually, perhaps in mid-life or later, one brings the ego-self axis to consciousness and begins a transpersonal rapprochement.

Existential psychology – Existential psychologists believe that it's not only important to identify and reduce the symptomatology of mental illnesses, addictions, relationship issues, and other psychological issues, but to go beyond the symptoms, addressing how a person defines *meaning*, purpose, and a life well lived. Existential psychology combines the big questions of philosophy with the tenets of psychology, exploring how individuals live out their day-to-day lives within the context of these enigmas. Existential psychology is one of the basic foundations of transpersonal psychology.

Flow experience – Term devised by Mihaly Csikszentmihalyi for experiences in which the person is totally involved in an activity, is fully immersed in a feeling of energized focus, full involvement, and enjoyment in the process of the activity.

Fourth Way tradition – Georges Gurdjieff's Work is to develop our capacity to exercise free will in the way we live life. Most people are 'asleep' in ego illusion, Gurdjieff warned, and his mission was to provide ways to assist people to 'wake up' from that unconscious slumber. It combines what Gurdjieff saw as three established traditional 'ways' or schools of self-development, those of the mind, emotions and body, or of yogis, monks and fakirs respectively.

Gestalt psychology – The term Gestalt may be defined as an object, idea, or experience being more than the sum of its parts. Gestalt therapy is a psychotherapeutic approach developed by Fritz Perls (1893–1970). It focuses on insight into gestalt patterns in patients and their relations to the world, focuses on here-and-now experience rather than on the past, and often uses role-playing and experimenting with new behaviors to aid the resolution of past conflicts. Gestalt therapy is a foundational contribution to transpersonal therapy.

Higher unconscious or superconscious – Roberto Assagioli's term for the realm of the unconscious that is the source of spiritual experience. The contents of the higher unconscious are not easily accessible to conscious awareness, and normally remain only potentially conscious. However, that realm is glimpsed in creative inspiration, spiritual insight, and peak experiences. To the extent that this domain of our psyche is repressed, along with its companion realm the lower unconscious, we are much less able to engage the heights and depths, the agonies and ecstasies, the joys and sorrows, of human existence.

Holotropic – Term devised by Stan Grof meaning *oriented toward wholeness* or *moving toward wholeness*, in the same way that *heliotropism* refers to the property of plants to always move in the direction of the sun. The concept also carries the implication of the whole being contained in each of its parts.

Horizontal path – A route to transpersonal development that involves an expansion of our sense of self outward into the wider world. This involves our senses, engages our bodies, and draws us into relationship with the environment and with other living beings. See vertical path.

Humanistic psychology – an approach to psychology that emphasizes feelings and emotions, an emphasis on the whole person, a recognition that the therapist's positive regard for the client is instrumental in affecting change, and that better understanding of oneself comes through observation of oneself. Humanistic psychology was developed in reaction to psychoanalysis and behaviorism, the dominant psychologies of the first half of the 20th century. Transpersonal psychology grew from the seed of humanistic psychology, adding spiritual and subtle energy dimensions.

Hypnotherapy – Hypnotherapy is a form of psychotherapy used to create subconscious change in a client in the form of new responses, thoughts, attitudes, behaviors or feelings. It is undertaken with a subject in a hypnotic trance. The trance state allows the conscious ego to relax its customary defenses and limited thinking, and to open access to deeper levels of creativity, expanded memory, somatic awareness, and contact with inner core resources. Hypnotherapy is differentiated from hypnosis, which is the simple technique of inducing an individual into a suggestible trance state.

Idealized self – A false self system based on the introjection of others' standards and expectations, and unconsciously intended to defend against the reality of the inevitability of suffering in this world. The idealized self-image is always smart, attractive, popular, good, and above all happy. And so you are convinced from a very early age that if you try hard enough, one day you will become that self. However, the idealized self is an illusion, and only distracts you from devoting your energies to nurturing and accepting the real self.

Immanence – The experience of being fully present in the physical world, whether human or divine. Immanence suggests that the spiritual world permeates the mundane, that the divine encompasses or is manifested in the material world. Immanence is often contrasted with transcendence, in which energy is used to move outside of and beyond the physical world.

Individuation – Jung's term for the process of psychological integration that leads toward realization of the archetype of the Self. It is a developmental process of transformation whereby the personal and collective unconscious are brought into consciousness to be assimilated into the whole personality. It is the development of the psychological individual as a being distinct from the general, collective psychology.

Integral psychology – The psychological system taught by Sri Aurobindo, and later elaborated by Ken Wilber. The goal of an integral psychology is to honor and embrace every legitimate aspect of human consciousness, psychology, and therapy. Wilber's psychological model includes waves of development, streams of development, states of consciousness, and the self, and follows the course of each from subconscious to self-conscious to superconscious.

Introjection – The process in which an individual replicates in himself behaviors, attributes or other fragments of the surrounding world, especially of other people. It is the opposite psychical process from projection, i.e., unconsciously placing out onto the world an internally held belief or attribute. For example, a parent may project onto her daughter the ambition to be a ballerina, and the daughter may introject her mother's desire.

Kundalini – In Yoga and Tantra, a vital energy that resides at the base of the spinal column and can be aroused and channeled up through the chakras, leading eventually to spiritual enlightenment. Kundalini is the primordial energy component of the esoteric subtle body, which consists of *nadis* (energy channels), *chakras* (psychic centers), and *prana* (subtle energy). Kundalini energy can be aroused intentionally through meditation and asana yoga practice. It can also erupt spontaneously, and can be a disorienting surprise, called spiritual emergency by Stan and Christina Grof.

Liminal – Liminality refers to occupying a place in between, e.g., between conscious and unconscious or between an awake state and sleep, or occupying a position at, or on both sides of, a boundary or threshold. It is outside of time, nonlinear. It can also refer in anthropology to the quality of ambiguity or disorientation that occurs in the middle stage of rituals, when participants no longer hold their pre-ritual status but have not yet begun the transition to the status they will hold when the ritual is complete.

Lower unconscious – Roberto Assagioli's term for the realm of the unconscious that is the (Freudian) unconscious of primitive impulses, repressed ideation, and emotionally charged complexes, the realm of our early wounding. The contents of the lower unconscious are not easily accessible to conscious awareness, and normally remain only potentially conscious. However, that realm is glimpsed in dreams, indulging compulsive or addictive impulses, . To the extent that this domain of our psyche is repressed, along with its companion realm the higher unconscious, we are much less able to engage the heights and depths, the agonies and ecstasies, the joys and sorrows, of human existence.

Lucid dreaming – A lucid dream is any dream in which one is aware that one is dreaming and not in the state of consensus reality, even though the experience may seem realistic and vivid. Lucid dreaming is a form of conscious mental processing, observable through increased amounts of activity in the brain's parietal lobes, absent during REM and non-REM sleep.

Middle unconscious – Roberto Assagioli's term for the realm of the unconscious that is the area of the personality in which we integrate the experiences, learnings, gifts, and skills which form the foundation of our conscious expression in the world. It forms the infrastructure of our conscious life. Without a place to store and retrieve all the procedural memories necessary for everyday living, our awareness would be so filled with the many individual elements that we could not express a larger pattern. We could not walk if we were thinking of all the individual movements, nor speak a language when constantly preoccupied with the rules of grammar. This same process operates to build up complete identity systems within the personality called subpersonalities.

Mystical experience – Direct experience of a transcendent reality or divinity or realities beyond perceptual or intellectual apprehension that are directly accessible by subjective experience. There are seven accepted characteristics of mystical experiences[701]: 1) ineffability (inability to capture the experience in ordinary language), 2) noetic quality (the notion that mystical experiences reveal an otherwise hidden or inaccessible knowledge), 3) transiency (the simple fact that mystical experiences last for a relatively brief period of time), 4) passivity (the sense that mystical experiences happen to someone; that they are somehow beyond the range of human volition and control), 5) unity of opposites (a sense of Oneness, Wholeness or Completeness), 6) timelessness (a sense that mystical experiences transcend time), and 7) a feeling that one has somehow encountered "the true self" (a sense that mystical experiences reveal the nature of our true, cosmic self: one that is beyond life and death, beyond difference and duality, and beyond ego and selfishness).

Narrative dimensions of knowing – Bruner, a cognitive psychologist, articulated the distinction between the narrative and the paradigmatic (or abstract) dimensions of knowing. The narrative mode tells a specific story, is based on the spatial and temporal location of an experience, placing it in the qualifying set and setting, and is therefore context-rich. See paradigmatic (or abstract) dimensions of knowing.

Near-death experiences – Near-death experiences (NDE) are a personal experience associated with impending death, encompassing multiple sensations possibly including detachment from the body, feelings of levitation, total serenity, security, warmth, the experience of absolute dissolution, and the presence of a transcendent light. NDE is considered an altered state of consciousness, and is thought to be highly relevant to the study of survival after physical death.

Nondual – Nonduality is a state of consciousness or being in which there is no awareness of the distinction between subject and object, or self and other. It is a sense of "nonseparation", the sense that all things are interconnected and not separate, while at the same time all things retain their individuality. There are no opposites, only relationships.

Numinous – Numinous describes a direct ineffable experience of the holy or sacred. The term was coined by Rudolf Otto in his book *The Idea of the Holy* in 1917, and used extensively by Carl Jung. A numinous experience invokes fascination, awe, and apprehension, perhaps even trepidation, i.e., a sense of inadequacy to cope with such a profound and powerful presence. Yet it cannot be ignored. Coming from the collective unconscious, the numinous is uncontrollable and outside conscious volition. Jung observed that it can feed the "hunger of the soul" and provide feelings of liberation and relief.

Ontology – Philosophical beliefs or study concerned with examining and determining what is real, the nature of being and becoming.

Organic inquiry - William Braud summarizes an unconventional transpersonal research approach, informed and inspired by feminist, Jungian, spiritual, and mystical traditions. Organic inquiry is an emerging approach to qualitative research on psychospiritual growth, in which the researcher crosses the egoic threshold into a *liminal* realm to gather useful experience unavailable to the individual ego in ordinary reality. The liminal is a state beyond ego where the ego is barely perceptible, a less structured and less familiar state, where experience may be witnessed, but not created or controlled by ego.

Out-of-body experiences – An out-of-body experience is one that typically involves a sensation of floating outside one's body and, in some cases, perceiving one's physical body from a place outside the body, e.g., looking down from above and seeing one's body. Out-of-body experiences are considered altered states of consciousness, and are of interest in parapsychology as possibly related to the survival after bodily death.

Paradigmatic (or abstract) dimensions of knowing - The paradigmatic-abstract mode aims at being context-free in order to gain the power to generalize beyond any particular set and setting. Narratives are based on the logic of plausibility, or on a mythos that suspends common-sense categories and expands imagination. Narratives and stories conjure a response from the listener or reader, and that response allows for a level of understanding that may not be possible without being in the state resulting from the response; that is, narratives provide access to *state-specific understanding*. Abstract paradigmatic thinking relies on the logic of rationality and consistency and makes use of formal abstractions, concepts, constructs, general information, and prototypic knowledge independent of particular context. See Narrative dimensions of knowing.

Parapsychology – A research discipline that scientifically investigates evidence of the paranormal phenomena, specifically these three kinds of unusual events: extra-sensory perception (ESP); mind-matter interaction (also known as psychokinesis); and survival after bodily death, including near-death experiences, apparitions, and reincarnation.

Past-life experiences – Relived memories of past lives or incarnations, usually accessed through hypnotic regression techniques. In the 2nd century BCE, the Hindu scholar Patañjali discussed the idea of the soul becoming burdened with an accumulation of impressions as part of the karma from previous lives. Patañjali called the process of past-life regression *prati-prasav* (literally "reverse birthing"), and saw it as addressing current problems through memories of past lives.

Peak experience – Term used by Maslow for moments of profound inspiration, awe and fulfillment, perhaps quasi-mystical and mystical experiences carrying an intense sense of well-being and an awareness of "ultimate truth" or profound meaningfulness.

Perennial philosophy – The belief that all religions share a common doctrinal and experiential core, popularized by Aldous Huxley in his book *The Perennial Philosophy* published in 1945. It has been instrumental in Ken Wilber's development of Integral Psychology.

Perinatal – Perinatal signifies the time, usually a number of weeks, immediately before and after birth. It is a profoundly impactful period in a human being's development. See prenatal.

Personal – A stage of development following the pre-personal, based on mental-egoic consciousness and the individual personality. A small minority of human beings develop beyond the personal level into the transpersonal level of functioning.

Personality – "A basic assumption of transpersonal psychology is that there is more to you than your personality. Your personality is your sense of a separate, different, unique identity. Your personality is but one facet, however, of the self—the total identity—and perhaps not even a central facet. The very word "transpersonal" means through or beyond the personality. To be totally identified with one's personality may be evidence of psychopathology. One therapeutic goal is to align the personality within the total self so that it functions appropriately. These ideas fly in the face of the commonly accepted idea that the be-all and end-all of life is to improve your personality. A goal, within the context of transpersonal therapy, is to encourage and develop those tendencies which allow an individual to disidentify from the restrictions of the personality and to apprehend their identity with the total self."[702]

Phenomenology – Phenomenology is the first-person study of conscious experience. Phenomenology is primarily concerned with the systematic reflection on and study of the structures of consciousness and the phenomena that appear in acts of consciousness. Phenomenology provides an important basis for the current development of various approaches to qualitative research in transpersonal psychology.

Plateau experience – Maslow suggested that as we age physically or develop to higher stages of optimal functioning, the intensity of peak moments gives way to a more sustained state of serenity that he called plateau-experiences. Unlike peak-experiences, plateaus can be cultivated through conscious, diligent effort.

Positive psychology – Positive psychology is the scientific study of human flourishing, an applied approach to optimal functioning, and the study of the strengths and virtues that enable individuals, communities and organizations to thrive.

Prenatal – Prenatal signifies the time of incubation in the mother's womb before birth. It is a profoundly impactful period in a human being's development. See perinatal.

Pre-personal – The pre-personal is a level of development before the emergence of mental-egoic consciousness and the individual personality. At the pre-personal level of development the universe revolves around *I, me and mine*; the determining factor in moment-to-moment experience is pleasure vs. pain, reward vs. punishment; individuals identify with only certain acceptable aspects of the 'ego' and project, deny, or repress other aspects. Hence a split occurs and a boundary is drawn between the 'persona' (acceptable aspects) and the 'shadow' (unacceptable aspects), which results in a greatly narrowed self-image.

Primal therapy – Primal Therapy was developed by Dr. Arthur Janov. Repressed pain divides the self in two and each side wars with the other. One is the real self, loaded with needs and pain that are submerged; the other is the unreal self that attempts to deal with the outside world by trying to fulfill unmet needs with neurotic habits or behaviors such as obsessions or addictions. The split of the self is the essence of neurosis and therapy is based on the rubric that "Feeling pain is the end of suffering."

Primal wound – Term used by Firman & Gila for the fundamental damage caused to the child's sense of self which results from the failure of adult caretakers to empathize with and mirror accurately the child's experience. Primal wounding breaks the fundamental relationships not only with oneself and other people, but also with the natural world and a sense of transpersonal meaning represented by the Divine or Ultimate Reality.

Projection – The process in which an individual unconsciously places out onto the world, especially onto another person, an internally held belief or attribute. It is the opposite psychical process from introjection. For example, a parent may project onto her daughter the ambition to be a ballerina, and the daughter may introject her mother's desire.

Psi-related experiences – Anomalous experiences inexplicable by ordinary reality, such as precognition, telepathy, clairvoyance, psychokinesis (or mind-over-matter), psychic healing, out-of-body experiences, and poltergeists. Psi is actually the 23rd letter of the Greek alphabet and first letter of the word psyche. To qualify as psi-related, an experience must involve interactions that are qualitatively different from our normal ways of exchanging with the world (verbal and nonverbal communication, sensations, bodily movements).

Psyche – The mind, soul, or spirit, as opposed to the body. In psychology, the *psyche* is the center of thought, feeling, and motivation, consciously and unconsciously directing the body's reactions to its social and physical environment. In Greek mythology, Psyche was a young woman who loved and was loved by Eros and was united with him after Aphrodite's jealousy was overcome. She subsequently became the personification of the soul.

Psychoidal – The psychoidal level of the unconscious is an imaginal realm postulated by Jung to be so deeply and collectively unconscious that it challenges the ego's demand for control and authority. The psychoid has to do with a realm of experience of deep regression and primary process, where the capacity to distinguish inner and outer, subject and object, fantasy and reality is blurred; the realm of paradox, of the instinctual, animal, primordial within – the archetypes that animate us.

Psychosynthesis – a form of psychotherapy developed by Roberto Assagioli that focuses on three levels of the unconscious – lower, middle, and higher unconscious, or superconscious. The goal of the treatment is the re-creation or integration of the personality. The goal of Psychosynthesis is "self-realization", not only repairing past damage done but also building a healthier future. Jung once commented, "If there is a 'psychoanalysis' there must also be a 'psychosynthesis' which creates future events according to the same laws."

Self – In Jungian psychology, the authentic, uncluttered, unhindered essence of the person—the coming forth of the pure being as a result of self-actualization. The self is the ego's origin and source of energy and stability, the container for the ego's personal sense of selfhood.

Self-actualization – the achievement of one's full potential through creativity, independence, spontaneity, and a grasp of the real world. Self-actualization, according to Abraham Maslow, represents growth of an individual toward fulfillment of the highest needs; in particular those for meaning in life. Carl Rogers spoke of man's tendency to actualize himself, to become his potentialities.

Self-streams – According to Ken Wilber, the self has three different lines or streams: (1) the frontal self or ego, (2) the deeper psychic being or soul, and (3) the transcendent witness, Self, or Spirit.

Shamanism – Shamanism is an indigenous spiritual tradition in which the shaman undergoes a journey to the spirit world to bring back knowledge or power to heal the community. The journeys between worlds usually involves creating an altered state of consciousness through ritual or psychoactive plants which gives him access to and influence in the spirit world. Shamanism is actually a way of life, focused on connection with nature and promoting the well-being of all creation.

Soul – "Soul reminds us that there is a deeper, more primordial world than our logical processes. We know the soul when we are stirred by a poem, moved by a piece of music, touched by a painting. Soul is the deep resonance that vibrates within us at such moments. Thus, the soul can be touched, felt, and known but never defined."[703]

Spirit attachment – Psychological or physical disturbances caused by or reflecting the presence of the attachment of a spirit entity to a person. The attachment can be with a splinter of a living person, or with someone who has passed on to the next life. It can be with a disembodied spirit or spirits who are seeking to meet unnatural needs through a living human being. It can be with the remnant of the person's own spirit attempting to complete unfinished business or unfulfilled agreements from a past incarnation.

Spiritual emergency – Term used by Stan and Christina Grof for disturbing and overwhelming crises that may be indistinguishable from psychosis, but which present an opportunity for transformation and spiritual growth: spiritual emergence. One paradigm for the experience is to perceive it as a spontaneous Kundalini activation without sufficient emotional, somatic and spiritual preparation.

Spiritual healing experiences – Spiritual healing is the restoration of wholeness or wellness to one's experience by recognizing, accepting, and realizing the presence of divinity in the individual, and removing the toxins of distorted beliefs about oneself that have separated the person from wholeness.

Spiritual materialism – Term used by Chogyam Trungpa for a form of self-deception in which spirituality becomes a subtle means to fulfill egocentric desires.

Spiritual narcissism – Term used by Jorge Ferrer for a focus on the achievement of spiritual benefits for oneself.

Spirituality – Spirituality is the process of personal transformation, either in accordance with traditional religious ideals, or, increasingly, oriented on subjective experience and psychological growth independently of any specific religious context.

Subtle energy – Ancient traditions reference subtle energies (e.g. qi, chi, prana, etheric energy, mana, orgone, life force, homeopathic resonance) that are believed to underlie the workings of traditional healing modalities. The existence of such energies is not acknowledged by today's scientific model, which explicitly accounts for just four fundamental forces (strong and weak nuclear, electromagnetic, and gravitational force). See psi-related experiences.

Subtle self – Ken Wilber's term for the deeper psychic being (soul).

Synchronicity – Jung's term for external events that occur in meaningful coincidence with processes in the psyche. These are "coincidences" that have a numinous feel to them, too meaningful to be random.

Tao – Tao is the eternal source of everything, and all change as well. Tao is a Chinese concept signifying 'way', 'path', or sometimes more loosely, 'principle'. Within the context of traditional Chinese philosophy and religion, the Tao is the intuitive knowing about life which cannot be grasped full heartedly as a concept only, but known nonetheless as the present living experience of one's everyday being. In Taoism, the object of spiritual practice is to 'become one with the Tao' or to harmonize one's will with Nature in order to achieve 'effortless action' (Wu wei).

Third Force – Maslow's term for humanistic psychology, offering an alternative to the two primary forces in psychology in the first half of the twentieth century, psychoanalysis and behaviorism.

Trance – An altered state of consciousness in which the person's attentiveness to the external environment is reduced and introspection is increased. Examples of trance states are hypnosis, meditation, daydreaming, deep relaxation, enchantment with fantasy, or a flow state.

Transcendence – Transcendence is existence or experience beyond the normal or physical level. It is one aspect of the concept pair transcendence/immanence, where transcendence refers to aspects of existence (human or divine) that is outside of and beyond the world, whereas immanence refers to aspects that are manifest in the world. Transcendent experience opens the individual to a new more poignantly meaningful perspective. After he survived a heart attack, Abraham Maslow felt as if "everything gets doubly precious, gets piercingly important. You get stabbed by things, by flowers and by babies and by beautiful things...every single moment of every single day is transformed." Transpersonal psychology values ego transcendence, elevating the personal identification beyond the personality and ego.

Transcendent actualization – The process of developing a higher level of experience, an acceptance of the subordination of the ego to the Self, the most authentic core of a person. Instead of being centered on oneself and the contents of the ego (sensory, mental, and emotional experiences), one turns toward and accommodates to the Self and its contents (spiritual intuitions, inspirations, altruistic impulses, ethical considerations).

Transcendent function – The natural tendency of the psyche to creatively resolve oppositions and to unify conscious and unconscious contents, according to Carl Jung.

Transpersonal ecology – An approach that emphasizes the importance of expanding our concern and sense of self out to achieve a wider and deeper identification with the natural world, the environment, to recognize our interdependence and to experience a personal loving intimate relationship.

Transpersonal growth – Transpersonal growth refers to the intrapsychic awareness of beings and events based on spiritual intuitions, ethical considerations, inspirations, and higher order feelings; and motivation based on the unification of the dualities of the personality and the realization of profound or spiritual values.

Transpersonal identity – Transpersonal identity consists of the ego living in touch with the Self as a source of love, wisdom, and creative inspiration, recognizing the superordinate status of the Self.

Transpersonal psychology – Transpersonal psychology is a school of psychology that integrates the spiritual and transcendent aspects of the human experience within the framework of a modern psychology studying human growth and development to its full potential. As a model for the realization of this human potential, transpersonal psychology focuses on developing the positive influences as well as on repairing the diseases and defenses of the human psyche. The transpersonal psychology model integrates the spiritual, social, emotional, intellectual, physical and creative being into one complete element and addresses all of these components equally for the purpose of growth and development, and of therapeutic treatment. The major subject areas of the field can be summed up in three themes: beyond-ego psychology, integrative/holistic psychology, and psychology of transformation.[704]

Transpersonal self – Term used by Roberto Assagioli as synonymous with higher self. Self is experienced most essentially as a sense of *avocation* or *calling*, providing direction and meaning not only for individual unfoldment, but for living out our relationships with other people, nature, and the planet as a whole. Self does not belong to the individual, but rather the individual belongs to Self.

Unconscious – The part of the psyche lying far below consciousness that is inaccessible to the conscious mind, and not easily raised into consciousness. The unconscious cannot be directly observed with the conscious mind, but it has its own means of communication (such as dreams or slips of the tongue). It deeply affects behavior and emotions, and even conscious thought. "The unconscious is an autonomous psychic entity....It is and remains beyond the reach of subjective arbitrary control, a realm where nature and her secrets can be neither improved upon nor perverted, where we can listen but may not meddle."[705] Jung viewed the unconscious mind as an active source of wisdom, "the unconscious mind of man sees correctly even when conscious reason is blind and impotent."[706]

Vertical path – A route to transpersonal development that involves an elevation of our sense of self upward beyond the physical world. The vertical progression gives you altitude, resulting in broadening your spiritual horizons. See horizontal path.

Endnotes

---

[1] British Psychological Society
[2] Institute of Transpersonal Psychology
[3] Grof, 1985, p. 197
[4] Rodrigues, 2010, pp. 48-49
[5] Frager & Fadiman, 2005
[6] cited in Fadiman et al., 2003, p. 119
[7] Hartelius et al., 2007, p. 135
[8] Cunningham, 2007, p. 42
[9] Sutich, 1973
[10] Cunningham 2007, p. 45
[11] Cardena, Lynn, & Krippner, 2000
[12] Hay, 2006; Newport & Strasberg, 2001
[13] Neumann, 1954, quoted in Clark, 1977, p. 70
[14] Scotton, Chinen, & Battista, 1996
[15] Taylor, 1996, p. 21
[16] Maslow, 1968
[17] Grof, 2008, p. 47
[18] Maslow, 1999/1961, p. 125
[19] Assagioli, 1965
[20] Rank, 1924
[21] Jung, 1960
[22] Friedman & Pappas, 2006, p. 49
[23] Abram, 1996, pp. 213-214
[24] Gibson, 2000, p. 183
[25] Jung, 1970
[26] Montgomery, 1991
[27] Palmer, 1998
[28] Kalton, 2000, p. 190
[29] Eliade, 1957, p. 87
[30] James, 1890
[31] James, 1902/1980, p. 388
[32] Freud, 1939
[33] Jung, 1928/1934, para. 203
[34] Torbert, 2002
[35] ACIM, 1976, p. 18
[36] Gurdjieff, 1963
[37] Aurobindo, 1970
[38] Miovic, 2004, p. 111

[39] Singer, 1983, p. 207
[40] Jung, 1988, p. 99
[41] Jung, 1925, para. 335
[42] Main, 2012
[43] Hall and Lindzey, 1978
[44] Fox, 1995, p. 231
[45] Lutyens, 1975, p. 195
[46] Butcher, 1986, p. 37
[47] Krishnamurti, 1973, p. 195
[48] Reich, 1949
[49] Lowen, 1975, p. 66
[50] Hartmann, 1961, 1965
[51] Frederick, 2014
[52] Ferrer, 2002
[53] Frankl, 1963
[54] Frankl, 1967, p. 8
[55] Frankl, 1967, p. 9
[56] Frankl, 1955, 1963
[57] May, 1967
[58] May, 1958, p. 11, emphasis in original
[59] Bradford, 2007, pp. 23-24
[60] Watts, 1961
[61] Grof, 1985, 1987
[62] Grof, 1980
[63] Grof, n.d. a
[64] Grof, n.d. b
[65] Tart, 1975
[66] Gibson, n. d.
[67] Wilber, 1983, p. 83
[68] Bidwell, 1999, p. 83
[69] Wilber, 1995, p. 262
[70] Blavatsky, 1889
[71] Huxley, 1945
[72] Baker Miller, 1978; Jordan & Hartling, 2002
[73] Lerman, 1986
[74] Brooks, 2010, p. 33
[75] Brooks & Crouch, 2010, pp. 28-29
[76] Brooks, 2010, p. 33
[77] Brooks, 2010, p. 37
[78] Brooks, 2010, p. 44
[79] Anderson, 2000
[80] Clements et al., 1999
[81] Brooks, 2010, p. 45

[82] Myers, 1985, p. 34

[83] Nobles, 1972, 1980; Zahan, 1979

[84] Ogbonnaya, 1994, p. 75, emphasis added

[85] Myers, 1985, p. 35

[86] Asante, 1984, p. 168

[87] Fromm & Suzuki, 1960

[88] Miovic, 2004, p. 110

[89] Walsh & Vaughan, 1993a

[90] Vaughan, Wittine, and Walsh, 1996

[91] Sovatsky, 2009

[92] Grof & Grof, 1989

[93] Laenen, 1998/2001

[94] Idel, 2009

[95] Garb, 2011

[96] Ferrer, 2002, 116–117

[97] Makes Marks, 2007, pp. 30-31

[98] Makes Marks, 2007, p. 29

[99] Arasteh, 1972

[100] Arasteh, 1965

[101] Knabb & Welsh, 2009

[102] Arasteh, 1965, p. 200

[103] Arasteh, 1965

[104] Mayer, 2015

[105] Reich, 1949

[106] Gendlin, 1978

[107] Gendlin, 2004; Hartman & Zimberoff, 2008

[108] Callahan, 2001

[109] Craig, 2008

[110] Krieger, 1975

[111] Shamdasani, 1996/1932

[112] Gregory, 2012

[113] Cohen, 2003

[114] Watkins, 1998

[115] Johnson, 1986

[116] Caplan et al., 2013

[117] Gubi, 2008

[118] Krippner, 2012

[119] NCCAM, 2005, p. 1

[120] Mayer, 2007

[121] Pulos, 2002, p. 174

[122] Seiden, & Lam, 2010, p. 95

[123] Scholem, 1991, 1995

[124] Cutsinger, 2003

[125] Khan, 1982
[126] Woodroffe, 1919/2003
[127] Lakshmanjoo, 2000; Reps & Senzaki , 1957/1998
[128] Norbu, 1992
[129] Gyatso, 2003
[130] Chia & Huang, 2005; Kohn & Wang, 2009; Wilhelm, 1931/1962
[131] Eagle Feather, 2007
[132] Powell, 1969
[133] Stavish, 2008
[134] Matthews & Matthews, 1986
[135] Regardie, 1981
[136] Steinbrecher, 1988
[137] Ashcroft-Nowicki, 1987
[138] Gendlin, 1978/2007
[139] Mark, 2009
[140] Reich, 1949
[141] Monroe, 1979; Rogo, 1986; Vieira, 2002
[142] Lahood, 2007, p. 37
[143] Levy-Bruhl, 1910
[144] Morris, 1991, p. 169
[145] e.g., Ferrer, 2002; Heron, 1998; Tarnas, 1991
[146] Laughlin, McManus, & Shearer, 1993, p. 190
[147] Winkelman, 2000
[148] Bugental, 1964
[149] Greening, 2006
[150] Rogers, 1961
[151] Karpman, 1968
[152] Zimberoff, 1989/2011
[153] Gainer & Torem, 1993; Torem & Gainer, 1995
[154] Schwartz, 1995
[155] Watkins & Watkins, 1997
[156] Maslow, 1968, 1971
[157] May, 1969
[158] Perls, 1969a, 1969b
[159] Grof, 1985, 1987
[160] Palmer & Hubbard, 2009, p. 30
[161] Gerard, 1964
[162] Battista, 1996, p. 52
[163] Assagioli, 1965, pp. 17-19
[164] Assagioli, 1965, p. 19
[165] Assagioli, 1965, p. 87
[166] Assagioli, 2000, p. 19
[167] Firman, 2011

[168] van Dierendonck et al., 2005
[169] Assagioli, 1965
[170] Assagioli, 1988
[171] Assagioli, 1976, p. 73
[172] Wilber, 2000
[173] Rowan, 2005, pp. 55-88
[174] Wade, 1996
[175] Rowan, 2012b
[176] Firman & Gila, 2002
[177] Assagioli, 1965, p. 22
[178] Crampton, 1974
[179] Appel, 2014
[180] Andersen, 2005; Epstein, 1984; Kabat-Zinn, 1982; Salmon et al., 2004
[181] Lutz et al., 2008
[182] Firman, 2011
[183] Rowan, 1990, p. 72
[184] Wannamaker, n.d., para. 7
[185] Assagioli, 1973
[186] Rosselli & Vanni, 2014, p. 10
[187] Sartre, 1956
[188] Solomon, 1972
[189] Neitzsche, 1958
[190] Solomon, 2000
[191] Heidegger, 1962
[192] Sartre, 1956
[193] Yalom, 1980, 1989
[194] Kierkegaard, 1970
[195] Tillich, 1957
[196] Buber, 1927/1970
[197] May, 1969
[198] Hartman & Zimberoff, 2003
[199] Rowan, 2012, p. 113
[200] Rowan, 2012, p. 114
[201] Schneider, 2003; Schneider & May, 1995
[202] Bugental, 1965, 1978
[203] Van Dusen, 1965
[204] Gendlin, 1962, 1978
[205] Schneider & May, 1995, p. 152
[206] Bradford, 2007
[207] Bradford, 2007, p. 28
[208] Bugental, 1978, pp. 36–37
[209] Bugental, 1978, p. 36
[210] Deikman, 1982

[211] Schoen, 1991

[212] Metzner, 1998, p. 28

[213] Fenner, 2003

[214] Perls, 1969a, 1969b

[215] Levendula, 1963

[216] Perls, 1969a, 1969b, 1970

[217] Latner, 1973

[218] Latner, 1973, pp. 122-123

[219] Reich, 1949, p. 45

[220] Reich, 1949, p. 20

[221] Becker, 1993

[222] Yontef, 1993

[223] Walsh & Vaughan, 1980, pp. 169-170

[224] Levy, 1983, p. 46

[225] Jung, 1996, pp. 28-29

[226] Hartman & Zimberoff, 2003a

[227] Perry, 1970; Hall, 1989

[228] Hartman & Zimberoff, 2012

[229] Fonagy, 2001, p. 109

[230] Jung, 1955, p. 189

[231] Hall, 1989, p. 43

[232] Jung, 1978, p. 358

[233] Knox, 2004, p. 57

[234] Sandner & Beebe, 1984, p. 298

[235] Giannini, 2004, p. 33

[236] Wilber, 1981, p. 9

[237] Wilber, 1997, pp. 142-144

[238] Wilber, 1995, p. 262

[239] Wilber, 1995, p. 256

[240] Keutzer, 1984, p. 869

[241] Walsh, 1989, p. 5

[242] Harner, 2013

[243] Winkelman, 2012, pp. 57-58

[244] Walsh, 2007

[245] Eliade, 1964/1951

[246] Winkelman, 2010, 2011

[247] Walsh, 2007

[248] Winkelman, 2012, p. 56

[249] Walsh, 2012, p. 108

[250] Maurer et al., 1997, p. 143

[251] Cardena, 1988a, 1988b, 1996

[252] Cardena, 1988a, p. 298

[253] Walsh, 2012, p. 107

[254] Markides, 1985, 1987, 1990
[255] Markides, 2008, p. 181
[256] Markides, 2008, p. 179
[257] Markides, 2005, pp. 127–147
[258] Wilber, et.al., 1986
[259] Vaughan, 2010, pp. 3-4
[260] Grof, 2008, p. 49
[261] Tart, 2008
[262] Frederick, 2014, p. 42
[263] Frederick, 2014, p. 43
[264] Frederick, 2014, p. 44
[265] Frederick, 2014, p. 43
[266] Krippner, 2009
[267] Bourguignon & Evascu, 1977
[268] Kierkegaard, 1980
[269] Baumeister, 1998
[270] Markus & Kityama, 1991
[271] DeCicco & Stroink, 2007
[272] Hill, 2006; Walsh & Vaughan, 1993b
[273] Friedman, 1983
[274] Boorstein, 1994; Pappas & Friedman, 2007; Walsh & Vaughan, 1993b; Wilber, 1979
[275] DeCicco & Stroink, 2007, p. 84
[276] Markus & Kitayama, 1991
[277] DeCicco & Stroink, 2007
[278] Boyer, 2002, p. 16
[279] Garcia-Romeu, 2010
[280] Welwood, 1984
[281] Stevens, 1984/1952, pp. 446-448
[282] Epstein, 1988, p. 62
[283] Epstein, 1988, p. 62
[284] Engler, 1983, p. 48
[285] Cloninger et al., 1993, p. 975
[286] Csikszentmihalyi, 1990
[287] Maslow, 1971
[288] Csikszentmihalyi, 1993
[289] Maslow, 1968
[290] Maslow, 1943, p. 382
[291] Maslow, 1971, p. 44
[292] Maslow, 1971a
[293] Maslow, 1994/1970, p. 79
[294] Maslow, 1971
[295] Maslow, 1971, p. 281

[296] Maslow, 1996, p. 31
[297] Maslow, 1971b, pp. 273-285
[298] Reed, 2003, p. 147
[299] Bauer & Wayment, 2008, pp. 8-9
[300] Bauer & Bonanno, 2001
[301] Helgeson & Fritz, 1999
[302] Bauer & Wayment, 2008
[303] Kelly, 1955
[304] Engler, 1984
[305] Edinger, 1972, p. 5
[306] Reinert, 1997
[307] Cole & Pargament, 1999, p. 179).
[308] Lefcourt, 1983
[309] Oberle, 1991
[310] Gagan, 1998, p. 143-144
[311] quoted in Epstein, 1993, p. 122
[312] Jung, 1959, p. 125
[313] Perls et al., 1951
[314] Goleman, 1975
[315] Kalff, 1983
[316] Jung, 1975
[317] Ross, 1991
[318] Zimberoff & Hartman, 1999
[319] Nagy, 1991, p. 57
[320] Plato, *The Phaedo*, quoted in Edinger, 1985, pp. 169-170
[321] Wickramasekera, 2013, p. 492
[322] Rowan, 2005, p. 3
[323] Rowan, 2005
[324] Zahi, 2009, p. 267
[325] Capafons, 2004; Wark, 2006
[326] Bányai, Zseni, & Tury,1997
[327] Yapko, 2011, p. 31.
[328] Winkelman, 2012
[329] Critchley et al., 2004
[330] Seeley et al., 2007
[331] Barabasz & Barabasz, 2008; Oakley & Halligan, 2010
[332] Winson, 1990
[333] Spiegel, 1996
[334] Larson & Lynch, 1986
[335] Tart, 2008
[336] Teicher, 2000
[337] de Lange et al., 2008
[338] Corbetta & Shulman, 2002

[339] Buckner & Carroll, 2007

[340] Spiegel, 2008

[341] Zahi, 2009

[342] Hugdahl, 1996

[343] Lazar et al., 2005

[344] Newberg & Iversen, 2003

[345] Egner, Jamieson, & Gruzelier, 2005

[346] Lutz et al., 2004

[347] Kets de Vries, 2014

[348] Schatzman, 1983

[349] Kets de Vries, 2014, pp. 88-89

[350] Schenk, 2006

[351] Hartman & Zimberoff, 2008a

[352] Jensen, 2001

[353] Bartocci & Dein, 2005

[354] Hillman, 1979, p. 94

[355] Hillman, 1979, p. 98

[356] Dossey, 1989, p. 9

[357] Jacoby, 1985, p. 205

[358] Tedlock, 1999

[359] Tedlock, 2004

[360] Domhoff, 2003

[361] Steiner, 1995

[362] Friedman, 2004

[363] Moss, 2002

[364] Friedman, 2004

[365] Davis, 2000, p. 3

[366] Sanchez & Vieira, 2007, p. 51

[367] Martin, 1997, 2002

[368] Deikman, 1982

[369] Safran & Segal, 1990

[370] Langer, 1989

[371] Bohart, 1983

[372] Krishnamurti, 1964

[373] Hick, 2008, p. 5

[374] Kabat-Zinn, 1990

[375] Shapiro, Schwartz, & Bonner, 1998

[376] Segal, Williams, & Teasdale, 2002

[377] Vieten, Amorok, & Schlitz, 2005, pp. 4-5

[378] Schwartz, 2000

[379] d'Aquili & Newberg, March 2000

[380] d'Aquili & Newberg, 1993, 1999

[381] Gimello, 1978, p. 178

[382] d'Aquili & Newberg, 1998
[383] d'Aquili & Newberg, 1998, pp. 195-196
[384] d'Aquili & Newberg, 1998, p. 197
[385] Tart, 2008
[386] Passmore & Marianetti, 2007
[387] Yeager, 2007
[388] Pelletier, 1979, p. 33
[389] Rock, 2012
[390] Amiotte, 1992 as quoted in Voss et al., 1999
[391] Voss et al., 1999, p. 234
[392] Voss et al., 1999, p. 235-236
[393] Voss et al., 1999, p. 236
[394] Gagan, 1998, p. 132
[395] Johnson, 1986, p. 21
[396] Johnson, 1986, p. 158
[397] Raff, 2000, p. 51
[398] Jung, 1973
[399] von Franz, 1979
[400] Johnson, 1986
[401] Johnson, 1986, p. 183-184
[402] Clark, 1977, p. 73
[403] Clark, 1977, p. 72
[404] Walsh & Vaughan, 1980, pp. 18-19
[405] Walsh, 2013, p. 3
[406] Cloninger et al., 1993
[407] Assagioli, 1965
[408] Fadiman, 1980, p. 180
[409] Clark, 1977
[410] Grof, 2000
[411] Cortright, 2007
[412] Peres, Simão & Nasello, 2007
[413] Saldanha, 1997
[414] Rodrigues, 2010, pp. 46-47
[415] Rodrigues, 2010, pp. 47-48, emphasis in the original
[416] Rodrigues, 2010, pp. 50-51
[417] Assagioli, 1967
[418] Fadiman, 1980, p. 177
[419] Frankl, 1965
[420] Haley, 1963
[421] Berne, 1961, 1964
[422] Zimberoff, 1989
[423] Welwood, 1990
[424] Jung, 1960

[425] Chogyam Trungpa, 1991, p. 149
[426] Goodman, 2005
[427] Maguire, 2001, p. 131
[428] Jung, 1960, p. 44
[429] Bolen, 1979
[430] Bazzano, 2010
[431] Kristeller, 2011, p. 199
[432] Chögyam Trungpa, 2015, p. 128
[433] Assagioli, 1965, p. 35
[434] Allison, 1974
[435] Comstock, 1987, 1991
[436] Gainer & Torem, 1993
[437] Torem and Gainer, 1995
[438] Kluft, 1989
[439] Watkins & Watkins, 1997
[440] Frederick, 2014, p. 40
[441] Frederick, 2014, p. 42
[442] Frederick, 2014, pp. 42-43
[443] Jung, 2009
[444] Jung, 1961
[445] Jung, 1961, p.183
[446] McNeal & Frederick, 1993
[447] Frederick & McNeal, 1999; Krakauer, 2001, 2006; Rossman, 1987
[448] Frederick & McNeal, 1999
[449] Feinstein & Krippner, 2006
[450] Ginandes, 2006
[451] Brown, 2011; Brown & Fromm, 1986
[452] Frederick, 2003
[453] Phillips & Frederick, 1995
[454] Frederick & McNeal, 1999
[455] Hartmann, 1961, 1965
[456] Hartmann, 1961, p. 3
[457] Morton & Frederick, 1999
[458] Frederick, 2014
[459] Frederick, 2014, p. 50
[460] Comstock, 1991
[461] Torem & Gainer, 1995
[462] Gainer & Torem, 1993
[463] Heery, 1989
[464] Krakauer, 2006
[465] Jung, 1961
[466] Zimberoff & Hartman, 2014
[467] Chögyam Trungpa, 2002, 3

[468] Zimberoff & Hartman, 1998

[469] Zimberoff & Hartman, 1999b

[470] Maslow, 1971, p. 34

[471] Maslow, 1971, p. 38

[472] Frankl, 1960

[473] Pascual-Leone, 1990

[474] Frankl, 1967, p. 9

[475] Crumbaugh & Maholick, 1964

[476] Jung, 1961, p. 297

[477] Aspinwall & Staudinger, 2003; Mayerson, 2013

[478] Steckler, 1992, pp. 42-44

[479] Yapko, 1984

[480] Bandler & Grinder, 1975

[481] Armatas, 2011

[482] McConkey, 1986

[483] Hornyak, 2004

[484] Brown & Fromm, 1986

[485] Hornyak, 2004

[486] Palmer & Dryden, 1995

[487] Boorstein, 2000, p. 412

[488] Frager, 1974

[489] Adams, 2010, p. 3

[490] Romanyshyn, 2012, p. 107-108, italics in original

[491] Braud, 2006

[492] Gardner, 1983; Goleman, 1994

[493] Tart, 1975

[494] Frager, 1974, p. 164

[495] Huxley, 1945/1970, pp. viii, ix

[496] Louchakova, 2005, p. 90

[497] Louchakova, 2005

[498] Louchakova, 2005, p. 100-101

[499] Denzin & Lincoln, 1994

[500] Louchakova, 2005

[501] Deslauriers, 1992

[502] McMahon, 1998

[503] Hartman & Zimberoff, 2008a

[504] Braud, 2006, p. 144

[505] Ruumet, 1997

[506] Friedman & MacDonald, 1997, p. 112

[507] Friedman & MacDonald, 1997, p. 113

[508] Friedman, 1983

[509] Friedman & MacDonald, 1997, pp. 116-117

[510] Davis, 2009, p. 4

[511] Braud & Anderson, 1998

[512] Fischer, 2006, p.6

[513] Glaser, 1978

[514] Braud, 2006, p. 141

[515] Rychlak, 1993

[516] Thompson, Locander, & Pollio, 1989, p. 142

[517] Solloway & Fisher, 2007, p. 72

[518] Knapp, 1976; Shostrom, Knapp, & Knapp, 1976

[519] Bruner, 1986

[520] Deslauriers, 1992

[521] Price-Williams, 1975

[522] Faithorn, 1992

[523] Anderson & Braud, 2011

[524] Wertz & Charmaz, 2011

[525] Braud, 2004

[526] Braud, 2004, pp. 18-19

[527] Clements, 2004, p. 31

[528] Clements, 2004, p. 30

[529] Louchakova, 2005, p. 99

[530] Deslauriers, 1992

[531] Levy, 1983, p. 46

[532] Jung, 1966

[533] Jung, 1966, paras. 389-390

[534] Porterfield, 2004

[535] Jung, 1966, para. 391

[536] Welwood, 1984

[537] Jung, 1966, para. 384

[538] Walach, 2008, p. 47

[539] Walach, 2013, p. 68, emphasis in the original

[540] Wilber, 1977

[541] Maslow, 1994/1970

[542] Markides, 2005

[543] Arasteh, 1965

[544] Plotkin, 2003

[545] Teilhard de P. Chardin, 1973/1966, p. 42

[546] Assagioli, 1971

[547] Frankl, 1997

[548] Bruitzman, 2013

[549] Loevinger, 1993, p. 2

[550] Wilber, 2009

[551] Loevinger, 1969, p. 85

[552] Loevinger, 1976, p. 9

[553] Thorne, 1993, p. 53

[554] Block, 1971

[555] Westen, 1998

[556] Blasi, 1993, p. 17

[557] Blasi, 1993, p. 18

[558] Manners & Durkin, 2001, p. 542

[559] McCrae & Costa, 1980

[560] Helson & Roberts, 1994; White, 1985

[561] Westenberg & Block, 1993

[562] Westenberg & Block, 1993

[563] White, 1985

[564] Carlozzi et al., 1983; Westenberg & Block, 1993

[565] Helson & Roberts, 1994; Helson & Wink, 1987; White, 1985

[566] White, 1985, p. 572

[567] McAdams, Ruetzel, & Foley, 1986

[568] Loevinger, 1976

[569] Chandler et al., 2005

[570] Cook-Greuter, 1990; Loevinger & Wessler, 1970

[571] Cook-Greuter, 2013

[572] Maslow, 1954/1970

[573] Cook-Greuter, 2000

[574] Pfaffenberger, 2013

[575] Cook-Greuter, 2000, p. 3

[576] Cook-Greuter, 2000, p. 9-10

[577] Cook-Greuter, 2000, p. 11

[578] Helson & Srivastava, 2001; Westenberg & Block, 1993

[579] Noam, 1988, 1993

[580] Labouvie-Vief, 1993; Labouvie-Vief & Diehl, 1998

[581] Helson & Roberts, 1994

[582] Loevinger, 1976

[583] Mols, Vingerhoets, Coebergh, & van de Poll-Franse, 2009

[584] Tedeschi & Calhoun, 2004, p. 1

[585] O'Leary & Ickovics, 1995

[586] Carver, 1998

[587] O'Leary & Ickovics, 1995

[588] Affleck & Tennen, 1996

[589] Calhoun and Tedeschi, 1998

[590] Gardner, 1983

[591] Gardner, 1999, pp. 41-43

[592] Gardner, 1999, p. 52

[593] Berne, 1961, 1964

[594] Perls, 1969a, 1969b

[595] Wilber, 1998

[596] Freud, 1939

[597] Sheldon & Lyubomirsky, 2006
[598] Salman, 2000, p. 78
[599] Campbell, 1991, p. 123
[600] Serrano, 1966, p. 50
[601] Jung, 1964, pp. 144-145
[602] Wilber, 1998, pp. 25-26
[603] McAdams, 1998, pp. 29-30
[604] Jacobs et al., 2003
[605] Pascual-Leone, 1990
[606] Damon & Hart, 1988; Harter, 1998
[607] Hillman, 2000
[608] Beck, 2007
[609] Alexander et al., 1990, p. 314
[610] Maslow, 1971a
[611] Loevinger, 1976, p. 26
[612] McAdams, 1998, p. 38
[613] MacIntyre, 1984
[614] Alexander et al., 1990
[615] Miller & Cook-Greuter, 1994, p. 134
[616] Taft, 1969
[617] Bugental, 1965, p. 33
[618] Fordham, 1985, p. 21
[619] Markus & Nurius, 1986; Ruvolo & Markus, 1992
[620] Sheldon & Lyubomirsky, 2006
[621] King & Raspin, 2004
[622] Kuhl & Helle, 1986
[623] King, 1998
[624] Wilber, 1998
[625] Pfaffenberger, 2013
[626] Noam, 1998
[627] King & Hicks, 2007, p. 31
[628] Waterman, 1993
[629] Deci & Ryan, 2008, p. 2
[630] Jung, 1933
[631] Allport, 1961
[632] Assagioli, 1965
[633] Maslow, 1968
[634] Rogers, 1961
[635] Ryff, 1989
[636] Bauer, McAdams, & Pals, 2008
[637] Bauer & Wayment, 2008
[638] Taft, 1969
[639] Kegan, 1982, 1994

[640] Kegan, 1994, p. 32
[641] Thorne et al., 2004
[642] Bluck & Gluck, 2004
[643] Bauer & McAdams, 2004
[644] Hy & Loevinger, 1996
[645] Deci & Ryan, 2000
[646] Kegan, 1994, p. 34
[647] Kegan, 1994, p. 31
[648] Baxter Magolda, 2008, 2009
[649] Jung, *Collected Works*, 14, ¶778, italics in the original)
[650] Wright, 1995, p. 6
[651] Wright, 1995, p. 7
[652] Hamachek, 1985
[653] Maslow, 1970
[654] Edinger, 1961
[655] Stern, 1985
[656] Damasio, 1994
[657] Fordham, 1985
[658] Urban, 2005
[659] Bremner, 1994, p. 25
[660] Bremner, 1994, p. 47
[661] Fordham, 1985
[662] Stern, 1985; Fonagy et al., 2002
[663] Jung, 1971, para. 706
[664] Frederick, 2014
[665] Hartmann, 1961, 1965
[666] Edinger, 1961
[667] Edinger, 1961, p. 3
[668] Edinger, 1961, p. 6
[669] Edinger, 1974
[670] Edinger, 1974, p. 6
[671] Edinger, 1961, pp. 8-9
[672] Edinger, 1961, p. 18
[673] Isakower, 1938
[674] Hartmann, et al., 1987; Levin, Galin & Zywiak, 1991
[675] Hartmann, 1991; Hartmann, Elkin & Garg, 1991
[676] Rogers, 1961
[677] Maslow, 1970
[678] Hamachek, 1985
[679] Hartmann, 1991
[680] Cowen & Levin, 1995
[681] Hamachek, 1985
[682] Wolf, 1982

[683] Blos, 1962

[684] Esman, 1983; Hartmann,1950

[685] Loeb, 1975

[686] Maslow, 1993

[687] Assagioli, 1987, 1991

[688] Hamel et al., 2003, pp. 5-6

[689] Assagioli, 1991

[690] Hamel et al., 2003, p. 8

[691] Assagioli, 1991

[692] Von Franz, 1971, p. 17

[693] Raff, 2000

[694] Assagioli, 1991

[695] Unno, 2015

[696] Hamel et al., 2003, p. 9

[697] Hamel et al., 2003, pp. 12-13

[698] Fordham, 1985, p. 12, taken from Jung, 1961, pp. 187–8

[699] Fordham, 1985, p. 33

[700] Singer, 2006, pp. 26–27

[701] Shrader, 2008

[702] Fadiman, 1980, p. 177

[703] Sperry & Shafranske, 2005, p. 137

[704] Hartelius et al., 2007

[705] Jung, 1944, p. 46

[706] Jung, 1952, p. 24

References

Abram, D. (1996). *The Spell of the Sensuous: Perception and Language in a More-Than-Human World*. New York: Vintage Books.

ACIM. (1976). *A Course in Miracles*. Mill Valley, CA: Foundation for Inner Peace.

Adams, A. (2010). Integral education for a conscious evolution. *ReVision: A Journal of Consciousness and Transformation, 32*(1), 2-6.

Affleck, G., & Tennen, H. (1996). Construing benefits from adversity: Adaptational significance and dispositional underpinnings. *Journal of Personality, 64*, 899-922.

Alexander, C. N., Davies, J. L., Dixon, C. A., Dillbeck, M. C., Oetzel, R. M., Druker, S. M., Muehlman, J. M., & Orme-Johnson, D. W. (1990). Growth of higher stages of consciousness: Maharishi's Vedic psychology of human development. In C. N. Alexander & E. J. Langer (Eds.), *Higher Stages of Human Development: Perspectives on Adult Growth*, 386-340. New York: Oxford University Press.

Allison, R. B. (1974). A new treatment approach for multiple personalities. *American Journal of Clinical Hypnosis, 17*, 15-32.

Allison, R.B., & Schwarz, T. (1980). *Minds in Many Pieces*. New York: Rawson, Wade.

Allport, G. W. (1961). *Pattern and Growth in Personality*. New York: Holt, Rinehart, & Winston.

Alpert, J. (1973). Mother right: A new feminist theory. *Ms., 2*(2), 52-55, 88-94.

Amiotte, A. (April 28, 1992). *Lakota Cosmology* [videotape]. Guest lecture at Sinte Gleska University, Mission, SD.

Andersen, D. T. (2005). Empathy, psychotherapy integration, and meditation: A Buddhist contribution to the common factors movement. *Journal of Humanistic Psychology, 45*, 483-502.

Anderson, R. (1998). Intuitive inquiry: A transpersonal approach. In W. Braud & R. Anderson (Eds.), *Transpersonal Research Methods for the Social Sciences: Honoring Human Experience*, 69-94. Thousand Oaks, CA: Sage.

Anderson, R. (2000). Intuitive inquiry: Interpreting objective and subjective data. *ReVision: A Journal of Consciousness and Transformation*, 22(4), 31-39.

Anderson, R. (2001). Embodied writing and reflections on embodiment. *Journal of Transpersonal Psychology*, 33, 83-98.

Anderson, R., & Braud, W. (2011). *Transforming Self and Others through Research. Transpersonal Research Methods and Skills for the Human Sciences and Humanities*. Albany, NY: State University of New York Press.

Appel, P. R. (2014). Psychosynthesis: A transpersonal model for hypnotically mediated psychotherapy. *American Journal of Clinical Hypnosis*, 56, 249-268.

Arasteh, A. (1965). *Final Integration in the Adult Personality*. Netherlands: E. J. Brill.

Arasteh, A. (1972). *Rumi the Persian: Rebirth in Creativity and Love*. Tucson, AZ: Omen Press.

Asante, M. K. (1984). The African American mode of transcendence. *The Journal of Transpersonal Psychology*, 16(2), 167-177.

Ashcroft-Nowicki, D. (1987). *Highways of the Mind: The Art and History of Pathworking*. Northamptonshire, UK: The Aquarian Press.

Aspinwall, L. G., & Staudinger, U. M. (Eds). (2003). *A Psychology of Human Strengths: Fundamental Questions and Future Directions for a Positive Psychology*. Washington DC: American Psychological Association.

Assagioli, R. (1965). *Psychosynthesis: A Manual of Principles and Techniques*. New York: Viking Press.

Assagioli, R. (1967). *Jung and Psychosynthesis* – A series of three lectures given in 1966 at the Istituto di Psicosintesi, Florence, Italy. New York, NY: Psychosynthesis Research Foundation (v. 19).

Assagioli, R. (1973). Le nuove dimensioni della psicologia (la terza, quarta e quinta forza nella psicologia). I Lezione – 1973. Corso di lezioni sulla psicosintesi – Istituto di Psicosintesi, Firenze [The New Dimensions of Psychology (the Third, Fourth and Fifth Force in Psychology) Lesson I – 1973. Course of Lessons on Psychosynthesis]. Firenze: Istituto di Psicosintesi.

Assagioli, R. (1976). Unpublished Notes on Jung (Unpublished manuscript). In Assagioli archive: 3.5.5, 41; 10.2.1, 73; 10.2.2, 73; 10.2.3, 73; 11.1–15, 75; 76; 77. Firenze: Istituto di Psicosintesi.

Assagioli, R. (1987). *L'acte de Volonté*. Montréal: Centre de Psychosynthèse de Montréal.

Assagioli, R. (1988). *Lo Sviluppo Transpersonale* [Transpersonal Development]. Roma: Casa Editrice Astrolabio.

Assagioli, R. (1991). *Transpersonal Development. The Dimension Beyond Psychosynthesis.* San Francisco: The Aquarian Press.

Assagioli, R. (2000). *Psychosynthesis*, 12th ed. Amherst, MA: Synthesis Center Press.

Aurobindo, S. (1970). *The Life Divine*. 5th ed. Pondicherry, India: Sri Aurobindo Ashram Trust, [published serially 1914–19; revised first edition published 1939–40].

Baker Miller, J. (1978). *Toward a New Psychology of Women*. Boston, MA: Beacon Press.

Bányai, E., Zseni, A., & Tury, F. T. (1997). Active-alert hypnosis in psychotherapy. In J. Rhue, S. Lynn, & I. Kirsch (Eds.), *Handbook of Clinical Hypnosis.* Washington, DC: American Psychological Association.

Barabasz, A. F., & Barabasz, M. (2008). Hypnosis and the brain. In M. R. Nash, & A. J. Barnier (Eds.), *The Oxford Handbook of Hypnosis: Theory, Research, and Practice*, 337-364. Oxford, UK: Oxford University Press.

Bartocci, G., & Dein, S. (2005). Detachment: Gateway to the world of spirituality. *Transcultural Psychiatry*, 42(4), 545-569.

Basu, S. (2000). *I*. Pondicherry, India: Sri Aurobindo Ashram Trust.

Bateson, G. (1972). *Steps to an Ecology of Mind.* New York: Ballantine Books.

Battista, J. (1996). Abraham Maslow and Roberto Assagioli: Pioneers of transpersonal psychology. In B. Scotten, A. Chinnen, & J. Battista (Eds.), *Textbook of Transpersonal Psychiatry and Psychology*, 52-61. New York: Basic Books.

Bauer, J. J., & Bonanno, G. A. (2001). Doing and being well (for the most part): Adaptive patterns of narrative self-evaluation during bereavement. *Journal of Personality*, 69, 451-482.

Bauer, J. J., & McAdams, D. P. (June 2004). Personal growth in adults' stories of life transitions. *Journal of Personality*, 72(3), 573-602.

Bauer, J. J., & Wayment, H. A. (2008). The psychology of the quiet ego. In J. J. Bauer, & H. A. Wayment (Eds.), *Transcending Self-Interest: Psychological Explorations of the Quiet Ego. Decade of Behavior*, 7-19. Washington, DC: American Psychological Association.

Bauer, J. J., McAdams, D. P., & Pals, J. L. (2008). Narrative identity and eudaimonic well-being. *Journal of Happiness Studies*, 9(1), 81-104.

Baumeister, R. F. (1998). The self. In D. T. Gilbert, S. T. Fiske, & G. Lindzey (Eds.), *The Handbook of Social Psychology*, 4th ed., 680-740. New York: McGraw-Hill.

Baxter Magolda, M. B. (2008). Three elements of self-authorship. *Journal of College Student Development, 49*(4), 269–284.

Baxter Magolda, M. B. (2009). *Authoring Your Life: Developing an Internal Voice to Navigate Life's Challenges*. Sterling, VA: Stylus.

Bazzano, M. (Apr 2010). Mindfulness in context. *Therapy Today*, 21(3) , 32-36.

Beck, C. J. (2007). *Everyday Zen*. New York: HarperOne.

Beck, P. V., Walters, A. L., and Francisco, N. (1996). *The Sacred: Ways of Knowledge, Sources of Life*. Tsaile, AZ: Navajo Community College Press.

Becker, E. (Fall, 1993). Growing up rugged: Fritz Perls and Gestalt therapy. *The Gestalt Journal*, 16(2). Retrieved from http://www.gestalt.org/becker.html

ben-Jochannon, Y. (1970). *African Origins of Major Western Religions*. New York: Alkebulan Books.

Benson, H. (1975). *The Relaxation Response*. New York: William Morrow.

Berne, E. (1961). *Transactional Analysis in Psychotherapy*. New York: Grove Press, Inc.

Berne, E. (1964). *Games People Play – The Basic Hand Book of Transactional Analysis*. New York: Ballantine Books.

Bertalanffy Von, L. (1968). *General Systems Theory*. New York: Braziller.

Bidwell, D. R. (1999). Ken Wilber's transpersonal psychology: An introduction and preliminary critique. *Pastoral Psychology*, 48(2), 81-90.

Blasi, A. (1993). The theory of ego development and the measure. *Psychological Inquiry*, 4(1), 17-19.

Blavatsky, H. P. (1889). *The Key to Theosophy*. Mumbai, India: Theosophy Company.

Block, J. (1971). *Lives through Time*. Berkeley, CA: Bancroft.

Blos, P. (1962). *On Adolescence*. New York: Free Press.

Bluck, S., & Gluck, J. (June 2004). Making things better and learning a lesson: Experiencing wisdom across the lifespan. *Journal of Personality*, 72(3), 543-572.

Bohart, A. (Apr 1983). *Detachment: A Variable Common to Many Psychotherapies?* Paper presented at the 63rd annual convention of the Western Psychological Association, San Francisco.

Bolen, J. (1979). *The Tao of Psychology: Synchronicity and the Self.* New York: Harper &Row.

Boorstein, S. (2000). Transpersonal psychotherapy. *American Journal of Psychotherapy*, 54(3), 408-423.

Bourguignon, E., & Evascu, T. (1977). Altered states of consciousness within a general evolutionary perspective: A holocultural analysis. *Behavior Science Research*, 12, 199-216.

Boyer, P. (2002). *The Evolutionary Origin of Religious Thought.* New York: Running Press Book Publishers.

Bradford, G. K. (2007). The play of unconditioned presence in existential-integrative psychotherapy. *Journal of Transpersonal Psychology*, *39*(1), 23-47.

Bradford, G. K. (2012). On the question of sanity: Buddhist and Existential perspectives. *Journal of Transpersonal Psychology*, 44(2), 224-239.

Braud, W. (2004). An introduction to Organic Inquiry: Honoring the transpersonal and spiritual in research praxis. *Journal of Transpersonal Psychology*, 36, 18-25.

Braud, W. (2006). Educating the 'more' in holistic transpersonal higher education: A 30+ year perspective on the approach of the Institute of Transpersonal Psychology. *Journal of Transpersonal Psychology*, 38(2), 133-158.

Braud, W., & Anderson, R. (1998). *Transpersonal Research Methods: Honoring Human Experience.* Thousand Oaks, CA: Sage.

Bremner, J. (1994). *Infancy.* Oxford: Blackwell.

British Psychological Society. Retrieved from http://transpersonalpsychology.org.uk/.

Brooks, C. (2010). Unidentified allies: Intersections of feminist and transpersonal thought and potential contributions to social change. *International Journal of Transpersonal Studies*, *29*(2), 33-57.

Brooks, C., & Crouch, C. (2010). Editorial introduction to special topic section: Transpersonal feminism. *International Journal of Transpersonal Studies*, *29*(2), 28-32.

Brown, D. P. (2011). New England Society of Clinical Hypnosis 56th Annual Workshop. Day 2. *How to Treat Attachment Pathology.* May 15, 2011. Newton Wellesley Hospital, Newton, MA.

Brown, D. P. & Fromm, E. (1986). *Hypnotherapy and Hypnoanalysis.* Hillsdale, NJ: Lawrence Erlbaum Associates.

Bruitzman, G. (Aug-Nov 2013). Searching for an integral vision: Light bearers, freedom fighters and prisoners in premodern, modern and postmodern times. *Integral Leadership Review.*

Bruner, J. (1986). *Actual Minds, Possible Worlds.* Cambridge, MA: Harvard University Press.

Buber, M. (1927/1970). *I and Thou* (W. Kaufmann, Trans.). New York: Scribner.

Buckner, R. L., & Carroll, D. C. (2007). Self-projection and the brain. *Trends in Cognitive Sciences, 11*, 49-57.

Bugental, J. (1964). The third force in psychology. *Journal of Humanistic Psychology, 4*(1), 19-26.

Bugental, J. (1965). *The Search for Authenticity: An Existential-Analytic Approach to Psychotherapy.* New York: Holt, Rinehart & Winston.

Bugental, J. (1978). *Psychotherapy and Process.* Reading, MA: Addison-Wesley.

Butcher, P. (1986). The phenomenological psychology of J. Krishnamurti. *Journal of Transpersonal Psychology, 18*(1), 35-50.

Calhoun, L. G., & Tedeschi, R. G. (1998). Beyond recovery from trauma: Implications for clinical practice and research. *Journal of Social Issues, 54*(2), 357-371.

Callahan, R. (2001). *Tapping the Healer Within: Using Thought Field Therapy to Instantly Conquer Your Fears, Anxieties, and Emotional Distress.* New York: Contemporary Books.

Campbell, J. (1991). *Reflections on the Art of Living: A Joseph Campbell Companion* (D. K. Osbon Ed.). New York: HarperCollins Publishers.

Capafons, A. (2004). Waking hypnosis for waking people: Why in Valencia? *Contemporary Hypnosis, 21*(3), 136-145.

Caplan, M., Portillo, A., & Seely, L. (2013). Yoga psychotherapy: The integration of Western psychological theory and ancient yogic wisdom. *Journal of Transpersonal Psychology, 45*(2), 139-158.

Cardeña, E. (1988a). Deep hypnosis and shamanism: Convergences and divergences. *Proceedings of the Fourth International Conference on the Study of Shamanism and Alternate Modes of Healing,* 290-302. (Produced by A-R Editions, Inc, 315 W. Gorham Street, Madison, WI 53703.)

Cardeña, E. (1988b). *The phenomenology of quiescent and physically active hypnosis.* Paper presented at the meeting of the Society for Clinical and Experimental Hypnosis, Asheville, North Carolina.

Cardena, E. (1996). Just floating in the sky: A comparison of shamanic and hypnotic phenomenology. In R. Quekekbherge, & D. Eigner (Eds.), 6th Jahrbuch fr TranskulturelleMedizinundPsychotherapie, 367-380. Berlin: VWB.

Cárdena, E., Lynn, S. J., & Krippner, S. (Eds.). (2000). *Varieties of Anomalous Experience: Examining the Scientific Evidence.* Washington, DC: American Psychological Association.

Carlozzi, A. F., Gaa, J. P., & Liberman, D. B. (1983). Empathy and ego development. *Journal of Counseling Psychology, 30,* 113-116.

Carver, C. S. (1998). Resilience and thriving: Issues, models, and linkages. *Journal of Social Issues, 54*(2), 245-266.

Chandler, H. M., Alexander, C. N., & Heaton, D. P. (2005). The Transcendental Meditation program and postconventional self-development: A 10-year longitudinal study. *Journal of Social Behavior and Personality, 17,* 93–121.

Chia, M., & Huang, T. (2005). *The Secret Teachings of the Tao Te Ching.* Rochester, VT: Destiny Books.

Chögyam Trungpa. (1991). *Crazy Wisdom.* Boston: Shambhala Publications.

Chögyam Trungpa. (2002). *Cutting Through Spiritual Materialism.* Boston, MA: Shambhala New Edition.

Chögyam Trungpa. (2015). *Mindfulness in Action: Making Friends with Yourself through Meditation and Everyday Awareness.* Boston, MA: Shambhala Publications.

Chögyam Trungpa, & Goleman, D. (2005). *The Sanity We Are Born With: A Buddhist Approach to Psychology.* Boston, MA: Shambhala Publications.

Clark, F. V. (1977). Transpersonal perspectives in psychotherapy. *Journal of Humanistic Psychology, 17*(2), 69-81.

Clements, J. (2004). Organic Inquiry: Toward research in partnership with spirit. *Journal of Transpersonal Psychology, 36*(1), 26-49.

Clements, J., Ettling, D., Jenett, D., & Shields, L. (1999). *Organic Inquiry: If Research Were Sacred.* Unpublished manuscript.

Cloninger, C. R., Svrakic, D. M., & Przybeck, T. R. (1993). A psychobiological model of temperament and character. *Archives of General Psychiatry, 50*(12), 975-990.

Cohen, K. (May/June 2003). Healing through ancient traditions: Qigong and Native American medicine. *Alternative Therapies*, 9(3), 83-91.

Cole, B. S., & Pargament, K. I. (1999). Spiritual surrender: A paradoxical path to control. In W. R. Miller, et al. (Eds.), *Integrating Spirituality into Treatment: Resources for Practitioners*, 179-198. Washington, DC: American Psychological Association.

Comstock, C. (1987). Internal self helpers as centers. *Integration, 3*(1), 3-12.

Comstock, C. (1991). The inner self helper and concepts of inner guidance: Historical antecedents, its role within dissociation, and clinical utilization. *Dissociation, 4*, 165-177.

Cook-Greuter, S. (1990). Maps for living: Ego-development stages from symbiosis to conscious universal embeddedness. In M. L. Commons, C. Armon, L. Kohlberg, F. A. Richards, T. A. Grotzer, & J. D. Sinnott (Eds.), *Adult Development vol. 2, Models and Methods in the Study of Adolescent and Adult Thought*, 79-104. New York: Praeger.

Cook-Greuter, S. R. (1995). *Comprehensive Language Awareness: A Definition of the Phenomenon and a Review of its Treatment in the Postformal Adult Development Literature.* Cambridge, MA: Harvard University Graduate School of Education.

Cook-Greuter, S. (2000). Mature ego development: A gateway to ego transcendence? *Journal of Adult Development*, 7(4), 227-240.

Corbetta, M., & Shulman, G. L. (2002). Control of goal-directed and stimulus-driven attention in the brain. *National Review of Neuroscience*, 3, 201–215.

Cortright, B. (1997). *Psythotherapy and Spirit: Theory and Practice in Transpersonal Psychotherapy.* Albany, NY: State University of New York Press.

Cortright, B. (2007). *Integral Psychology.* Albany, NY: State University of New York Press.

Cousineau, P. (2003). *The Way Things Are: Conversations with Huston Smith on the Spiritual Life.* Berkeley, CA: University of California Press.

Cowen, D., & Levin, R. (1995). The use of the Hartmann Boundary Questionnaire with an adolescent population. *Dreaming*, 5(2), 105-114.

Craig, G. (2008). *The EFT Manual.* Energy Psychology Press.

Crampton, M. (1974). Psychological energy transformations: Developing positive polarizatlon. *Journal of Transpersonal Psychology*, 6(1), 39-56.

Critchley, H. D., Wiens, S., Rotshtein, P., et al. (2004). Neural systems supporting interoceptive awareness. *Nature Neurosciences*, 7, 189-195.

Crumbaugh, J. C., & Maholick, L. T. (1964). An experimental study in existentialism: The psychometric approach to Frankl's concept of noogenic neurosis. *Journal of Clinical Psychology*, 20(2), 200-207.

Csikszentmihalyi, M. (1990). *Flow: The Psychology of Optimal Experience*. New York: HarperPerrenial.

Csikszentmihalyi, M. (1993). *The Evolving Self: A Psychology for the Third Millennium*. New York: HarperCollins.

Cunningham, P. F. (2007). The Challenges, Prospects, and Promise of Transpersonal Psychology. *International Journal of Transpersonal Studies*, 26, 41-55.

Cutsinger, J. (2003). The ladder of divine ascent: The yoga of hesychasm. In B. Dieker & J. Montaldo (Eds.), *Merton and Hesychasm: The prayer of the Heart in the Eastern Church*, 75-89. Louisville, KY: Fons Vitae.

d'Aquili, E. G., & Newberg, A. B. (1993). Religious and mystical states: A neuropsychological model. *Zygon: Journal of Religion and Science*, 28, 177–199.

d'Aquili, E. G., & Newberg, A. B. (1998). The neuropsychological basis of religions, or why God won't go away. *Zygon: Journal Of Religion & Science*, 33(2), 187.

d'Aquili, E., & Newberg, A. B. (1999). *The Mystical Mind: Probing the Biology of Religious Experience*. Minneapolis, MN: Fortress Press.

d'Aquili, E. G., & Newberg, A. B. (March 2000). The neuropsychology of aesthetic, spiritual, and mystical states. *Zygon: Journal of Religion and Science*, 35(1), 39-51.

Damasio, A. (1994). *Descartes' Error*. New York: Grosett/Putnam.

Damon, W., & Hart, D. (1988). *Self-Understanding in Childhood and Adolescence*. New York: Cambridge University Press.

Daniels, M. (2005). *Shadow, Self, Spirit: Essays in Transpersonal Psychology*. Charlottesville, VA: Imprint Academic.

Davis, J. (Spring 2000). We Keep Asking Ourselves, What Is Transpersonal Psychology? *Guidance & Counseling*, 15(3), 3.

Davis, J. (2009). Complementary research methods in Humanistic and Transpersonal Psychology: A case for methodological pluralism. *Humanistic Psychologist, 37*(1), 4-23.

Deci, E. L., & Ryan, R. M. (2000). The 'what' and 'why' of goal pursuits: Human needs and the self-determination of behavior. *Psychological Inquiry, 11*(4), 227-268.

Deci, E. L., & Ryan, R. M. (2008). Hedonia, eudaimonia, and well-being: An introduction. *Journal of Happiness Studies, 9,* 1–11.

DeCicco, T. L., & Stroink, M. L. (2007). A third model of self-construal: The metapersonal self. *International Journal of Transpersonal Studies, 26,* 82-104.

Deikman, A. J. (1982). *The Observing Self: Mysticism and Psychotherapy.* Boston, MA: Beacon Press.

de Lange, F. P., Koers, A., Kalkman, J. S., Bleijenberg, G., Hagoort, P., van der Meer, J. W. M., et al. (2008). Increases in prefrontal cortical volume following cognitive behavioral therapy in patients with chronic fatigue syndrome. *Brain, 13*(8), 2172-2180.

Denzin, N. K., & Lincoln, Y. S. (Eds.). (1994). *Handbook of Qualitative Research.* Thousand Oaks, CA: Sage.

Desjardins, A. (1972). *Les chemins de la Sagesse* (Tomes, I, II, III). Paris: La Table Ronde.

Deslauriers, D. (1992). Dimensions of knowing: Narrative, paradigm, and ritual. *ReVision: A Journal of Consciousness and Transformation, 14*(4), 187–193.

Diop, C. A. (1974). *The African Origin of Civilization: Myth or Reality.* New York: Lawrence Hill and Company.

Domhoff, G. W. (2003). *Senoi Dream Theory: Myth, Scientific Method, and the Dreamwork Movement.* Retrieved from: http://dreamresearch.net/Library/senoi.html

Dow, J. (1986). Universal aspects of symbolic healing: A theoretical synthesis. *American Anthropologist, 88*(1), 56-69.

Dworkin, A. (1981). *Pornography: Men Possessing Women.* New York: Perigee.

Eagle Feather, K. (K. Smith). (2007). *Toltec Dreaming: Don Juan's Teachings on the Energy Body.* Rochester, VT: Bear and Company.

Edinger, E. F. (Jan 1961). The Ego-Self Paradox. *Journal of Analytical Psychology, 6*(1), 69-75.

Edinger, E. F. (1972). *Ego and Archetype: Individuation and the Religious Function of the Psyche.* Boston: Shambala Publications.

Edinger, E. F. (1985). *Anatomy of the Psyche*. LaSalle, IL: Open Court.

Egner, T., Jamieson, G. A., & Gruzelier, J. (2005). Hypnosis decouples cognitive control from conflict monitoring processes of the frontal lobes. *Neuroimage*, 27, 143-149.

Eliade, M. (1957). *The Sacred and the Profane*. New York: Harcourt, Brace, and World.

Eliade, M. (1964/1951). *Shamanism: Archaic Techniques of Ecstasy*. New York: Pantheon.

Engler, J. (1983). Vicissitudes of the self according to psychoanalysis and Buddhism: A spectrum model of object relations development. *Psychoanalysis and Contemporary Thought*, 6(1), 29-72.

Epstein, M. (1984). On the neglect of evenly suspended attention. *Journal of Transpersonal Psychology*, 16, 193-205.

Epstein, M. (1988). The deconstruction of the self: Ego and "egolessness" in Buddhist insight meditation. *Journal of Transpersonal Psychology*, 20(1), 61-69.

Epstein M. (1995). Release: the Buddha's third truth; Nowhere standing: the Buddha's fourth truth; Bare attention; The psychodynamics of meditation. In *Thoughts without a Thinker*. New York: Basic Books, 75-155.

Esman, A (1983). The stimulus barrier. *Psychoanalytic Study of the Child*, 38, 193-207.

Fadiman, J. (1980). The transpersonal stance. In R. Walsh & F. Vaughan (Eds.), *Beyond Ego,* 175-181. Los Angeles: Tardier.

Fadiman, J., Grob, C., Bravo, G., Agar, A., & Walsh, R. (2003). Psychedelic research revisited. *Journal of Transpersonal Psychology*, 35, 111-125.

Faithhorn, L. (1992). Three ways of ethnographic knowing. *ReVision: A Journal of Consciousness and Transformation*, 15(1), 23-27.

Feinstein, D., & Krippner, S. (2006). *The Mythic Path: Discovering the Guiding Stories of Your Past—Creating a Vision for Your Future* (3rd ed.). Santa Rosa, CA: Energy Psychology Press/Elite Books.

Fenner, P. (2003). Nonduality and therapy: Awakening the unconditioned mind. In J. Prendergast, P. Fenner, & S. Krystal (Eds.), *The Sacred Mirror: Nondual Wisdom and Psychotherapy*, 23-36. St. Paul, MN: Paragon House.

Ferrer, J. (2002). *Revisioning Transpersonal Theory: A Participatory Vision of Human Spirituality*. Albany, NY: State University of New York Press.

312

Firman, D. (2011). *Transpersonal psychology: An introduction to psychosynthesis.* Retrieved from http://counselingoutfitters.com/ vistas/vistas11/Article_49.pdf

Firman, J. (1993). *Je et Soi. Nouvelles perspectives en psychosynthèse* [I and Self. Re-Visioning Psychosynthesis]. Sainte-Foy: Le Centre d'intégration de la personne de Québec.

Firman, J., & Gila, A. (2002). *Psychosynthesis: A Psychology of the Spirit.* New York: State University of New York Press.

Fischer, C. T. (2006). Humanistic psychology and qualitative research: Affinity, clarifications, and invitations. *Humanistic Psychologist, 34*(1), 3-11.

Flint, G. O. (2006). *Theory and Treatment of Your Personality: A Manual for Change.* Vernon, B.B.: NeoSolteric Enterprises.

Fonagy, P. (2001). *Attachment Theory and Psychoanalysis.* New York: Other Press.

Fonagy, P., Gergely, G., Jurist, E. & Target, M. (2002). *Affect Regulation, Mentalization, and the Development of the Self.* New York: Other Press.

Fordham, M. (1985). *Explorations into the Self.* London: Academic Press.

Fox, M. (1995). *Wrestling with the Prophets.* San Francisco: Harper SanFrancisco.

Frager, R. (1974). A proposed model for a graduate program in Transpersonal Psychology. *Journal of Transpersonal Psychology, 6,* 163-166.

Frager, R., & Fadiman, J. (2005). *Personality and Personal Growth* (6th ed.). Upper Saddle River, NJ: Prentice Hall.

Frankl, V. (1955). *The Doctor and the Soul.* New York: Knopf.

Frankl, V. E. (1960). Beyond self-actualization and self-expression. *Journal of Existential Psychiatry, 1,* 5-20.

Frankl, V. E. (1963). *Man's Search for Meaning: An Introduction to Logotherapy.* New York: Pocket Books.

Frankl, V. E. (1967). *Psychotherapy and Existentialism: Selected Papers on Logotherapy.* New York: Simon & Schuster.

Fraser, G. (1991). The dissociative table technique: A strategy of working with ego states in dissociative disorders and ego state therapy. *Dissociation, 4,* 205-213.

Fraser, G. A., & Curtis, J. C. (Nov 1984). *A Subpersonality Theory of Multiple Personality.* Presented at the First International Conference of Multiple Personality Disorder and Dissociation, Chicago, Illinois.

Frederick, C. (2003). *You Are Always in my Heart: Grief as a Resource.* Paper presented at the First World Congress of Ego State Therapy. March 22, 2003, Bad Orb, Germany.

Frederick, C. (2005). Selected topics in ego state therapy [Monograph]. *International Journal of Clinical and Experimental Hypnosis, 53,* 339-428.

Frederick, C. (2010). Members' clinical corner focus article and expert commentary. Expert commentary: Gifts from the center core. Retrieved from http://www.isst-d.org/membersonly/MCC/MCC_2011_05_Frederick_Commentary.pdf

Frederick, C. (2014). The Center Core in Ego State Therapy and other hypnotically facilitated psychotherapies. *American Journal of Clinical Hypnosis, 56,* 39–53.

Frederick, C., & McNeal, S. (1999). *Inner strengths: Contemporary psychotherapy and hypnosis for ego-strengthening.* Mahwah, NJ: Lawrence Erlbaum Associates.

Freud, S. (1939). *Moses and Monotheism.* SE 23, 3–137.

Friedman, H. (1983). The self-expansiveness level form: A conceptualization and measurement of a transpersonal construct. *Journal of Transpersonal Psychology,* 15(1), 37-50.

Friedman, H., & MacDonald, D. (1997). Towards a working definition of transpersonal assessment. *Journal of Transpersonal Psychology, 29,* 105-122.

Friedman, H., & Pappas, J. (2006). Self-expansiveness and self-contraction: Complementary processes of transcendence and immanence. *The Journal of Transpersonal Psychology,* 38(1), 41-54.

Friedman, R. (2004). Dream-telling as a request for containment: Reconsidering the group-analytic approach to the work with dreams. *Group Analysis,* 37(4), 508-524.

Fromm, E., & Suzuki, D. T. (1960). *Zen and Psychoanalysis.* New York: Harper & Row.

Gagan, J. M. (1998). *Journeying: Where Shamanism and Psychology Meet.* Santa Fe, NM: Rio Chama Publications.

Gainer, M. J., & Torem, M. S. (1993). Ego state therapy for self-injurious behavior. *American Journal of Clinical Hypnosis, 35,* 257-266.

Garb, J. (2011). *Shamanic Trance in Modern Kabbalah.* Chicago, IL: University of Chicago Press.

Garcia-Romeu, A. (2010). Self-transcendence as a measurable transpersonal construct. *Journal of Transpersonal Psychology*, 42(1), 26-47.

Gardner, H. (1983). *Frames of Mind: The Theory of Multiple Intelligences*. New York: Basic Books.

Gardner, H. (1999). *Intelligence Reframed: Multiple Intelligences for the 21st Century*. New York: Basic Books.

Gendlin, E. T. (1962). *Experiencing and the Creation of Meaning*. New York: Macmillan.

Gendlin, E. T. (1978/2007). *Focusing*. New York: Bantam Books.

Gendlin, E. T. (2004). *Let Your Body Interpret Your Dreams*. Chicago: Chiron Publications.

Gerard, R. (1964). *Psychosynthesis: A Psycho-therapy for the Whole Man*. Amherst, MA: Psychosynthesis Distribution.

Giannini, J. L. (2004). *Compass of the Soul: Archetypal Guides to a Fuller Life*. Gainesville, FL: Center for Applications of Psychological Type.

Gibson, L. (n. d.) Ontology of the Shadow. Retrieved from http://www.stanislavgrof.com/pdf/Ontology%20of%20the%20Shadow%20full%20paper.pdf.

Gibson, T. L. (2000). Wholeness and transcendence in the practice of pastoral psychotherapy from a Judeo-Christian perspective. In P. Young-Eisendrath and M. E. Miller (Eds.), *The Psychology of Mature Spirituality*, 175-186. Philadelphia, PA: Taylor & Francis Inc.

Gilligan, S. G. (1987). *Therapeutic trances: The cooperation principle in Ericksonian hypnotherapy*. New York: Brunner/Mazel.

Gimello, R. (1978). Mysticism and meditation. In S. Katz (Ed.), *Mysticism and Philosophical Analysis*. New York: Oxford University Press.

Ginandes, C. (2006). Six players on the inner stage: Using ego state therapy with the medically ill. *International Journal of Clinical and Experimental Hypnosis, 54*(2), 113-129.

Glaser, B. G. (1978). *Theoretical Sensitivity*. Mill Valley, CA: Sociology Press.

Goleman, D. (1975). The Buddha on meditation and states of consciousness. In C. Tart, (Ed.), *Transpersonal Psychologies*, 203-230. New York: Harper & Row.

Goleman, D. (1977). *The Meditative Mind*. New York: Perigree.

Goleman, D. (1994). *Emotional Intelligence*. New York: Bantam Books.

Goodman, R. (1992). *Lakota Star Knowledge: Studies in Lakota Stellar Theology* (2nd ed.). Rosebud, SD: Sinte Gleska University.

Goodman, S. (Spring 2005). Wisdom Crazy: An Interview with Steven Goodman. *Inquiring Mind*, retrieved from http://www.inquiringmind.com/Articles/WisdomCrazy.html.

Greening, T. (2006). Five basic postulates of humanistic psychology. *Journal of Humanistic Psychology*, 46(3), 239-239.

Grof, S. (1980). *LSD Psychotherapy*. Sarasota, FL: Hunter House.

Grof, S. (1985). *Beyond the Brain*. Albany, NY: State University of New York Press.

Grof, S. (1987). *The Adventure of Self Discovery*. Albany, NY: State University of New York Press

Grof, S. (2000). *Psychology of the Future*. Albany, NY: State University of New York Press.

Grof, S. (2008). Brief History of Transpersonal Psychology. *International Journal of Transpersonal Studies, 27*, 46-54.

Grof, S. (n.d. a). Ervin Laszlo's Akashic Field and the Dilemmas of Modern Consciousness Research. Retrieved from http://www.stanislavgrof.com/pdf/Ervin_Laszlo.pdf

Grof, S. (n.d. b). Holotropic Research and Archetypal Astrology. Retrieved from http://www.stanislavgrof.com/pdf/05_Archai_Grof_Holotropic_Research.pdf

Grof, S., & Grof, C. (Eds.) (1989). *Spiritual Emergency: When Personal Transformation Becomes a Crisis.* Los Angeles: Tarcher.

Gregory, B. (2012). The integration and application of tai chi principles with mind-body hypnotherapy. *Australian Journal of Clinical & Experimental Hypnosis, 40*(1), 51-72.

Gubi, P. M. (2008). *Prayer in Counselling and Psychotherapy: Exploring a Hidden Meaningful Dimension.* London: Jessica Kingsley Publishers.

Gurdjieff, G. I. (1963). *Meetings with Remarkable Men*. New York: E. P. Dutton & Co.

Gyatso, G. K. (2003). *Tantric Grounds and Paths: How to Enter, Progress on, and Complete the Vajrayana Path*. Glen Spey, NY: Tharpa Publications.

Haley, J. (1963). *Strategies of Psychotherapy*. New York: Grune & Stratton.

Hall, C. S., & Lindzey, G. (1978). *Theories of Personality*. New York: Wiley.

Hall, J. A. (1989). *Hypnosis: A Jungian Perspective*. New York: The Guilford Press.

316

Hamachek, D. E. (Oct 1985). The self's development and ego growth: Conceptual analysis and implications for counselors. *Journal of Counseling and Development*, 64(2), 136-142.

Hamel, S. (1997). *Étude exploratoire du besoin de transcendance et des modalités de satisfaction chez des étudiant(e)s universitaires en psychologie.* Unpublished Doctoral Dissertation, Université de Montréal, Qc, Canada.

Hamel, S., Leclerc, G., & Lefrançois, R. (2003). A psychological outlook on the concept of transcendent actualization. *The International Journal for the Psychology of Religion*, 13(1), 3-15.

Harner, M. (1982). *The Way of the Shaman.* New York: Bantam.

Harner, M. (2013). *Cave and Cosmos: Shamanic Encounters with Spirits and Heavens.* Berkeley, CA: North Atlantic Books.

Hartelius, G., Caplan, M., & Rardin, M. A. (2007). Transpersonal psychology: Defining the past, divining the future. *The Humanistic Psychologist*, 35(2), 135–160.

Harter, S. (1998). The development of self-representations. In W. Damon (Series Ed.) & N. Eisenberg (Vol. Ed.), *Handbook of Child Psychology: Vol. 3. Social, Emotional, and Personality Development* (5th Ed.), 553-617. New York: Wiley.

Hartman, D., & Zimberoff, D. (2003). The existential approach in Heart-Centered therapies. *Journal of Heart-Centered Therapies*, 6(1), 3-46.

Hartman, D., & Zimberoff, D. (2003a). Ego states in Heart-Centered therapies. *Journal of Heart-Centered Therapies*, 6(1), 47-92.

Hartman, D. & Zimberoff, D. (2008a). Dream Journey: A new Heart-Centered therapies modality. *Journal of Heart-Centered Therapies*, 11(1), 33-90.

Hartman, D. & Zimberoff, D. (2008b). Higher stages of human development. *Journal of Heart-Centered Therapies*, 11(2), 3-95.

Hartman, D., & Zimberoff, D. (2010). Immanent transcendence, projection and re-collection. *Journal of Heart-Centered Therapies*, 13(2), 3-66.

Hartman, D., & Zimberoff, D. (2012). A trauma-weakened ego goes seeking a bodyguard. *Journal of Heart-Centered Therapies*, 15(1), 27-71.

Hartman, D., & Zimberoff, D. (2014). *From Therapy to Life Mastery: Coaching, Natural Next Step from Hypnotherapy.* Issaquah, WA: Wellness Press.

Hartmann, E. (1991). *Boundaries in the Mind: A New Psychology of Personality.* New York: Basic Books.

Hartmann, E., Elkin, R., & Gag, M. (1991). Personality and dreaming: The dreams of people with very thick or very thin boundaries. *Dreaming*, 1, 311-324.

Hartmann, E., Russ, D., Oldfield, M., Sivan, I., & Cooper, S. (1987). Who has nightmares? The personality of the lifelong nightmare sufferer. *Archives of General Psychiatry*, 44, 49-56.

Hartmann, H. (1950). Psychoanalysis and developmental psychology. *Psychoanalytic Study of the Child*, 5,7-17.

Hartmann, H. (1961). *Ego Psychology and the Problems of Adaptation*. New York: International Universities Press.

Hartmann, H. (1965). *Essays on Ego Psychology*. New York: International Universities Press.

Hay, D. (2006). *Something There*. Philadelphia: Templeton Foundation Press.

Heery, M. W. (1989). Inner voice experiences: An exploratory study of thirty cases. *Journal of Transpersonal Psychology*, 21(1), 73-82.

Heidegger, M. (1962/1927). *Being and Time* (J. Macquarrie & E. Robinson, Trans.). New York: Harper & Row. (Original work published in 1927).

Helgeson, V. S., & Fritz, H. L. (1999). Unmitigated agency and unmitigated communion: Distinctions from agency and communion. *Journal of Research in Personality*, 33, 131-158.

Helson, R., & Roberts, B. W. (1994). Ego development and personality change in adulthood. *Journal of Personality and Social Psychology*, 66, 911-920.

Helson, R., & Srivastava, S. (Jun 2001). Three paths of adult development: Conservers, seekers, and achievers. *Journal of Personality & Social Psychology*, 80(6), 995-1010.

Helson, R., & Wink, P. (1987). Two conceptions of maturity examined in the findings of a longitudinal study. *Journal of Personality and Social Psychology*, 53, 531-541.

Heron, J. (1998). *Sacred Science: Person-Centered Inquiry into the Spiritual and the Subtle*. Ross-on-Wye, England: PCCS Books.

Hick, S. F. (2008). Cultivating therapeutic relationships: The role of mindfulness. In S. F. Hick & T. Bien (Eds.), *Mindfulness and the Therapeutic Relationship*, 3-33. New York: Guilford Press.

Hill, D. L. (2006). Sense of belonging as connectedness, American Indian worldview, and mental health. *Archives of Psychiatric Nursing*, 20, 210-216.

Hillman, J. (1979). *The Dream and the Underworld*. New York: HarperPerennial.

Hillman, J. (2000). *The Force of Character: And the Lasting Life*. New York: Ballantine Books.

Hugdahl, K. (1996). Cognitive influences on human autonomic nervous system function. *Current Opinion in Neurobiology*, 6, 252-258.

Huxley, A. (1970/1945). *The Perennial Philosophy*. New York: Harper & Row. (Original work published in 1945)

Huxley, A. (1998/1932). *Brave New World* (First Perennial Classics ed.). New York: HarperCollins Publishers. (Original work published in 1932)

Huxley, A. (2011/1954). *The Doors of Perception*. London: Thinking Ink. (Original work published in 1954)

Hy, L. X., & Loevinger, J. (1996). *Measuring Ego Development (2nd ed)*. Mahwah, NJ: Lawrence Erlbaum.

Idel, M. (2009). Mystical weeping. Jewish Heritage Online Magazine. Retrieved from http://jhom.com/topics/tears/mystical.html

Institute of Transpersonal Psychology. Retrieved from http://www.sofia.edu/about/history/.

Isakower, I. (1938). A contribution to the patho-psychology of phenomena associated with falling asleep. *International Journal of Psychoanalysis*, 19, 331-345.

Jacobs, J. E., Bleeker, M. M., & Constantino, M. J. (2003). The self-system during childhood and adolescence: Development, influences, and implications. *Journal of Psychotherapy Integration*, 13(1), 33-65.

Jacoby, M. A. (1985). *Longing for Paradise: Psychological Perspectives on an Archetype*. Boston, MA: Sigo Press.

James, G. (1954). *Stolen Legacy*. New York: Philosophical Library.

James, W. (1890). *Principles of psychology* (Vol. 1). New York: Holt.

James, W. (1902/1980). *Varieties of Religious Experience*. London: Fontana.

James, W. (1912/1976). Essays in radical empiricism. Cambridge, MA: Harvard University Press. (Original work published 1912)

Jensen, D. (April 2001). Saving the indigenous soul: An interview with Martin Prechtel. *The Sun Magazine*, 381.

Johnson, R. A. (1986). *Inner Work: Using Dreams and Active Imagination for Personal Growth*. New York: HarperCollins.

Jordan, J. V., & Hartling, L. M. (2002). New developments in relational-cultural theory. In M. Ballou & L. S. Brown (Eds.), *Rethinking Mental*

Health and Disorder: Feminist Perspectives, 48-70. New York: Guilford Press.

Jung, C. G. (1925). 'Marriage As a Psychological Relationship', *CW17*.

Jung, C. G. (1928/1934). *The Relations between the Ego and the Unconscious. CW* 7, paras. 202–406.

Jung, C. G. (1933). *Modern Man in Search of a Soul* (W. S. Dell & C. F. Baynes, Trans.). New York: Harcourt, Brace & World.

Jung, C. G. (1939). *The Integration of the Personality.* New York: Farrar & Rinehart.

Jung, C. G. (1955). "Wotan," *Civilization in Transition, Collected Works, Vol. 10*. Princeton, NJ: Princeton University Press.

Jung, C. G. (1960/1931). The structure of the psyche. In S. H. Read, M. Fordham, & G. Adler (Eds.), R.F.C. Hull (Trans.), *The Collected Works of C. G. Jung*, Vol. 8, 139–158. New York: Pantheon Books. (Original work published 1931)

Jung, C. G. (1960). The structure and dynamics of the psyche: The transcendent function. In R. F. C. Hull (Trans.) *The collected works of C. G. Jung, Vol. VIII*, 67-91. Bollingen Series XX. Princeton, NJ: Princeton University Press.

Jung, C. G. (1961). *Memories, Dreams, Reflections*. (R. Winston & C. Winston, Trans.). New York: Vintage Books.

Jung, C. G. (1964). *Collected Works: Vol. 10. Psychology of Religion: East and West*. Bollingen Series 20. Princeton, NJ: Princeton University Press.

Jung, C. G. (1966). "The Mana Personality." *The Collected Works of C. G. Jung: Two Essays on Analytical Psychology*. Vol. 7, second ed. Princeton: Bollingen, para 384.

Jung, C. G. (1967). *Collected Works: Vol. 13. Alchemical Studies*. Bollingen Series 20. Princeton, NJ: Princeton University Press.

Jung, C. G. (1970). *Psychoanalysis and the Cure of Souls*. In *Psychology and Religion West and East*. New York: Pantheon Press.

Jung, C. G. (1971). Phenomenology of the self. In J. Campbell & R.F.C. Hull (Eds., Trans.), *The Portable Jung*, 139-162. New York: Penguin Books.

Jung, C. G. (1973). *C. G. Jung Letters*, Vol. 1, Gerhard Adler, Aniel Jaffe (Eds.), trans. By R.F.C. Hull. Bollingen Series XCV: 1, Princeton, NJ: Princeton University Press.

Jung, C. G. (1975). *Letters*. Selected and edited by G. Adler & A. Jaffe. Vol. 2 (1951-1961). Princeton, NJ: Princeton University Press.

Jung, C. G. (1978). *C. G. Jung Speaking*, W. McGuire (Ed.). Thames & Hudson, London: Picador.

Jung, C. G. (1980). *The Symbolic Life*, translated by R. F. C. Hull. In *The Collected Works* 18, 2nd ed., Bollingen Series XX. Princeton, NJ: Princeton University Press.

Jung, C. G. (1988). *Jung's Seminar on Nietzsche's Zarathustra* (Ed. J. Jarrett). Princeton, NJ: Princeton University Press, 1934-1939.

Jung, C. G. (1996). *The Psychology of Kundalini Yoga: Notes of the Seminar Given in 1932 by C. G. Jung*, Sonu Shamdasani (Ed.). Bollingen Series XCIX. Princeton, NJ: Princeton University Press.

Jung, C. G. (2009). *The Red Book*, edited by Sonu Shamdasani. New York: W. W. Norton & Company.

Kabat-Zinn, J. (1982). An outpatient program in behavioral medicine for chronic pain patients based on the practice of mindfulness meditation: Theoretical considerations and preliminary results. *General Hospital Psychiatry, 4*, 33-47.

Kabat-Zinn, J. (1990). *Full Catastrophe Living: Using the Wisdom of Your Body and Mind to Face Stress*. New York: Delacorte.

Kalff, M. (1983). The negation of ego in Tibetan Buddhism and Jungian psychology. *Journal of Transpersonal Psychology*, 15(2), 103-124.

Kalton, M. C. (2000). Green spirituality: Horizontal transcendence. In P. Young-Eisendrath and M. E. Miller (Eds.), *The Psychology of Mature Spirituality*, 187-200. Philadelphia, PA: Taylor & Francis Inc.

Karpman, S. (Apr 1968). Script drama analysis. *Transactional Analysis Bulletin*, 7(26).

Kasprow, M.C., & Scotton, B.W. (Winter 1999). A review of transpersonal theory and its application to the practice of psychotherapy [Review]. *Journal of Psychotherapy Practice & Research*, 8(1), 12-23.

Kegan, R. (1982). *The Evolving Self: Problem and Process in Human Development*. Cambridge, MA: Harvard University Press.

Kegan, R. (1994). *In Over Our Heads: The Mental Demands of Modern Life*. Cambridge, MA: Harvard University Press.

Kelly, G. A. (1955). *A Theory of Personality: The Psychology of Personal Constructs*. New York: Norton.

Keutzer, C. S. (1984). Transpersonal psychotherapy: Reflections on the genre. *Professional Psychology: Research And Practice*, 15(6), 868-883.

Khan, V. I. (1982). *Introducing Spirituality into Counseling and Therapy*. Lebanon Springs, NY: Omega Press.

Kierkegaard, S. (1970). *The Concept of Dread*. Princeton, NJ: Princeton University Press.

Kierkegaard, S. (1980). The Sickness unto Death. (edited and translated by H. V. Hong and E. H. Hong). *The Kierkegaard Writings XIX*. Princeton, NJ: Princeton University Press.

King, L. A. (1998). Personal goals and personal agency: Linking everyday goals to future images of the self. In M. Kofta, G. Weary, & G. Sedek (Eds.), *Personal Control in Action: Cognitive and Motivational Mechanisms*, 109–128. New York: Plenum.

King, L. A., & Hicks, J. A. (Summer 2007). Lost and found possible selves: Goals, development, and well-being. *New Directions for Adult & Continuing Education*, 114, 27-37.

King, L. A., & Raspin, C. (Jun 2004). Lost and found possible selves, subjective well-being, and ego development in divorced women. *Journal of Personality*, 72(3), 603-632.

Kluft, R. P. (1989). Playing for time: Temporizing techniques in the treatment of multiple personality disorder. *American Journal of Clinical Hypnosis. 32*, 90-98.

Knabb, J. J., & Welsh, R. K. (2009). Reconsidering A. Reza Arasteh: Sufism and Psychotherapy. *Journal of Transpersonal Psychology*, *41*(1), 44-60.

Knapp, R. (1976). *Handbook for the Personal Orientation Inventory*. San Diego, CA: Educational and Industrial Testing Service.

Knox, J. (2004). Developmental aspects of analytical psychology: New perspectives from cognitive neuroscience and attachment theory - Jung's model of the mind. In J. Cambray & L. Carter (Eds.), *Analytical Psychology*, 56-82. New York: Brunner-Routledge.

Kohn, L., &Wang, R. R. (Eds.). (2009). *Internal Alchemy*. Magdalena, NM: Three Pines Press.

Koplowitz, H. (1984). A projection beyond Piaget's formal operations stage: A general system stage and a unitary stage. In M. L. Commons, F. A. Richards, & C. Armon (Eds.), *Beyond Formal* Operations, 279-295. New York: Praeger.

Koplowitz, H. (1990). Unitary consciousness and the highest development of mind: The relation between spiritual development and cognitive development. In M. L. Commons, C. Armon, L. Kohlberg, F. A.

Richards, T. Grotzer, & J. D. Sinnott (Eds.), *Adult Development, vol. 2*, 105-111. New York: Praeger.

Kornfield, J., & Walsh, R. (1993). Meditation: Royal road to the transpersonal. In R. Walsh & F. Vaughan (Eds.), *Paths Beyond Ego: The Transpersonal Vision*, 56–69. New York: Penguin Putnam.

Krakauer, S. Y. (2001). *Treating Dissociative Disorder: The Power of the Collective Heart*. Ann Arbor, MI: Edwards Brothers.

Krakauer, S. Y. (2006). The two-part film technique: Empowering dissociative clients to alter cognitive distortions and maladaptive behaviors. *Journal of Trauma and Dissociation, 72*, 19-57.

Krieger, D. (1975). Therapeutic Touch: The imprimatur of nursing. *American Journal of Nursing, 75(5)*.

Krippner, S. (2009). Indigenous health care practitioners and the hypnotic-like healing procedures. *Journal of Transpersonal Research*, 1(1), 7-18.

Krippner, S. (2012). Shamans as healers, counselors, and psychotherapists. *International Journal of Transpersonal Studies*, 31(2), 72-79.

Krippner, S., & Welch, P. (1992). *Spiritual Dimensions of Healing: From Native Shamanism to Contemporary Health Care*. New York: Irvington Publishers.

Krishnamurti, J. (1964). The problem of freedom. In D. Rajagopal (Ed.), *Krishnamurti: Think on These Things*, 9-17. New York: HarperCollins.

Krishnamurti, J. (1973). *You Are the World: Authentic Report of Talks and Discussions in American Universities*. New York: Harper and Row.

Kristeller, J. (2011). Spirituality and meditation. In J. D. Aten, M. R. McMinn, & E. L. Worthington, (Eds.), *Spiritually Oriented Interventions for Counseling and Psychotherapy*, 197-227. Washington, DC: American Psychological Association.

Kuhl, J., & Helle, P. (1986). Motivational and volitional determinants of depression: The degenerated intention hypothesis. *Journal of Abnormal Psychology*, 95, 247–251.

Labouvie-Vief, G. (1993). Ego processes in adulthood: A comment on Jane Loevinger. *Psychological Inquiry*, 4, 34-37.

Labouvie-Vief, G., & Diehl, M. (1998). The role of ego development in the adult self. In P. M. Westenberg, A. Blasi, & L. D. Cohn (Eds.), *Personality Development: Theoretical, Empirical, and Clinical Investigations of Loevinger's Conception of Ego Development*, 219-235. Mahwah, NJ: Lawrence Erlbaum.

Laenen, J. H. (1998/2001). *Jewish Mysticism: An Introduction.* (D. E. Orton, Trans.). Louisville, KY: Westminister John Knox Press.

Lahood, G. (2007). One hundred years of sacred science: Participation and hybridity in transpersonal anthropology. *Revision,* 29(3), 37-48.

Lakshmanjoo, Swami. (2000). *Kashmir Shaivism: The Secret Supreme.* Culver City, CA: Universal Shaiva Fellowship.

Langer, E. (1989). *Mindfulness.* New York: Addison-Wesley.

Larson, J., & Lynch, G. (1986). Induction of synaptic potentiation in hippocampus by pattered stimulation involves two events. *Science,* 232, 985-988.

Latner, J. (1973). *The Gestalt Therapy Book.* New York: Bantam Book.

Laughlin, C., McManus, J., & Shearer, J. (1993). Toward a transpersonal anthropology. In R. Walsh & F. Vaughn (Eds.), *Paths Beyond Ego: The Transpersonal Vision,* 190-195. New York: Putnam.

Laughlin, K. Q. (Summer 2013). The Individuation Project: Implications of a new myth. *Quadrant: Journal of the C. G. Jung Foundation for Analytical Psychology,* 43(2), 33-49.

Lazar, S. W., Kerr, C. E., Wasserman, R. H., Gray, J. R., Greve, M., Treadway, T., et al. (2005). Meditation experience is associated with increased cortical thickness. *NeuroReport,* 16(17), 1893-1897.

Leary, M. R. (2004). *The Curse of the Self: Self-awareness, Egotism, and the Quality of Life.* Oxford, England: Oxford University Press.

Lefcourt, H. M. (1983). *Research with the Locus of Control Construct: Developments and Social Problems, Vol. 2* (1st ed.). New York: Academic Press.

Lerman, H. (1986). *A Mote in Freud's Eye.* New York: Springer.

Levendula, D. (1963). Principles of Gestalt Therapy in relation to hypnotherapy. *American Journal of Clinical Hypnosis,* 6(1), 22-26.

Levin, R, Galin, J., & Zywiak, B. (1991). Nightmares, boundaries, and creativity. *Dreaming,* 1, 63-73.

Levy, J. (Spring 1983). Transpersonal Psychology and Jungian Psychology. *Journal of Humanistic Psychology,* 23(2), 42-51.

Levy-Bruhl, L. (1910/1985). *How Natives Think.* Princeton, NJ: Princeton University Press.

Lips, H. M. (1999). *A New Psychology of Women: Gender, Culture and Ethnicity.* Palo Alto, CA: Mayfield.

Loeb, L. (1975). Intensity and stimulus barrier in adolescence. *Adolescent Psychiatry,* 4, 255-263.

Loevinger, J. (1969). Theories of ego development. In L. Breger (Ed.), *Clinical-cognitive Psychology: Models and Integrations*. Englewood Cliffs, NJ: Prentice-Hall.

Loevinger, J. (1976). *Ego Development: Conceptions and Theories*. San Francisco: Jossey-Bass.

Loevinger, J. (1993). Measurement of personality: True or false. *Psychological Inquiry*, 4(1), 1-16.

Loevinger, J. (1997). Stages of personality development. In R. Hogan, J. Johnson, & S. Briggs (Eds.), *Handbook of Personality Psychology*, 199-208. San Diego, CA: Academic.

Loevinger, J., & Wessler, R. (1970). *Measuring Ego Development: Vol. 1. Construction and Use of a Sentence Completion Test*. San Francisco: Jossey-Bass.

Louchakova, O. (2005). On advantages of the Clear Mind: Spiritual practices in the training of a phenomenological researcher. *Humanistic Psychologist*, 33(2), 87-112.

Lowen, A. (1975). *Bioenergetics*. New York: Coward, McCann & Geoghegan.

Luk, C. (Lu K'uan Yu). (1977). *Taoist Yoga: Alchemy And Immortality*. York Beach, ME: Samuel Weiser.

Lutyens, M. (1975). *Krishnamurti: The Years of Awakening*. New York: Farrar, Straus & Giroux.

Lutz, A., Gretschar, L. L., Rawlings, N., Ricard, M., & Davidson, R. J. (2004). Long-term meditators self-induce high-amplitude gamma synchrony during mental practice. *Neuroscience*, 101(46), 16369-16373.

Lutz, A., Slagter, H. A., Dunne, J. D., & Davidson, R. J. (2008). Attention regulation and monitoring in meditation. *Trends in Cognitive Science*, *12*, 163–169.

MacIntyre, A. (1984). *After Virtue: A Study in Moral Theory*. South Bend, IN.: University of Notre Dame Press.

MacKinnon, C. A. (1993). Feminism, Marxism, method, and the state: Toward a feminist jurisprudence. In P. B. Bart & E. G. Moran (Eds.), *Violence Against Women: The Bloody Footprints*, 201-227. Newbury Park, CA: Sage. (Original work published 1982)

Maguire, K. (2001). Working with survivors of torture and extreme experiences. In S. King-Spooner & C. Newnes (Eds.), *Spirituality and Psychotherapy*, 122-136. Ross-on-Wye: PCCS Books.

Main, S. (2012). 'The Other Half' of education: Unconscious education of children *Educational Philosophy and Theory*,44(1), 82-95.

Makes Marks, L. F. (2007). Great mysteries: Native North American religions and participatory visions. *Revision*, 29(3), 29-36.

Maldonado, J. R., & Spiegel, D. (1998). Trauma, dissociation, and hypnotisability. In J. D. Bremner & C. R. Marmar (Eds.), *Trauma, Memory and Dissociation*. Washington DC: American Psychiatric Press.

Manners, J., & Durkin, K. (2001). A critical review of the validity of ego development theory and its measurement. *Journal of Personality Assessment*, 77(3), 541-567.

Mark, C. (2009). *Energy Healing: The Practical Workbook*. London: Watkins Publishing.

Markides, K. C. (1985). *The Magus of Strovolos: The Extraordinary World of a Spiritual Healer*. London: Routledge and Kegan Paul—reprinted by Penguin Arkana 1990.

Markides, K. C. (1987). *Homage to the Sun: The Wisdom of the Magus of Strovolos*. New York: Penguin Arkana.

Markides, K. C. (1990). *Fire in the Heart: Healers, Sages, and Mystics*. New York: Paragon House—reprinted by Penguin Arkana.

Markides, K. C. (2005). *Gifts of the Desert: The Forgotten Path of Christian Spirituality*. New York: Doubleday.

Markides, K. C. (2008). Eastern Orthodox mysticism and transpersonal theory. *Journal of Transpersonal Psychology*, 40(2), 178-198.

Markus, H. R., & Kitayama, S. (1991). Culture and the self: Implications for cognition, emotion, and motivation. *Psychological Review*, 98, 224-253.

Markus, H., & Nurius, P. (1986). Possible selves. *American Psychologist*, 41, 954–969.

Martin, J. R. (1997). Mindfulness: A proposed common factor. *Journal of Psychotherapy Integration*, 7, 291-312.

Martin, J. R. (2002). The common factor of mindfulness – an expanding discourse: Comment on Horowitz (2002). *Journal of Psychotherapy Integration*, 12(2), 139-142.

Maslow, A. H. (1943). A theory of human motivation. *Psychological Review, 50*, 370–396.

Maslow, A. H. (1970/1954). *Motivation and Personality*. New York: Harper & Row.

Maslow, A. H. (1999/1961). Peak-experiences as acute identity experiences. In A. H. Maslow, *Toward a Psychology of Being* (3rd ed.), 113-125. New York: Wiley. (Reprinted from *American Journal of Psychoanalysis*, 1961, 21, 254-260).

Maslow, A. H. (1968). *Toward a Psychology of Being.* New York: Van Nostrand Reinhold.

Maslow, A. H. (1969). The farther reaches of human nature. *Journal of Transpersonal Psychology*, 1, 1-9.

Maslow, A. H. (1971). *The Farther Reaches of Human Nature.* New York: Penguin Books.

Maslow, A. H. (1971a). The creative attitude. In *The Farther Reaches of Human Nature*, 55-68. New York: Penguin Books.

Maslow, A. H. (1971b). Theory Z. In *The Farther Reaches of Human Nature*, 270-286. New York: Penguin Books.

Maslow, A. H. (1976). *Religions, Values, and Peak Experiences.* New York: Penguin. (Original work published in 1964)

Maslow, A. H. (1979). *The Journals of A. H. Maslow Vols. 1-2* (R. J. Lowry, Ed.). Monterey, CA: Brooks/Cole.

Maslow, A. H. (1993). *The Farther Reaches of Human Nature.* New York: Penguin Arkana. (Original work published in 1971)

Maslow, A. H. (1994). *Religions, Values, and Peak Experiences.* New York: Penguin Books (originally published in 1970).

Maslow, A. H. (1996). Critique of self-actualization theory. In E. Hoffman (Ed.), *Future Visions: The Unpublished Papers of Abraham Maslow*, 26-32. Thousand Oaks, CA: Sage.

Maslow, A. H. (1999). Peak-experiences as acute identity experiences. In A. H. Maslow, *Toward a Psychology of Being* (3rd ed.), 113-125. New York: Wiley. (Reprinted from *American Journal of Psychoanalysis*, 1961, 21, 254-260).

Matthews, J., & Matthews, C. (1986). *The Western Way: A Practical Guide to the Western Mystery Tradition* (2 Volumes). New York: Arkana.

Maurer, R. L. Sr., Kumar, V. K., Woodside, L., & Pekala, R. J. (1997). Phenomenological experience in response to monotonous drumming and hypnotizability. *American Journal of Clinical Hypnosis*, 40(2), 130-145.

May, R. (1958). The origins and significance of the Existential movement in psychology. In R. May, E. Angel, & H. Ellenberger (Eds.),

Existence: A New Dimension in Psychiatry and Psychology, 3-36. NY: Simon & Schuster.

May, R. (1967/1996). *Psychology and the Human Dilemma.* New York: W. W. Norton.

May, R. (1969). *Existential Psychology, Second edition.* New York: Random House.

Mayer, M. (2007). *Bodymind Healing Psychotherapy: Ancient Pathways to Modern Health.* Orinda, CA: Bodymind Healing Publications.

Mayer, M. (Jan 9, 2015). *Transforming Energy Psychology into a Comprehensive, Transpersonal Psychotherapy.* Retrieved from http://acepblog.org/2015/01/09/transforming-energy-psychology-into-a-comprehensive-transpersonal-psychotherapy/

Mayerson, N. M. (2013). *Signature Strengths: Validating the Construct.* Presentation to International Positive Psychology Association, Los Angeles, CA, 82-83.

McAdams, D. P. (1985). *Power, Intimacy, and the Life Story: Personological Inquiries into Identity.* New York: Guilford Press.

McAdams, D. P. (1998). Ego, trait, identity. In P. M. Westenberg, A. Blasi, & L. D. Cohn (Eds.), *Personality Development*, 27-38. Mahwah, NJ: Lawrence Erlbaum.

McAdams, D. P., Ruetzel, K., & Foley, J. M. (1986). Complexity and generativity at midlife: Relations among social motives, ego development, and adults' plans for the future. *Journal of Personality and Social Psychology*, 50(4), 800-807.

McCrae, R. R., & Costa, P. T. (1980). Openness to experience and ego level in Loevinger's Sentence Completion Test: Dispositional contributions to developmental models of personality. *Journal of Personality and Social Psychology, 39,* 1179–1190.

McMahon, J. D. S. (1998). The anatomy of ritual. In B. Batey (Ed.), *Gateways to Higher Consciousness: 1998 Annual Conference Proceedings of the Academy of Religion and Psychical Research*, 49-56. Bloomfield, CT: Academy of Religion and Psychical Research.

McNeal, S., & Frederick, C. (1993). Inner strength and other techniques for ego-strengthening. *American Journal of Clinical Hypnosis, 35,* 170-178.

Metzner, R. (1998). *The Unfolding Self: Varieties of Transformational Experience.* Novato, CA: Origin Press.

Miller, M., & Cook-Greuter, S. (1994). From postconventional development to transcendence: Visions and theories. In M. Miller & S.

Cook-Greuter (Eds.), *Transcendence and Mature Thought in Adulthood: The Further Reaches of Adult Development*, xv-xxxiv. Lanham, MD: Rowman & Littlefield.

Miovic, M. (2004). An Introduction to Spiritual Psychology: Overview of the Literature, East and West. *Harvard Review of Psychiatry* (Taylor & Francis Ltd), 12(2), 105-115.

Mols, F., Vingerhoets, A. J., Coebergh, J. W., & van de Poll-Franse, L. V. (2009). Well-being, posttraumatic growth and benefit finding in long-term breast cancer survivors. *Psychology & Health, 24*(5), 583-595.

Monroe, R. (1979). *Journeys Out of the Body*. New York: Broadway Books.

Montgomery, C. (1991). The care-giving relationship: Paradoxical and transcendent aspects. *Journal of Transpersonal Psychology*, 23, 91-104.

Morris, B. (1991). *Western Conceptions of the Individual*. New York: St. Martin's Press.

Morton, P., & Frederick, C. (1999). Re-alerting in the middle of a tightrope: Promoting conscious/unconscious complementarity during the integration. *Hypnos, 26*, 5-13.

Moss, E. (2002). Working with dreams in a bereavement therapy group. *International Journal of Group Psychotherapy*, 52(2), 151-171.

Myers, L. J. (1985). Transpersonal psychology: The role of the Afrocentric paradigm. *The Journal of Black Psychology, 12*(1), 31-42.

Nagy, M. (1991). The *lumen naturae*: Soul of the psychotherapeutic relationship. In K. Gibson, D. Lathrop, & E. M. Stern (Eds.), *Carl Jung and Soul Psychology*, 55-61. Binghamton, NY: Harrington Park Press.

Nasr, S. H. (1992). Foreword. In M. H. Yazdi (Ed.), *The Principles of Epistemology in Islamic Philosophy: Knowledge by* Presence, vii–xiii. Albany, NY: State University of New York Press.

NCCAM. (2005). *Energy Medicine: An Overview*. In Backgrounder. Washington, DC: National Center for Complementary and Alternative Medicine, National Institutes of Health.

Neumann, E. (1954). *The Origins and History of Consciousness*. New York: Pantheon.

Newberg, A. B., & Iversen, J. (2003). The neural basis of the complex mental task of meditation: Neurotransmitter and neurochemical considerations. *Medical Hypotheses*, 61(2), 282-291.

Newport, F., & Strausberg, M. (June 8, 2001). Americans' belief in psychic and paranormal phenomena is up over last decade. *Gallup News Service.* Retrieved from www.gallup.com/poll/releases /pr010608.asp

Nietzsche, F. (1958). *Thus Spake Zarathustra.* New York: Random House.

Noam, G. G. (1988). The self, adult development, and the theory of biography and transformation. In D. K. Lapsley & F. C. Powers (Eds.), *Self, Ego, and Identity: Integrative Approaches,* 202-237. New York: Springer-Verlag.

Noam, G. G. (1993). Ego development: True or false? *Psychological Inquiry,* 4, 43-48.

Noam, G. (1998). Solving the ego development-mental health riddle. In P. M. Westenberg, A. Blasi, L. D. Cohn (Eds.), *Personality Development: Theoretical, Empirical, and Clinical Investigations of Loevinger's Conception of Ego Development,* 271-295. Mahwah, NJ: Erlbaum.

Nobles, W. (1972). African philosophy: Foundations for black psychology. In. R. Jones (Ed.), *Black Psychology.* New York: Harper and Row.

Nobles, W. (1980). Extended self: Re-thinking the so-called Negro self concept. In R. Jones, (Ed.), *Black Psychology* (2nd ed.) New York: Harper and Row.

Norbu, N. (1992). *Dream Yoga and the Practice of Natural Light.* Ithaca, NY: Snow Lion Publications.

Oakley, D. A., & Halligan, P. W. (2010). Psychophysiological foundations of hypnosis and suggestion. In S. J. Lynn, J. W. Rhue, & I. Kirsch (Eds.), *Handbook of Clinical Hypnosis,* 79-118.Washington, DC: American Psychological Association.

Oberle, K. (1991). A decade of research in Locus of Control: What have we learned. *Journal of Advanced Nursing,* 16, 800-806.

Ogbonnaya, A. O. (1994). Person as community: An African understanding of the person as intrapsychic community. *Journal of Black Psychology,* 20(1), 75-87.

O'Leary, V. E., & Ickovics, J. R. (1995). Resilience and thriving in response to challenge: An opportunity for a paradigm shift in women's health. *Women's Health: Research on Gender, Behavior, and Policy,* 1, 121-142.

Palmer, H., & Hubbard, P. (2009). A contextual introduction to Psychosynthesis. *Journal of Transpersonal Research,* 1(1), 29-33.

Palmer, P. (1998). *The Courage to Teach.* San Francisco: Jossey-Bass.

330

Pappas, J. D., & Friedman, H. L. (2007). The construct of self-expansiveness and the validity of the Transpersonal Scale of the Self-Expansiveness Level Form. *The Humanistic Psychologist, 35*(4). 323-347.

Pascual-Leone, J. (1990). Reflections on life-span intelligence, consciousness, and ego development. In C. N. Alexander & E. J. Langer (Eds.), *Higher Stages of Human Development: Perspectives on Adult Growth*, 258-285. New York: Oxford University Press.

Peres, J., Simão, M., & Nasello, A. (2007): Espiritualidade, religiosidade e sicoterapia. *Revista de Psiquiatria Clinica*, 34, supl. 1, 136-145.

Perls, F. S. (1969a). *Gestalt Therapy Verbatim*. Lafayette, CA: Real People Press.

Perls, F. S. (1969b). *In and Out the Garbage Pail*. Lafayette, CA: Real People Press.

Perls, F. S. (1970). Four lectures. In J. Fagen & I. Shepherd (Eds.), *Gestalt Therapy Now*. Palo Alto, CA: Science and Behavior Books.

Perry, J. W. (1970). Emotions and Object Relations. *The Journal of Analytical Psychology*, 15(1), 1-12.

Pfaffenberger, A. H. (2013). Exploring the pathways to postconventional personality development. *Integral Leadership Review*. Retrieved from http://integralleadershipreview.com/9061-exploring-the-pathways-to-postconventional-personality-development/.

Phillips, M., & Frederick, C. (1995). *Healing the Divided Self: Clinical and Ericksonian Hypnotherapy for Dissociative and Post-Traumatic Conditions*. New York: W. W. Norton.

Plotkin, B. (2003). *Soulcraft: Crossing into the Mysteries of Nature and Psyche*. Novato, CA: New World Library.

Porterfield, S. (2004). Manufactured mana: American culture and the mass media. *2004 International Conference, Jungian Society for Scholarly Studies*, Newport, Rhode Island. Retrieved from http://www.thejungiansociety.org/Jung%20Society/Conferences/Confe rence-2004/Manufactured-Mana.html

Powell, A. E. (1969). *The Etheric Double*. Wheaton, IL: The Theosophical Publishing House.

Prabhavananda, S., & Isherwood, C. (Trans.). (1972). *The Song of God: Bhagavad Gita* (3rd ed.). Hollywood, CA: Vedanta Society.

Price-Williams, D. R. (1975). *Explorations in Cross-Cultural Psychology*. San Francisco: Chandler & Sharp.

Pulos, L. (2002). Integrating energy psychology and hypnosis. In Gallo, F. P. (Ed.), *Energy Psychology In Psychotherapy: A Comprehensive Sourcebook. The Norton Energy Psychology Series.*, 167-178. New York: W. W. Norton & Co.

Raff, J. (2000). *Jung and the Alchemical Imagination.* Lake Worth, FL: Nicolas-Hays, Inc.

Rank, O. (1924/1952). *The Trauma of Birth.* New York: Robert Brunner.

Reed, P. G. (2003). The theory of self-transcendence. In M. J. Smith & P. Liehr (Eds.), *Middle Range Theories in Nursing*, 145-165. New York: Springer.

Regardie, I. (1981). *The One Year Manual: Twelve Steps to Spiritual Enlightenment.* York Beach, ME: Samuel Weiser, Inc.

Reich, W. (1949). *Character Analysis.* New York: Orgone Institute Press. (originally published 1933 in Germany)

Reichenbach, H. (1938). *Experience and Prediction.* Chicago: University of Chicago Press.

Reinert, D. F. (1997). The Surrender Scale: Reliability, factor structure, and validity. *Alcoholism Treatment Quarterly*, 15(3), 15-32.

Reps, P., & Senzaki, N. (1957/1998). *Zen Flesh, Zen Bones: A Collection of Zen and Pre-Zen Writings.* Boston, MA: Tuttle.

Rock, A. J. (2012). Introduction to special topic section: Shamanism. *International Journal of Transpersonal Studies*, 31(2), 42-46.

Rodrigues, V. (2010). On consciousness-modifying (transpersonal) psychotherapy. *Journal of Transpersonal Research*, 2(1), 44-61.

Rogers, C. R. (1961). *On Becoming a Person.* Boston: Houghton Mifflin.

Rogo, D. S. (1986). *Leaving the Body: A Complete Guide to Astral Projection. A Step-by-Step Presentation of Eight Different Systems of Out-of-Body Travel.* New York: Prentice Hall.

Romanyshyn, R. (2012). Complex education: Depth psychology as a mode of ethical pedagogy. *Educational Philosophy and Theory*, 44(1), 96-116.

Ross, S. A. (1991). Freedom from possession: A Tibetan Buddhist view. *Journal of Social Behavior and Personality*, 6(6), 415-426.

Rosselli, M., & Vanni, D. (2014). Roberto Assagioli and Carl Gustav Jung. *Journal of Transpersonal Psychology*, 46(1), 7-34.

Rossman, M. L. (1987). *Healing Yourself: A Step-by-Step Program for Better Health Through Imagery.* New York: Walker and Company.

Rowan, J. (1990). *Subpersonalities: The People Inside Us.* New York: Routledge.

Rowan, J. (2005). *The Transpersonal: Spirituality in Psychotherapy and Counselling* (2nd ed.). East Sussex: Routledge.

Rowan, J. (2012). Existentialism and the transpersonal. *Existential Analysis*, 23(1), 113-119.

Rowan, J. (2012b). Mind, body and soul. *Therapy Today*, *23*(10), 22-25.

Ruumet, H. (1997). Pathways of the soul: A helical model of psychospiritual development. *Presence: The Journal of Spiritual Directors International*, 3(3), 6-24.

Ruvolo, A. P., and Markus, H. R. (1992). Possible selves and performance: The power of self-relevant imagery. *Social Cognition, 10,* 95-124.

Rychlak, J. F. (1993). A suggested principle of complementarity for psychology. *American Psychologist*, 48, 933–942.

Ryff, C. D. (1989). Happiness is everything, or is it? Explorations on the meaning of psychological well-being. *Journal of Personality and Social Psychology, 57,* 1069-1081.

Safran, J. D., & Segal, Z. V. (1990). *Interpersonal Process in Cognitive Therapy*. New York: Basic Books.

Saldanha, V. (1997). *A Psicoterapia Transpessoal*. Campinas, Brazil: Editora Komedi.

Salman, S. (2000). The wisdom of psychological creativity and amor fati. In P. Young-Eisendrath & M. E. Miller (Eds.), *The Psychology of Mature Spirituality: Integrity, Wisdom, Transcendence*, 77-86. New York: Routledge.

Salmon, P., Sephton, S., Weissbecker, I., Hoover, K., Ulmer, C., & Studts, J. L. (2004). Mindfulness meditation in clinical practice. *Cognitive and Behavioral Practice*, *11*, 434-446.

Sanchez, N., & Vieira, T. (2007). *Take Me to Truth: Undoing the Ego*. Winchester, UK: O Books.

Sanders, R. E., Thalbourne, M. A., & Delin, P. S. (2000). Transliminality and the telepathic transmission of emotional states: An exploratory study. *Journal of the American Society for Psychical Research*, 94, 1–24.

Sandner, D. F., & Beebe, J. (1984). Psychopathology and analysis. In M. Stein (Ed.), *Jungian Analysis*. Boulder, CO and London: Shambhala.

Sartre, J. P. (1956). *Being and Nothingness* (H. Barnes, Trans.). New York: Philosophical Library.

Schneider, K. (2003). Existential-humanistic psychotherapies. In A. Gurman & S. Messer (Eds.), *Essential Psychotherapies*, 149-181. New York: Guilford Press.

Schneider, K. & May, R. (Eds.). (1995). *The Psychology of Existence: An Integrative, Clinical Perspective.* New York: McGraw-Hill.

Schoen, S. (1991). Psychotherapy as sacred ground. *Journal of Humanistic Psychology*, 31(1), 51-55.

Scholem, G. (1991). On the mystical shape of the Godhead: Basic concepts in Kabbalah. New York: Schocken Books.

Scholem, G. (1995). *Major Trends in Jewish Mysticism.* New York: Schocken Books.

Schumacher, E. F. (1978). *A Guide for the Perplexed.* New York: Harper & Row.

Schwartz, A. J. (2000). *The Nature of Spiritual Transformation: A Review of the Literature.* Metanexus Institute. Retrieved from http://www.metanexus.net/spiritual_transformation/research/pdf/STSR P-LiteratureReview2-7.PDF.

Schwartz, R. C. (1995). *Internal Family Systems Therapy.* New York: Guilford Press.

Scotton, B. W., Chinen, A. B., & Battista, J. R. (Eds.). (1996). *Textbook of Transpersonal Psychiatry and Psychology.* New York: Basic Books.

Seeley, W. W., Menon, V., Schatzberg, A. F., et al. (2007). Dissociable intrinsic connectivity networks for salience processing and executive control. *Journal of Neuroscience*, 27, 2349-2356.

Segal, Z. V., Williams, J. M. G., & Teasdale, J. D. (2002). *Mindfulness-based Cognitive Therapy for Depression: A New Approach to Preventing Relapse.* New York: Guilford Press.

Seiden, D. Y., & Lam, K. (2010). From Moses and monotheism to Buddha and behaviorism: Cognitive behavior therapy's transpersonal crisis. *Journal of Transpersonal Psychology*, 42(1), 89-113.

Senge, P. (1990). *The Fifth Discipline: The Art and Practice of the Learning Organization.* New York: Currency Doubleday.

Serrano, M. (1966). *C. G. Jung and Herman Hesse: A Record of Two Friendships.* New York: Schocken Books.

Shamdasani, S. (Ed.). (1996/1932). *The Psychology of Kundalini Yoga: Notes of the Seminar Given in 1932 by C. G. Jung.* Princeton, NJ: Princeton University Press.

Shapiro, D. H., & Walsh, R. N. (Eds.). (1984). *Meditation: Classic and Contemporary Perspectives.* New York: Aldine.

Shapiro, S. L., Schwartz, G., & Bonner, G. (1998). Effects of mindfulness-based stress reduction on medical and premedical students. *Journal of Behavioral Medicine*, 21, 581-599.

Sheldon, K. & Lyubomirsky, S. (2006). How to increase and sustain positive emotion: The effects of expressing gratitude and visualizing best possible selves. *The Journal of Positive Psychology. Special Issue: Positive Emotions. 1(2)*, 73-82.

Shostrom, E. L., Knapp, L., Knapp, R. (1976). *Actualizing Therapy: Foundations for a Scientific Ethic*. San Diego, CA: Educational and Industrial Testing Service.

Shrader, D. W. (2008). Seven Characteristics of Mystical Experiences. *Proceedings of the 6th Annual Hawaii International Conference on Arts and Humanities*. Honolulu, HI.

Singer, J. (1983). From Jungian analysis to transpersonal psychotherapy. *Psychiatric Hospital, 14*(4), 207-212.

Singer, T. (2006). Unconscious forces shaping international conflicts: Archetypal defenses of the group spirit from revolutionary America to confrontation in the Middle East. *The San Francisco Jung Institute Library Journal*, 25(4), 6-28.

Solloway, S. G., & Fisher, W. P. (2007). Mindfulness in measurement: Reconsidering the measurable in mindfulness practice. *International Journal of Transpersonal Studies, 26*, 58-81.

Solomon, R. C. (2000). *No Excuses: Existentialism and the Meaning of Life*. The Teaching Company Lecture Series.

Sovatsky, S. (2009). Kundalini and the complete maturation of the ensouled body. *Journal of Transpersonal Psychology, 41*(1), 1-21.

Spiegel, D. (1996). Hypnosis in the treatment of post-traumatic stress disorder. *Casebook of Clinical Hypnosis*, 99-112. Washington, DC: American Psychological Association.

Spiegel, D. (2008). Intelligent design or designed intelligence? Hypnotizability as neurobiological adaptation. In M. R. Nash, A. J. Barnier (Eds.), *The Oxford Handbook of Hypnosis: Theory, Research, and Practice*, 179-199. Oxford, United Kingdom: Oxford University Press.

Starhawk. (1999). *Spiral Dance: A Rebirth of the Ancient Religion of the Goddess* (20th anniversary edition). San Francisco, CA: HarperSanFrancisco. (Original work published 1979)

Stavish, M. (2008). *Between the Gates: Lucid Dreaming, Astral Projection, and the Body of Light in Western Esotericism*. San Francisco, CA: Weiser Books.

Steinbrecher, E. C. (1988). *The Inner Guide Meditation: A Spiritual Technology for the 21st Century*. York Beach, ME: Samuel Weiser, Inc.

Steiner, C. Medici de (1995). Analyzing children's dreams. *International Journal of Psycho-Analysis*, 76, 45-49.

Stern, D. (1985). *The Interpersonal World of the Infant*. New York: Basic Books.

Stevens, W. (1984/1952). *The Collected Poems of Wallace Stevens*. New York: Vintage Books.

Sutich, A. (1969). Statement of Purpose. *Journal of Transpersonal Psychology*, 1(1), 5-6.

Sutich, A. (1973). Transpersonal therapy. *Journal of Transpersonal Psychology*, 5(1), 1-14.

Sutich, A. (1976). The emergence of the transpersonal orientation: A personal account. *Journal of Transpersonal Psychology*, 8, 5-19.

Taft, R. (1969). Peak experiences and ego permissiveness: An exploratory factor study of their dimensions in a normal person. *Acta Psychologica*, 29, 35-64.

Tarnas, R. (1991). *The Passion of the Western Mind: Understanding the Ideas that Have Shaped Our Worldview*. New York: Harmony Books.

Tart, C. T. (1975). *States of Consciousness*. New York: E. P. Dutton & Co.

Tart, C. T. (2008). Accessing state-specific transpersonal knowledge: Inducing altered states. *Journal of Transpersonal Psychology*, 40(2), 137-154.

Taylor, E. (1996). William James and transpersonal psychiatry. In B. W. Scotton, A. B. Chinen, J. R. Battista (Eds.), *Textbook of Transpersonal Psychiatry and Psychology*, 21-28. New York: Basic Books.

Tedeschi, R. G., & Calhoun, L. G. (2004). Posttraumatic growth: Conceptual foundations and empirical evidence. *Psychological Inquiry*, 15(1), 1-18.

Tedlock, B. (1999). Sharing and interpreting dreams in Amerindian nations. In D. Shulman & G. Stroumsa (Eds.), *Dream Cultures: Explorations in the Comparative History of Dreaming*, 87-103. New York: Oxford University Press.

Tedlock, B. (2004). The poetics and spirituality of dreaming: A Native American enactive theory. *Dreaming*, 14(2-3), 183-189.

Teicher, M. (2000). Wounds time won't heal. *Cerebrum*, 2, 4.

Teilhard de P. Chardin. (1973). *On Happiness*. London: Collins, St. James Place. (Original work published 1966).

Thalbourne, M. A., Bartemucci, L., Delin, P. S., Fox, B., & Nofi, O. (1997). Transliminality: Its nature and correlates. *Journal of the American Society for Psychical Research*, 91, 305-331.

Thompson, C., Locander, W., & Pollio, H. (1989). Putting consumer experience back into consumer research: The philosophy and method of existential-phenomenology. *Journal of Consumer Research*, 16, 133-146.

Thorne, A. (1993). On contextualizing Loevinger's stages of ego development. *Psychological Inquiry*, 4(1), 53-55.

Thorne, A., McLean, K. C., Lawrence, A. M. (Jun 2004). When remembering is not enough: Reflecting on self-defining memories in late adolescence. *Journal of Personality*, 72(3), 513-542.

Tillich, P. (1957). *Dynamics of Faith*. New York: Harper & Brothers.

Torbert, W. R. (2002). In D. Fisher, D. Rooke, & W. R. Torbert (Eds.), *Personal and Organizational Transformations: Through Action Inquiry*. New York: Edge/Work Press.

Torem, M. S., & Gainer, M. J. (1995). The center core: Imagery for experiencing the unifying self. *Hypnos, 22,* 125-131.

Unno, T. (Summer 2015). Into the valley: The path of imperfection. *Tricycle, 24(4)*.

Urban, E. (2005). Fordham, Jung and the self: A re-examination of Fordham's contribution to Jung's conceptualization of the self. *Journal of Analytical Psychology*, 50, 571–594.

van Dierendonck, D., Garssen, B., & Visser, A. (2005). Burnout prevention through personal growth. *International Journal of Stress Management*, 12(1), 62-77.

Van Dusen, W. (1965). Invoking the actual in psychotherapy. *Journal of Individual Psychology*, 21, 66–76.

Vaughan, F. (2000). *The Inward Arc: Healing in Psychotherapy and Spirituality (2nd edition)*. Bloomington: iUniverse.com

Vaughan, F. (2010). Identity, maturity and freedom: Transpersonal and existential perspectives. *Journal of Transpersonal Research*, 2(1), 2-9.

Vaughan, F., Wittine, B., Walsh, R. (1996). Transpersonal psychology and the religious person. In E. P. Shafranske (Ed.), *Religion and the Clinical Practice of Psychology*, 483-509. Washington, DC: American Psychological Association.

Vieira, W. (2002). *Projectiology: A Panorama of the Experiences of the Consciousness Outside the Human Body*. Rio de Janeiro, Brazil: International Academy of Consciousness.

Vieten, C., Amorok, T., & Schlitz, M. (2005). Many paths, one mountain: A cross-traditional model of spiritual transformation. Paper presented at *Science and Religion: Global Perspectives*, sponsored by the Institute of Noetic Sciences and the Metanexus Institute, January 4-8, 2005, in Philadelphia, PA, pp. 4-5.

von Franz, M-L. (1971). *Marie L. von Franz and James Hillman:. Lectures on Jung's Typology.* Zurich: Spring Publications.

von Franz, M-L. (1979). Unpublished lecture, Panarian Conference, Los Angeles.

Wade, J. (1996). *Changes of Mind: A Holonomic Theory of the Evolution of Consciousness.* Albany: SUNY Press.

Walach, H. (2008). Narcissism: The shadow of transpersonal psychology. *Transpersonal Psychology Review*, 12(2), 47-59.

Walach, H. (2013). Criticisms of transpersonal psychology and beyond – The future of transpersonal psychology. In H. L. Friedman & G. Hartelius (Eds.), *The Wiley Blackwell Handbook of Transpersonal Psychology*, 62-87. London: John Wiley & Sons, Ltd.

Walsh, R. (1989). What is a shaman? Definition, origin and distribution. *Journal of Transpersonal Psychology*, 21(1), 1-11.

Walsh, R. (2007). *The World of Shamanism.* Woodbury, MN: Llewellyn Press.

Walsh, R. (2012). Experiences of 'Soul Journeys' in the World's Religions: The Journeys of Mohammed, Saints Paul and John, Jewish Chariot Mysticism, Taoism's Highest Clarity School, and Shamanism. *The International Journal of Transpersonal Studies*, 31(2), 103-110.

Walsh, R. (2013). Karma yoga and awakening service: Modern approaches to an ancient practice. *Journal of Transpersonal Research*, 5(1), 2-6.

Walsh, R., & Vaughn, F. (Eds.). (1980). *Beyond Ego: Transpersonal Dimensions in Psychology.* Los Angeles: J.P. Tarcher.

Walsh, R., & Vaughan, F. (Eds.) (1993a). *Paths Beyond Ego: The Transpersonal Vision.* Los Angeles: Tarcher.

Walsh, R., & Vaughan, F. (1993b). On transpersonal definitions. *Journal of Transpersonal Psychology*, 25(2), 199-207.

Wannamaker, A. B. (n.d.). *The Process of Healing and Growth in Psychosynthesis and Christian 'Healing of the Memories'.* Retrieved from www.else-egeland.org/abw2en.htm

Wark, D. M. (2006). Alert hypnosis: A review and case report. *American Journal of Clinical Hypnosis*, 48(4), 291-300.

Waterman, A. S. (1993). Two conceptions of happiness: Contrasts of personal expressiveness (eudaemonia) and hedonic enjoyment. *Journal of Personality and Social Psychology*, 64, 678–691.

Watkins, J. G., & Watkins, H. H. (1997). *Ego States: Theory and Therapy*. New York: W. W. Norton.

Watkins, M. (1998). *Waking Dreams*. Spring Publications.

Watts, A. (1936). *The Spirit of Zen: A Way of Life, Work and Art in the Far East*. New York: Grove Press.

Watts, A. (1957). *The Way of Zen*. New York: Pantheon Books.

Watts, A. (1961). *Psychotherapy East and West*. New York: Pantheon Books.

Welwood, J. (1984). Principles of inner work: Psychological and spiritual. *Journal of Transpersonal Psychology*, 16(1), 63-73.

Welwood, J. (1990). *Journey of the Heart: The Path of Conscious Love*. New York: HarperCollins.

Wertz, F. J., Charmaz, K., McMullen, L. M., Josselson, R., Anderson, R., & McSpadden, E. (2011). *Five Ways of Doing Qualitative Analysis: Phenomenological Psychology, Grounded Theory, Discourse Analysis, Narrative Research, and Intuitive Inquiry*. New York: Guildford Press.

Westen, D. (1998). Loevinger's theory of ego development in the context of contemporary psychoanalytical theory. In P. M. Westenberg, A. Blasi, and L. D. Cohn (Eds.), *Personality Development: Theoretical, Empirical and Clinical Investigations of Loevinger's Conception of Ego Development*, 59-69. Mahwah, N.J.: Erlbaum.

Westenberg, P. M., & Block, J. (1993). Ego development and individual differences in personality. *Journal of Personality and Social Psychology*, 65, 792-800.

White, M. S. (1985). Ego development in adult women. *Journal of Personality*, 53, 561-574.

White, R. A. (1998). Becoming more human as we work: The reflexive role of exceptional human experience. In W. Braud & R. Anderson (Eds.), *Transpersonal Research Methods for the Social Sciences: Honoring Human Experience*, 128-145. Thousand Oaks, CA: Sage.

Wickramasekera, I. I. (2013). Hypnosis and transpersonal psychology: Answering the call within. In H. L. Friedman, G. Hartelius (Eds.), *The Wiley-Blackwell Handbook of Transpersonal Psychology*, 492-511. Wiley-Blackwell.

Wilber, K. (1977). *The Spectrum of Consciousness*. Wheaton, IL: Quest Books.

Wilber, K. (1979). A developmental view of consciousness. *Journal of Transpersonal Psychology, 11*(1), 1-21.

Wilber, K. (1981). *Up from Eden: A Transpersonal View of Human Evolution.* Garden City, NY: Anchor Press/Doubleday.

Wilber, K. (1983). *Eye to Eye: The Quest for a New Paradigm.* New York: Anchor Books.

Wilber, K. (1995). *Sex, Ecology, Spirituality: The Spirit of Evolution.* Boston: Shambhala.

Wilber, K. (1997). *The Eye of the Spirit: An Integral Vision for a World Gone Slightly Mad.* Boston: Shambhala.

Wilber, K. (1998). *The Essential Ken Wilber.* Boston, MA: Shambhala Publications.

Wilber, K. (2000). *Integral Psychology: Consciousness, Spirit, Psychology, Therapy.* Boston, MA: Shambhala Publications.

Wilber, K. (2009). *States, Stages, and 3 Kinds of Self.* Retrieved from https://www.integrallife.com/video/states-stages-and-3-kinds-self

Wilber, K., Engler J., & Brown, D. (Eds.). (1986). *Transformations of Consciousness: Conventional and Contemplative Perspectives on Development.* Boston: Shambhala New Science Library.

Wilhelm, R. (1931/1962). *The Secret of the Golden Flower: A Chinese Book of Life.* (C. F. Baynes, Trans.). New York: Harcourt, Brace & World.

Wilshire, D. (1989). The uses of myth, image, and the female body in re-visioning knowledge. In A. M. Jaggar & S. R. Bordo (Eds.), *Gender/Body/Knowledge: Feminist Reconstructions of Being and Knowing,* 92-114. New Brunswick, NJ: Rutgers University Press.

Winkelman, M. (2000). *Shamanism: The Neural Ecology of Consciousness and Healing.* Westport, CT: Bergin and Garvey.

Winkelman, M. (2010). *Shamanism: A Biopsychosocial Paradigm of Consciousness and Healing.* Santa Barbara, CA: ABC-CLIO.

Winkelman, M. (Mar 2011). Shamanism and the evolutionary origins of spirituality and healing. *NeuroQuantology, 9*(1), 54-71.

Winkelman, M. (2012). Shamanism in cross-cultural perspective. *The International Journal of Transpersonal Studies, 31*(2), 47-62.

Winson, J. (Nov 1990). The meaning of dreams. *Scientific American,* 86-96.

Wolf, E. (1982). Adolescence: Psychology of the self and self objects. *Adolescent Psychiatry, 10,* 171-181.

Woodroffe, J. (Arthur Avalon). (1919/2003). *The Serpent Power*. Madras, India: Ganesh & Co.

Wright, P. A. (1995). Bringing women's voices to transpersonal theory. *ReVision, 17*(3), 3-10.

Yalom, I. D. (1980). *Existential Psychotherapy*. New York: Basic Books.

Yalom, I. D. (1989). *Love's Executioner: And Other Tales of Psychotherapy*. New York: Harper Collins.

Yapko, M. (Sept/Oct 2011). Suggesting mindfulness. *Psychotherapy Networker*, 29-33, 50-52.

Yontef, G. (1993). Gestalt therapy: An introduction. In *Awareness, Dialogue, and Process* published by The Gestalt Journal Press. Retrieved from http://www.gestalt.org/yontef.htm.

Zahan, D. (1979). *The Religion, Spirituality, and Thought of Traditional Africa*. Chicago: University of Chicago Press.

Zahi, A. (2009). Spiritual-transpersonal hypnosis. *Contemporary Hypnosis, 26*(4), 263-268.

Zimberoff, D. (1989/2011). *Breaking Free from the Victim Trap*. Issaquah, WA: Wellness Press.

Zimberoff, D., & Hartman, D. (1998). The Heart-Centered Hypnotherapy modality defined *Journal of Heart-Centered Therapies, 1*(1), 3-49.

Zimberoff, D., & Hartman, D. (1999). Personal transformation with Heart-Centered therapies. *Journal of Heart-Centered Therapies, 2*(1), 3-53.

Zimberoff, D., & Hartman, D. (1999b). Heart-Centered energetic psychodrama. *Journal of Heart-Centered Therapies, 2*(1), 77-98.

Zimberoff, D., & Hartman, D. (2003). Gestalt Therapy and Heart-Centered therapies. *Journal of Heart-Centered Therapies, 6*(1), 93-104.

Zimberoff, D., & Hartman, D. (2014). *Overcoming Shock: Healing the Traumatized Mind and Heart*. Far Hills, NJ: New Horizon Press.

Index

magician, 151, 203
mana, 50, 203-205, 279
Markides, Kyriacos C., 85
Maslow, Abraham, 9, 11, 15-16,
    23, 26, 32-33, 35, 54-55, 94-
    102, 125-126, 167, 169, 182,
    193, 210-211, 217, 226, 233,
    242-243, 274, 276, 278, 280
May, Rollo, 33-34, 35, 55, 63,
    182
Mayer, Michael, 49-50
Mayerson Foundation, 169
meditation, 10, 15, 16, 33, 44,
    46, 51, 59-60, 72, 82-84, 89,
    94-95, 100, 108, 116-117,
    119-121, 129, 132, 134-135,
    139, 150, 154-155, 161, 174,
    184-186, 198, 211, 219, 253
    Mindfulness, 146
memory, 28, 69, 76, 137, 149,
    172, 177, 187, 236, 250
    anticipated, 135, 178
    body, 90
    collective, 126
    consolidation, 117
    procedural, 118-119
    retrieval, 117
    traumatic, 147
Mitakuye Oyasin, 47
movement, 40, 43, 55, 67, 69, 71,
    97, 103, 182, 222
    Human Potential, 30
    transpersonal, 51
    descending, 247
    ascending , 247
multilocal participatory events,
    47
muscle testing, 50
narrative research, 198-199

near-death experience, 12, 24,
    35, 85, 132, 273
neurogenesis, 118
neuroplasticity, 118
Newberg, Andrew B., 132, 134
Nietzsche, Friedrich, 62-63
nonattachment, 65, 69
nondual, 34, 225, 273
numinous, 17, 72, 116, 160, 162,
    204-205, 273
organic inquiry, 41, 199-201, 273
out-of-body experience, 12, 24,
    51, 274
Oxherder, 253-263
participatory spiritual pluralism,
    30
peak experience, 11, 16, 27, 32-
    33, 59, 81, 95, 97, 100, 131,
    132, 198, 211, 227-228, 275
Perennial philosophy, 30, 37, 38-
    39, 46, 275
Perls, Fritz, 28, 29, 55, 66-67, 69,
    268
personal level of development,
    38, 81, 87-88, 92, 100, 176,
    192-193, 275
Personal Orientation Inventory
    (POI), 196
phenomenological psychology,
    183-185, 198, 201
plateau experience, 33, 95, 100,
    131, 211, 276
postambivalence, 103, 169, 209
pre- and perinatal, 27, 35, 55,
    148, 164, 275, 276
pre-personal level of
    development, 38, 81, 87, 276
Prechtel, Martin, 124
precognition, 12, 24, 245, 277

Made in the USA
Coppell, TX
22 January 2020

14870008R00193